Heading South to Teach

Heading South to Teach

THE WORLD OF

Susan Nye Hutchison,

1815–1845

KIM TOLLEY

The University of North Carolina Press *Chapel Hill*

This book was published with the assistance of the
Z. Smith Reynolds Fund of the University of North Carolina Press.

Manufactured in the United States of America

The paper in this book meets the guidelines for permanence
and durability of the Committee on Production Guidelines for
Book Longevity of the Council on Library Resources.

The University of North Carolina Press has been a member
of the Green Press Initiative since 2003.

Cover illustration: portrait of Susan Nye Hutchison courtesy of Richard H. Marks,
Greenville, N.C., and *American Stage Wagon Stopping at a Public House*,
line engraving, American, 1798, The Granger Collection, New York

Library of Congress Cataloging-in-Publication Data
Tolley, Kimberley.
Heading South to teach : the world of Susan Nye Hutchison, 1815–1845 / Kim Tolley.
    pages cm
Includes bibliographical references and index.
ISBN 978-1-4696-2433-4 (pbk : alk. paper) —
ISBN 978-1-4696-2434-1 (ebook)
1. Hutchison, Susan Nye. 2. Teachers—United States—Biography. 3. Women
teachers—United States—Biography. 4. Teachers—Southern States—Diaries.
5. Teaching—Southern States—History—19th century. 6. Education—Southern
States—History—19th century. 7. Education—United States—History—19th century.
8. Educational change—United States—History. I. Title.
LA2317.H88T65 2015
371.10092—dc23
[B]
2015010518

Contents

Illustrations and Tables

Acknowledgments

This book would not have been possible without significant support from individuals and institutions. I am indebted to the North Caroliniana Society at the University of North Carolina at Chapel Hill for funding the initial research for this project with an Archie K. Davis Research Fellowship in 2002. I am also grateful to the Faculty Development Committee at Notre Dame de Namur University for sponsoring some of my travel to archives and conferences. In particular, my thanks go to Stephen Cole, Marianne Delaporte, Lu Chang, Joanne Rossi, the late Klaus Musmann, and other participants at a 2008 Faculty Development brown bag luncheon for urging me to "write the book!"

One of the great pleasures of working on this project has been the chance to discuss ideas with colleagues from a variety of fields. I owe a debt of gratitude to a few people in particular. Nancy Beadie and I have talked about early national education history for nearly two decades, and her insights have proven invaluable. Her steady encouragement throughout the research and writing process and useful comments on an early partial draft of the manuscript helped me see it through to publication. Margaret A. Nash and I have long shared an interest in Susan Nye Hutchison, and the experience of coauthoring a book chapter with Margaret more than a decade ago first prompted my thinking about the role of teachers in the Second Great Awakening. Finally, I'm very grateful to John E. Murray for his generosity in agreeing to read through the entire late-stage manuscript and for his incredibly thorough and positive feedback.

Since the project's inception, fellow scholars have provided much constructive criticism. Ron Butchart and Lucia McMahon offered wonderfully detailed and critical feedback on the final manuscript. I also thank those who provided helpful comments on early drafts submitted as papers to conferences and journals: Margaret A. Nash, John J. McCusker, Hilary J. Moss, Robert Wolf, Barbara Beatty, James Albisetti, Mary Jo Maynes, James Leloudis, Mary Kelley, Stacey M. Robertson, David Mitch, and Sherman Dorn.

Other individuals provided support and encouragement at critical moments. In particular, Geraldine Jonçich Clifford shared not only input and advice about the publication process but also her unflagging confidence that the manuscript would find a home. I also thank Michael McGandy, Patricia Cline Cohen, and Mary Kelley for suggestions about finding a press that would provide the best fit. I am grateful to Charles Grench and Lucas Church for their role in bringing the manuscript to the University of North Carolina Press.

Some of Susan Nye Hutchison's North Carolina descendants were exceptionally generous in sharing surviving documents that remain in private hands. Susan's great-great-grandson, Richard H. Marks, and his wife, Lynne Marks, welcomed me to their home and allowed me to examine photocopies of family letters, photographs, and Susan's missing journal entries from 1818 and 1821. Susan's great-great-granddaughter, Agnes Marks Cooley, kindly provided additional information.

This book could not have been written without the many librarians and archivists who provided advice and assistance. Some stand out for going well above and beyond the call of duty. In particular, Betsy Strauss of the Amenia Historical Society and Linda Hocking of the Litchfield Historical Society patiently answered my many questions. Judy Costello, David Kreigh, and Mary Wegmann of Notre Dame de Namur's Gellert Library helped me navigate the world of microfilm orders.

I have been fortunate to have the help of first-rate editors and illustrators on this project. Ellen D. Goldlust's meticulous copyediting made this a far better book. Stephanie Wenzel adroitly managed the editing process, and Michelle Wallen's proofreading was impeccable. Nathan Tolley read through an early draft of the full manuscript and provided incredibly useful feedback about how to write for a broad audience. Emma Tolley created and formatted maps.

My deepest thanks go to my husband, Bruce Tolley, who read every single chapter multiple times and never ceased to provide critical feedback coupled with unfailing encouragement. If he ever grew tired of hearing me ramble on about the ups and downs of Susan's marriage and her experiences with education and slavery, he never showed it. He is—as always—my better half and best reader.

Heading South to Teach

Introduction

Susan Nye Hutchison hit rock bottom in the fall of 1833. In September, she closed her little school in Georgia and sold off her belongings to neighbors and friends. "Miss Miller bought of me my little work table which I bought a good while before my marriage," she wrote. "I felt sad at parting with the silent companion of many trials." After years of teaching to support her family, she decided to separate from her husband, an abusive wastrel. Near the end of October, she returned north to her parents' farm in New York with her two youngest sons and stepdaughter. Her church covered her traveling costs because she had not a penny to her name.[1]

Many women who fell into poverty simply experienced bad luck. Some became ill or injured and could no longer support themselves; others married men who were lost at sea or carried away by cholera. Some husbands gambled away their earnings, beat their wives, or abandoned their families. Women in such circumstances often turned to relatives for help, relying on parents, sisters, or brothers to care for some children or take in the entire family for a period. Susan Nye Hutchison fit this profile—three years earlier, she had sent her two eldest sons north to live with her parents and older brother on the family farm.[2]

In 1815, she had come south as an unmarried teacher, full of idealism, missionary zeal, and ambition to make her own way in the world. Now she retreated north to shelter in her parents' household with no money, five children to support, and no husband.

THIS BOOK RECOUNTS the life and times of Susan Nye Hutchison (1790–1867), a northern farmer's daughter who taught in North Carolina and Georgia throughout the era of religious revival known as the Second Great Awakening. The day she left her husband was the lowest point in her life, but her story neither begins nor ends there. Praying with slaves and free blacks in the streets of Raleigh, North Carolina; establishing an independent school in Augusta, Georgia; marrying and raising a family; separating from an abusive husband; founding schools and publishing her writings; secretly teaching slaves to read in defiance of the law—her journals and other archival records chart these experiences over a period of thirty years. On one level, this is the story of an ordinary yet remarkable woman who turned to teaching as a meaningful way to earn a living and led an extraordinary life. On another level, this book is about the significance of religion and education in antebellum American society and culture.

One of the most fascinating things about Susan Nye Hutchison is her career ambition. Ambition is a trait rarely ascribed to antebellum women, by either contemporaries or historians. Even in the twenty-first century, many individuals remain uncomfortable with the notion that a woman—especially one with children—could or should be as ambitious as a man in seeking recognition, financial comfort, and social influence. Susan herself reflected this discomfort at times. Raised to be modest and retiring, she sometimes acknowledged her own ambition with regret, even though in the end, that character trait helped her raise her family from poverty.[3]

I first discovered Susan in 1994, while researching a doctoral dissertation on the science education of young women in antebellum schools. Buried in an 1815 edition of the *Raleigh Register* was a brief mention of chemistry experiments conducted on the stage of the State House: "The experiments made by the Students in Chemistry did honor to Miss Nye."[4] Because this was the earliest record I had discovered of public science experiments by young women, I noted this event in my dissertation and then shelved my curiosity about "Miss Nye" as I graduated from the University of California at Berkeley and began a tenure-track teaching position. Several years later, a database search revealed the existence of Susan Nye Hutchison's journals in North Carolina. Intrigued, I traveled from California to visit the State Archives in Raleigh.

The writing on the first page drew me in. I traveled with Susan from rural New York to the South, learning about her teaching and lay ministry, her encounters with slavery, and her marriage, separation, and widowhood. Her journals presented a substantial first-person account of developments related to women's work, evangelism, social reform, family, education, and antislavery. Struggling to earn a living, trying to raise children while teaching full time, worrying about pleasing parents, students, and family members—Susan's experiences would be familiar to many working women in the twenty-first century. She established several schools in an era when men and women competed head-to-head for positions of leadership in incorporated female academies. Antebellum society placed limits on what she could achieve as a woman, yet she did not allow those limits to define her. I admired her grit.

HISTORICAL SIGNIFICANCE

As a female who rose to a position of authority in antebellum society and lifted her family out of poverty, Susan Nye Hutchison presents a paradox in women's history. A recurring theme in the historiography is backlash and declining opportunity. The first iteration appeared in the influential work of Elisabeth Anthony Dexter, whose *Colonial Women of Affairs* concludes that in contrast to the colonial era, women's economic opportunities contracted significantly after the American Revolution. Subsequent research cast doubt on the notion of the colonial period as a golden age for women, but recent scholarship has highlighted the way Americans retreated from the radicalism of the revolution and turned away from new ideas about women's social and political equality with men. For example, Rosemarie Zagarri has shown that just after the revolution, women participated informally in party politics and electoral activities, attending rallies, organizing political activities, and voicing their opinions on political issues; by 1828, however, male politicians came to view women's political engagement as unwelcome. Historians have documented a similar backlash against women's public speaking and preaching. For example, both Catherine A. Brekus and Susan Juster have identified a pattern of declining opportunities available to women preachers and exhorters during this period. Carolyn Eastman has claimed that in reaction against women's public speaking, American writers in the 1820s turned away from the notion of female education as intrinsically valuable and began advocating a differentiated course of study centered on domesticity.[5]

The thesis of backlash and decline fits well with the mid-nineteenth-century phenomenon that historian Barbara Welter called the Cult of True Womanhood and subsequent scholars have termed the Cult of Domesticity, an ideology in contemporary literature idealizing woman's role as wife and mother. Sarah Josepha Hale, editor of the *Ladies' Magazine* from 1828 to 1836, informed her readers that America did not want "those talents and acquirements, which have fitted women to rule empires and manage state intrigues; we want patterns of virtue, of intelligence, of piety and usefulness in private life." Whereas Hale presumably exempted herself from this sweeping statement, historian Nancy F. Cott has found expressions of this ideology in the diaries of some New England women. According to

Mary P. Ryan, by the late 1830s, *Mother's Magazine* advised "that it was woman's fate to 'pass her life in domestic privacy.'" Based on the correspondence and diaries of elite New England women, Lucia McMahon has claimed that by 1830, American writers had exchanged notions of women's "mere equality" with men for an ascendant ideology of female domesticity. Together, the revolutionary rhetoric of egalitarianism and the midcentury focus on domesticity bracket a compelling narrative arc. As historian Suzanne Lebsock has pointed out, it is easy to imagine "a female variation on the Rip Van Winkle theme": in 1790, the charismatic woman preacher takes a break and falls asleep after exhorting a crowd of hundreds on the Boston common, then wakes up in 1850 wearing stiff petticoats and embroidering lace doilies, cloistered in a quiet little cottage.[6]

But to what extent did nineteenth-century rhetoric about female domesticity affect the behavior and limit the opportunities of an ambitious woman who needed to work for a living? A growing body of research on the experiences of antebellum women has shown that although women faced ongoing social constraints, free women gained increasing autonomy from men. More women found wage work, fewer women married, and more married women acquired property outside their husbands' control. Scholars have explored the ways that middle-class women began to move into civil space, manage their own benevolent societies, petition state and federal governments, and become politically engaged in the antislavery, Indian removal, and temperance movements. Throughout the antebellum period, the numbers of females in common schools and academies increased in both the North and the South, and despite prescriptive messages about female domesticity, young women increasingly studied the same academic subjects as young men. Prior to the Civil War, women moved from teaching part time in summer schools to full-time, year-round work in common schools and academies, and some began to move up an emerging career ladder, from teacher to preceptress to school principal.[7]

Susan Nye Hutchison's story illustrates some of the tensions and contradictions between published rhetoric and actual experience. She lived through a period of rhetorical backlash against women's work and activism, yet she established and ran several incorporated academies. Despite the pronouncements of some evangelicals during the 1830s that women had no business stating their opinions on matters of church and state, she published essays on slavery and the division of the Presbyterian Church. Her experience provides a case study of the way one woman conformed to social mores in some respects but also resisted cultural constraints.

To date, few historians have made more than cursory use of her journals, and none has seemed aware of her published writings or the documentary sources that confirm the incorporation of her academy in Salisbury, the duration of her career as an academy principal in the South, or her eventual financial success. Scholars familiar with Susan's journals have mined them for the occasional quote about antebellum teaching, social mores, family life, or religion.[8]

Susan's journals are important because they open a window into a dimension of education history that has been largely unavailable. They provide the earliest and the most complete surviving account of a female teacher who migrated from the Northeast to the South during the early nineteenth century. Thousands of young northerners born just after the American Revolution left friends and family behind and headed west or south, sometimes risking their lives as they crossed rivers, mountains, deserts, and oceans. Some were drawn by a sense of adventure or a desire for fortune; others were impelled by religious zeal. Roughly 360,000 people—most of them men—headed south before 1860. Among them were ministers and educators such as the Reverend Martin Detargny of Princeton, who became Raleigh Academy's first principal. The women teachers who came south have been largely invisible in the historical record. As historian Christie Anne Farnham has put it, "These young women have not even left the legacy of a stereotype." Part of the problem is that although the records of some female students and schools have survived, the records of female teachers are relatively scarce in historical archives, especially for the years before 1830. Traces of academy founders are even more rare. Much of what we know about the female founders of incorporated academies is based on an extremely small sample of women.[9]

Based on very scant evidence, some historians have presented a dismal portrait of teaching in the antebellum South. In 1988, Elizabeth Fox-Genovese concluded, based on one primary source in which a woman expressed embarrassment that her daughter and other relatives had become teachers, that southerners viewed teaching as "not a fit occupation for a lady." Other scholars have cited Fox-Genovese in drawing the same conclusion. However, the notion that southerners generally disdained teaching appears to be largely unfounded. First, the typical white southern woman was neither a plantation mistress nor a southern belle. Although elite parents may have viewed women's work in teaching as a sign of the family's decline in prosperity, wealthy families capable of leaving their daughters a fortune or marrying them off to rich suitors represented only a small fraction of the population. Recent research has shown that year-round academy teaching in both North and South was relatively high-paying work for a woman needing to support herself; moreover, a female teacher could increase her earnings and move up in position over time, eventually becoming a department head or even the principal of a female school. Second, archival evidence has contradicted the idea that the South was less tolerant of female employment in teaching than was the North. Historian Anya Jabour has found that the letters and diaries of southern female academy students reveal a strong attachment to their teachers and a respect for the profession of teaching as "a genteel way of making a living." Similarly, Lebsock has found that entrepreneurial school keeping was a significant business for women in antebellum Petersburg, Virginia.[10]

Susan Nye Hutchison became a very successful educational entrepreneur during her last dozen years in North Carolina, presenting an important counterpoint to what we know about the more prominent women who worked in the North. Born in 1790, she was of the same generation as Mary Lyon (1787–1849), Emma Willard (1787–1870), and Catharine Beecher (1800–1878). Like these well-known women, Susan founded several schools and eventually rose to become the head of a state-chartered all-female academy, but she differed from these educators in several respects. For a start, she worked for thirty years in the South. She also had children. In contrast, Lyon and Beecher never married; Willard married but never had children. Because Beecher—and to some extent Willard and Willard's sister, Almira Hart Phelps—wrote about the importance of training young women for marriage and motherhood, some historians have concluded that antebellum female educators generally held similar beliefs about the importance of female domesticity. Yet Hutchison's journals and her schools' published courses of study never valorized domesticity over women's work outside the home. In this respect, she is particularly important as a divergent case in the context of this historiography. When added to the small chorus of other prominent women's voices, her words reveal a broader range of contemporary opinion about women's appropriate role in American society.[11]

Susan's journals are also significant in providing a grassroots perspective on the era of religious revival historians have called the Second Great Awakening. To date, broader scholarship on Jacksonian politics, evangelical religion, and the Market Revolution remains largely disconnected from the history of education. Scholars have tended to investigate the rise of religion and the development of an American middle class in the context of churches, camp revivals, meetinghouses, and families. The literature on the Second Great Awakening rarely mentions teachers and schools, even though, as historian Nancy Beadie has pointed out, schools were more universal agencies of association than were churches or reform societies. We still know relatively little about the involvement of women teachers in evangelism during the early national period.[12]

Scholars have offered different interpretations of the resurgence of popular religion during this era. Some have portrayed the Second Great Awakening as an outgrowth of the radicalism and social egalitarianism arising from the American Revolution. Others have focused on the conservative and reactionary developments that eventually led to schisms in the major Protestant denominations during the late 1830s and 1840s. Historians generally agree that after the Second Great Awakening, evangelical religion lost its liberal character. Christine Heyrman has argued that southerners rejected the more radical elements of evangelical religion as a threat to their hierarchical society and that evangelicalism in the South consequently developed a distinctive identity that sought to maintain the region's social order.[13]

This book interprets the Second Great Awakening as an educational and social movement that not only facilitated the spread of literacy and religion but also created meaningful community networks among ordinary men and women. Schools and religious organizations were highly integrated throughout this period. Bonding relationships formed in churches and schools and created strong supportive social networks within local communities; bridging relationships extended those connections to similar communities across the country. Hutchison's story reveals some of the ties that developed within and among the evangelical communities in the North and the South and illustrates the female teacher's role in developing those relationships. At the same time, her story also highlights the fragility of those bonds in the face of growing tensions over slavery.[14]

Ideological similarities and differences among evangelical Protestants in the North and South were never static but always shifting, from ecumenical collaboration to denominational competition, from shared discourse about gradual emancipation to division over the question of slaveholding. Susan wrote about these developments not only in her journals but also in published essays—one on the abolition movement and another on the impending division of the national Presbyterian Church. As a result, her writings provide an important record of the social and cultural changes unfolding in the South during this time.

SUSAN NYE HUTCHISON'S JOURNALS

Women's journals have benefits and drawbacks as primary source material. Benefits include the opportunity to gain a chronological narrative of events and an individual's reaction to social and cultural developments. Moreover, some diaries and journals have literary merit in their own right and can stand alongside published essays and novels as significant creative works. There are also some noteworthy drawbacks. Manuscripts sitting on the shelves of modern-day archives lack the historical context that once gave meaning to the writing. Journal entries sometimes appear to be random and highly subjective impressions of events with no coherent narrative structure. In addition, what seems like a private record may in fact have been written for a very specific audience.[15]

Women wrote in diaries and journals for multiple purposes and readers. Most writers whose words are preserved in historical archives hailed from wealthy families or were connected in some way to prominent men. A few were ordinary working women who jotted down brief impressions of daily events: for example, colonial midwife Martha Ballard used her diary to document the many births she attended. Students composed many of the antebellum women's diaries that have survived. Governesses and tutors and schools such as Litchfield Female Academy commonly assigned journal writing to encourage students to reflect on their learning and engage in self-examination. Thus, the audience for this kind of writing always included not only the author and possibly her friends but also her instructors. For example, Rachel Van Dyke's very literary diary entries, written from 1810 to 1811, include detailed notes in the margins from her male tutor. Scholars have explored the way some women "wrote themselves into being" in their diaries, a phrase that suggests an autobiographical motivation. Of course, many of the elite women whose diaries have been saved in historical archives had ample free time to continue to write long after they finished their education. In this regard, Susan Nye Hutchison's journals are exceptional: although she was highly educated, she did not come from a wealthy family, and during most of the years she wrote, she worked outside the home, even after having children. As might be expected, her writing resembles that of elite antebellum women but also differs in several respects.[16]

Susan Nye may have been motivated to begin a journal by a desire to create a permanent record of her new independent life. She penned her first entry the day she embarked to teach in North Carolina. Later, as she became caught up in the daily routines of work and family, her writing became less narrative and autobiographical and more pragmatic and focused on day-to-day events, more similar to Ballard's quotidian entries than to Van Dyke's introspective and literary compositions. Some of Susan's earliest entries about her travel south and the beginning of her evangelism in Raleigh reflect a detailed autobiographical narrative. These entries are lengthy and descriptive, averaging more than two hundred words per day over the first two months. But the amount of time and effort she put into writing gradually declined. By her fourth month in Raleigh, as she became caught up in the full-time work of teaching, her average journal entry fell to just under one hundred words, and over the following years, her writing became even briefer. By December 1840, the last month of her surviving journals, Susan's entries averaged thirty-one words. The shortest of those entries was a four-word reference to her third son's failing health—"Adam very bad indeed"—while the longest was a sixty-four-word entry about an angry dispute in which "many tears were shed" and her eldest son, Sylvanus, "shewed a dreadful temper."[17]

Susan's audience included her God, her descendants, and herself. The religious language in her journals connects to the religious fervor of the Second Great Awakening. One reason evangelical men and women kept journals during this period was to create a written record of their self-examination and progress toward salvation. On Sabbath days, Susan often inscribed a prayer, as she did on her twenty-fifth birthday: "I am this day 25. Oh, God of mercy, help me this holy Sabbath, to be in thy spirit. Help me to keep the day in fasting and prayer! Oh, that I may, what few days I have to live spend them more in the service of God." At other times she critically analyzed the state of her faith: "Sometimes I am led to doubt whether I have ever been converted and again I hope the Love of God is shed abroad in my heart—but alas I have lived in a backslidden state. . . . I have passed a day of more self examination than common—my heart is earthy." Similar entries recur throughout her journals.[18]

Like the diaries of other nineteenth-century men and women, Susan's journals contain descriptions of significant events embedded within the recurring details of daily routines. At times, her writing vividly brings an event to life, as when a fire swept across Augusta, Georgia, during a slave insurrection in the spring of 1829: "Today a most awful conflagration occurred in town. About half after 2 as we sat at table the cry of fire aroused us, at first a dark smoke arose but soon the blaze burst out and rising toward heaven swelled and spread till all the southeastern part of the city was one wide conflagration."[19]

She also wrote as a way of remembering events from the past, and such anniversary entries are helpful in reconstructing events when gaps occur in the journals. The first handwritten journal begins in April 1815 and continues through August 13, 1815; the remaining pages have been ripped out of the volume. Fragments of writing on the torn edges indicate that Susan continued to write after this last entry, but roughly one-third of the first journal is lost. The journal resumes eleven years later, on October 1, 1826. Susan continued to write entries more or less continuously through January 1, 1841, with smaller gaps occurring from December 19, 1834, to August 18, 1836, and from October 22, 1836, to January 1, 1837. These gaps pose a challenge, but a rough timeline of the missing portions of her life can be reconstructed from her entries noting the anniversaries of important events and from church records and newspaper announcements. For example, the excerpt below is reproduced as it appears in her journal, with the dates inserted on the left:

> February 1, 1834—Cousin Milton Barlow came here—I have not seen him since his return from the West—or rather our return from the South.
> 2—Cousin M returned to Dover.
> 4—I sent a letter to Mr. H in Savannah—the air is like April—
> 7—Again the snow is falling—
> 10—Another anniversary of my marriage. Nine years ago I was united to Mr. H with the prospect of a life of comfort—Then the blessing of the Lord fell upon our temporal goods and we had the lovely prospect of voyages and travels, visits and improvement and enjoyment—Alas how sadly blighted have been these anticipations.
> 12—Today is the anniversary of the day in which I went to reside with my husband at his boarding house—Last night I had a pleasant visit with Sister A and brother D at Mr. Swift's.[20]

Susan occasionally used her journals to communicate with future generations. After one very frustrating period with two defiant adolescent stepchildren, she wrote, "I wished to insert for the perusal of all descended from me, that unless they may deem it a special call of their God—they should not, for any temporal purpose (even though they feel disposed to perform every duty without reserve) that they should not be induced to become step-parents for I have found that it is not possible (without the direct help of the blessed spirit) to promote the good of others or to receive good ones-self."[21]

Susan's descendants not only read her journals but also took steps to preserve them. Sometime around 1938, two of her grandsons began to transcribe the twenty-six years of surviving journals. Stuart Nye Hutchison, a Presbyterian minister in Pittsburgh, created a 28-page word-for-word transcription of the first volume. Robert Stuart Hutchison of Charlotte transcribed 267 pages of extracts from the other volumes and prepared an abridged version for family members. Several decades later, these documents, together with the handwritten first volume, came to rest in the North Carolina State Archives in Raleigh and the Southern Historical Collection in the Wilson Library at the University of North Carolina at Chapel Hill.[22]

Susan's journals remain a central source for this study, but the papers and correspondence of some of her contemporaries, school records, newspapers, wills, court records, legislative reports, religious tracts, schoolbooks, and other sources provide supplementary documentation. Church records confirm the dates of her marriage and the births of her children and other events. Wherever possible, I have used additional primary sources to provide different perspectives on some of the places and phenomena about which she wrote, including the establishment of Raleigh Academy; the 1829 fires and slave insurrection in Augusta, Georgia; the practice of discipline in the evangelical churches; the rise of the common school movement in North Carolina; and the division of the Presbyterian Church. I have also tracked down her published essays.

As the investigation of one woman's life experience, this book presents a microhistory, a form of historical research that "asks large questions in small spaces." The small spaces in this case include the schools, churches, and towns where Susan Nye Hutchison worked, worshipped, and lived. Most social histories seek to uncover broad social trends and patterns by analyzing statistical data or by analyzing anecdotal data drawn from multiple archival sources. Such an approach enables social historians to develop broad generalizations but never allows for a fine-grained examination of events from a single perspective over time. Cognizant of the need for greater balance in the field, in a recent presidential address to the Social Science History Association, Andrew Abbott called on scholars to consider "the historicality of individuals" and to explore in greater detail the particular contexts that make individuals' choices appear significant over time. This book constitutes my response to Abbott's call. Although this is not a work of historical sociology, I have drawn on recent scholarship in that field to analyze and interpret some of the decisions Susan Nye Hutchison made at several critical junctures in her life.[23]

ORGANIZATION OF THE BOOK

This volume is organized into three sections based on the different life stages reflected in Susan's journals. The first section explores her early teaching career as a single woman in the context of the Second Great Awakening. Chapter 1 investigates some of the socioeconomic factors that drew her to teaching and the development of new social networks that facilitated the migration of young unmarried women across vast geographic distances. Chapter 2 explores Susan's teaching and ministry in Raleigh and the evolution of the Raleigh Academy curriculum. Susan's encounters with slavery and the inherent difficulty of reconciling Christian moral philosophy with the practice of continued slaveholding are the subject of chapter 3.

After moving to Augusta, Georgia, in 1823 and conducting her own school for a year, Susan married Adam Hutchison. Chapter 4 explores her marriage and return to teaching as a married woman. Chapter 5 analyzes her separation from her husband. These chapters illuminate the way marriage changed a woman's legal and social status and reveal the ongoing tension between gendered social mores and the reality of lived experience. Both chapters explore the way the Presbyterian Church community in Augusta regarded men and women's behavior in private and public spaces, allowing individuals a great deal of latitude in the privacy of the home but monitoring and occasionally intervening in behavior that unfolded in public.

A year after the Hutchisons' separation, Adam died, leaving Susan to support four young sons and a stepdaughter. As a widow, her legal and social status changed: she was now the head of her own household, with legal custody of her children and full control of her own financial affairs. Chapter 6 reconstructs her evolution from financially strapped New York schoolteacher to successful North Carolina school founder. Like many women educators of her era, as she gained a strong regional reputation, she became engaged with the politically charged issues of antislavery and the public school movement. Chapter 7 analyzes her published writing on slavery and the division of the Presbyterian Church and explores her risky decision to secretly teach slaves to read, in violation of North Carolina law. The book concludes by situating her experience in a larger context, exploring some of the educational legacies of the Second Great Awakening and identifying some of the opportunities and constraints female educators of the time encountered.

SUSAN NYE HUTCHISON's journey from New York to North Carolina and Georgia leads to some unusual manifestations of antebellum history. After all, few white women went out into southern streets to publicly pray with free blacks and slaves. Of the women who worked for a living—around 29 percent of native-born southern whites and 33 percent of northeastern whites by 1860—very few established their own incorporated academies.[24] Susan appears to have been one of the first women in the country to publish on slavery and abolition in the 1830s, and she was the first woman in North Carolina to submit a petition to the State Assembly on female education. In such ways her life is exceptional, yet in many respects her experience also reflects larger social and economic developments that offered free antebellum women new opportunities hedged by traditional social constraints.

Like many other young northern women born after the American Revolution, Susan Nye left her parents' farm to earn an independent living. She composed her first journal entry the day she left home, and this is where her story begins—in a wagon rumbling through the predawn darkness along a westward road to the Hudson River.

CHAPTER 1

From New York to North Carolina

Amenia, April 22, 1815

After a most affecting parting from my beloved brothers, sisters and friends, I kissed my little sleeping babes and before the sun shone upon my dear native hills bade them farewell, perhaps forever! The morning was beautifully pleasant, and my heart felt I know not how as I rode through a country endeared by ten thousand scenes of tenderest recollection. I may never see them again, said I, and my mother and father looked sad; I looked to heaven and was cheerful. As we reached Dover Plain, Brother Ebenezer's house was still closed. We roused them and entering, kindled a fire and drew round it. Breakfast was soon over for who bidding friends so dear adieu could feel a wish to lengthen the sad repast—Oh, my brother, my sister, my beautiful, my lovely little ones, we must be separated and shall we meet again? Called at Mr. Ketchem's, bade them adieu. Returning to Ebenezer's, gave and received the parting kiss and drove away. Oh a parting scene.

Before sunrise on April 22, 1815, twenty-four-year-old Susan Nye left her family's farm in rural New York. She and her parents traveled by wagon, following the road from South Amenia to Poughkeepsie, where Susan planned to board a ship and travel down the Hudson River to New York City. Near the village of Dover Plain, they stopped to say farewell to family and friends. Susan was aware she might never return home. She was heading south to teach in Raleigh, North Carolina.[1]

Later that day, she boarded the sloop that would carry her downriver to New York City. Travel by sea was the only viable option for anyone wishing to go from New York to North Carolina. Railroad lines did not yet exist. South of the new capital city of Washington, D.C., everyone went by horseback, because the journey by stagecoach was impossible. As Thomas Jefferson noted in 1801, "Of eight rivers between [Monticello] and Washington, five have neither bridges nor boats." The voyage to Raleigh would take about three weeks.[2]

That evening, Susan composed the first entry in her journal. Like many diarists during this period, she frequently alternated descriptive passages with religious phrases. Her narrative intersperses expressions of sorrow and anxiety about leaving home with religious sentiments designed to provide some spiritual comfort. After leaving Poughkeepsie by sloop, she wrote, "From the bosom of a tranquil home beneath the protection of the best of parents, I was thrown upon the watery element consigned to the care of strangers; but heaven was propitious." She wrote alone in her cabin while the other female passengers gathered for a game of cards or retired to sleep, and her first entry conveys a sense of sadness and unease at leaving friends and family behind: "The night was drizzly and dark. A heavy wind bore us rapidly from my peaceful home."[3]

Why would a young, single woman leave her home and undertake such a long voyage on her own? Family genealogical records indicate that Susan's female ancestors had traveled in the company of male relatives. For centuries, free unmarried women had leveraged traditional kinship relations to support their relocation from one geographic region to another. Some migrated great distances with their families or received shelter from relatives along the way; others arrived at their destinations to join established guardians who could help them start new lives. Historians have traditionally portrayed colonial women—whether in transit or rooted in place—as living a more enclosed and protected existence than did their male counterparts. The scant evidence from later entries in Susan's journal suggests that her mother fit this picture. Born in 1752, Sylvania Barlow Nye spent her entire life in Amenia. As a married woman, she raised children, managed the home, helped with the livestock and garden, socialized with neighboring women, and occasionally bartered homespun articles and farm products in town for necessities such as sugar or medicine. But unlike her mother, Susan did not remain at home within the domestic circle, and unlike her grandmother, she did not migrate under the protection of a male relative. Like scores of other young single women who headed south in the early national period, Susan Nye chose a different path.

ALMOST EVERYONE IN AMENIA knew the Nye family. Susan's father, Sylvanus (1753–1841), had served as a private in the county militia during the American Revolution. He married Sylvania Barlow (1752–1838), and after the war they settled on a farm near Sylvania's relatives in Amenia. The Barlows were an established farming family, having migrated from Massachusetts in the mid-eighteenth century. According to family lore, Sylvania's father, Moses, and his brother had worked as sailors in Sandwich, a town on Cape Cod. One day during an immense storm at sea, they vowed that

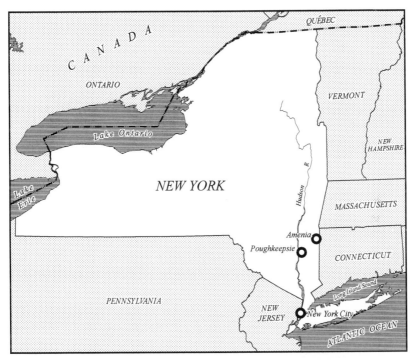

Map of New York State and surrounding locations. Adapted by Emma Tolley from a New York State outline map available from the Department of the Interior at www.nationalatlas.gov.

if they returned home safely, they would "cast their future fortune on the land." Having survived the tempest, they packed up their families in 1756 and sailed from Plymouth Harbor to New York and up the Hudson River to Poughkeepsie. From there they traveled overland by wagon to Amenia, where they took up farming. When Sylvania Barlow married Sylvanus Nye in 1774, arable land was still available in the area. They bought a place about six miles south of town and settled down to raise sheep and cattle; grow apples, wheat, and flax; and produce a family of eight children. Born on August 13, 1790, Susan was the seventh.[4]

Years later, when she lived for a time on the family farm with her children and brother, Susan wrote about the daily struggle to wrest a living from the land, but during the first decades of her parents' marriage, the farm was very profitable. The rolling land around Amenia was fertile. Early settlers cleared the forest, planted wheat, and built mills on nearby streams. The wars in Europe and the need for colonial military provisions created a strong demand for wheat and flour. Farmers loaded up their ox-drawn carts to haul wool, produce, and wheat products to the Poughkeepsie wharves, where sloops and schooners shipped provisions north and south on the Hudson River. Cattle drives down the valley brought beef to both military forces and city dwellers. One travel narrative described the Amenia Valley as "finely cultivated, fertile, and settled by a collection of thrifty farmers." In 1813, a correspondent for the *Gazetteer of the State of New York* claimed, "The farmers of Amenia possess more of agricultural opulence than any other town in Dutchess County."[5]

Susan Nye grew up during a period when a quiet revolution in female education was unfolding in the United States. Colonial sermons had emphasized the importance of teaching both men and women to read the Bible to increase their knowledge of God and chances of salvation, but colonists believed that the schooling of females was essentially a private matter, a concern of church and family rather than the state. Daughters generally learned at home from a family member, tutor, or governess. In Massachusetts, according to Horace Mann, "The first improvement in this respect consisted in smuggling in the girls, perhaps for an hour a day, after the boys had recited their lessons and gone home." By the mid-eighteenth century, increasing numbers of towns began to open "women's schools," employing female teachers to teach girls and young boys. Some parents arranged for their daughters to enroll in the all-male town schools, where they received instruction from the master at odd hours, before the boys arrived or after they left. Here and there in New York and elsewhere, private schools originally serving boys began to offer instruction beyond the elementary level to girls in separate departments. Educational opportunities for girls gradually expanded in town after town.[6]

When Susan and her younger sister, Amanda (1795–1876), were young, local district common schools in the area provided elementary instruction, and private schools and academies in some of the larger, more established towns offered subjects at higher levels. In most areas of the Northeast, a combination of local taxes and tuition, coupled in some areas with small state subsidies, provided the financial basis for "public" common schools. By the early nineteenth century, schools advertised their terms and courses of study in local newspapers, describing themselves variously as academies, seminaries, day schools, boarding schools, or ladies' select schools. Academies were legally incorporated and operated under the supervision of a board of trustees. Before colleges opened their doors to females in the mid-nineteenth century, many academies offered the highest level of education available for women.[7]

Families living in small northeastern towns and on farms often provided the financial support and motivation for the schooling of girls. Susan's father was a landowner, but he was not a wealthy man; he had no money to leave his children when he died. Given what is known of the Nyes, it is reasonable to assume they had pragmatic reasons for sending their daughters to school. During uncertain economic times, it was in the family's best interests to help unmarried daughters become self-supporting.[8]

With some study at an academy, a young woman could gain the skills to support herself in a variety of ways: she could keep the books for a business, work as a companion to an older woman, or teach school. Students often enrolled sporadically, alternating periods of attendance with work or independent study at home. A girl might study privately at home before enrolling for several terms, leave for a period to teach in a district school, and return when she had enough money for additional schooling. New Hampshire preacher Nancy Towle (1796–1876), just six years younger than Susan, wrote in her memoirs that "at the age of sixteen, seventeen, and twenty-one, I attended the academy in Hampton," and "at the age of eighteen, I engaged with much satisfaction in the laudable employment of schoolkeeping." Susan and Amanda Nye may have studied under similar conditions.[9]

Susan's journal never states where she obtained her education, but she probably attended Litchfield Female Academy in Connecticut. The school was only thirty miles from the Nye farm, and the stagecoach from Poughkeepsie to Litchfield went directly through Amenia and regularly stopped for passengers. In addition, the school had a very strong academic reputation and was one of the earliest and best-known institutions to provide an advanced education to young women. Sarah Pierce (1767–1852) established the school in 1792, and it ultimately drew students from at least sixteen states plus Canada, Ireland, and the West Indies. Although records are scanty, more than forty alumnae are known to have gone on to teach, and they migrated to at least fourteen states. Fifteen of these women opened their own schools, including most famously Catharine Beecher, who founded Hartford Female Seminary with her sister Mary in 1823. In fact, had Susan Nye not studied at a prestigious school such as Litchfield, she probably would not have received an offer of employment from Raleigh Academy. By 1814, the North Carolina school had such a strong reputation that it drew students from neighboring states, and it would not likely have hired a teacher who lacked credentials from a well-regarded higher school. Moreover, Susan had personal connections with students

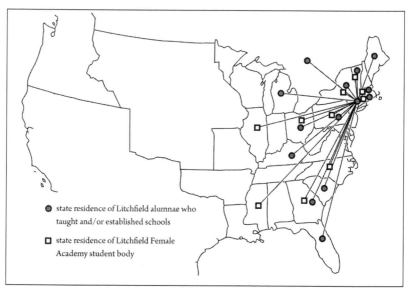

Geographical distribution of the student body and alumnae of Litchfield Female Academy, 1792–1833. Data derived from Brickley, "Sarah Pierce's Litchfield Female Academy," 60, 556. Map adapted by Emma Tolley from a U.S. outline map available from the Department of the Interior at www.nationalatlas.gov.

at Litchfield. At least twenty-four young women from Amenia attended Litchfield between 1793 and 1829, and among them was Amanda Nye, who was a resident student during the summer of 1816. Susan's good friend Arabella Bosworth was also an alumna.[10]

In addition to the personal connection through her sister and friend, Susan's religious sensibilities suggest an association with the school. At some point before she headed south to teach, she had experienced a religious conversion. Sarah Pierce would have described her as a "professing" or "awakened" Christian. In January 1815, she was the only member of her family to sign the Confession of Faith of Amenia's Presbyterian Church, and in a journal entry she wrote eighteen years later, she still worried that members of her father's family remained unconverted. Since the evidence suggests she did not find religion through her family, and since it appears she became a member of the church just before leaving New York, her "awakening" may well have occurred at school.[11]

Litchfield Academy encouraged religious revival among its pupils. The aim of religious education at Litchfield was the individual conversion of each student. An evangelical Congregationalist, Pierce believed that conversion would lead women to fulfill their God-given roles as social reformers. In parallel with the work of a minister, women could influence others "to support the Gospel, not only in their own city and country, but in evangelizing the heathen." The staff at the academy lectured students on the importance of "doing good," assigned readings in the lives of religious women, instructed students to reflect on their spiritual development through journal writing, and actively involved students in community service through the school's Benevolent Association. Like the female students at Litchfield, Susan Nye used her journal to engage in spiritual reflection and self-examination.[12]

The evangelism at Litchfield reflected the spirit of the age in which Susan grew up. After the Revolutionary War, some politicians and European observers expected Americans to embrace the secular radicalism of men such as Thomas Paine and abandon religion, and for a brief period, such developments seemed likely. The College of New Jersey (now Princeton University), which trained young Presbyterian men for the ministry, had shut down for three years during the fighting, and in 1782, rumors circulated that only two of its students professed themselves Christians. Yale College was in a similar condition. As Presbyterian minister Lyman Beecher later recalled, by 1795 the college church was "almost extinct," and the young men of the class "called each other Voltaire, Rousseau, D'Alembert, etc." During these years, Benjamin Franklin, Benjamin Rush, Judith Sargent Murray, and other writers drew on the ideas of Enlightenment philosophers to argue that educating girls was not only a practical and enlightened choice but also a political duty. Historian Linda K. Kerber has shown that both male and female authors promoted an ideology of "republican motherhood": the belief that females could assist the new republic by influencing sons and husbands to be public-spirited citizens. To observers such as Beecher, religion everywhere appeared to be in a state of decline. Nevertheless, although the war disrupted religion by destroying church buildings, scattering congregations, and politicizing everyday discourse, religious feeling endured. As historian Gordon S. Wood has noted, many of the country's radical founding fathers were astonished to discover that the democratic revolution not only presaged the rise of ordinary people but also foreshadowed the resurgence of popular Christianity in American society.[13]

Historians have called this era of religious resurgence the Second Great Awakening (1795–1837). Concerned that the new nation had lost its faith and moral compass, Protestant preachers began to travel from town to town to revive religion among the people. Starting in the mid-1790s,

Presbyterians, Methodists, and Baptists preached in the backwoods country in Kentucky and Tennessee before multitudes who traveled great distances to hear them. Rumors circulated that as many as twenty thousand people—an enormous number in an age when few cities had populations above five thousand—came to listen and pray at these revivals, camping out in the fields and woods.[14]

Although many scholars have emphasized the role of the clergy in stirring up religious fervor during this period, in some areas, like-minded lay members banded together in grassroots efforts to rebuild and strengthen their churches. During the Revolutionary War Susan Nye's little Congregational church in Amenia "let down their watch, neglected their discipline and ordinances and lay in broken Circumstances." For a decade, the congregation struggled to function without a regular minister. In 1795, members asked a local Baptist pastor to help with services and reached out to the Methodists as well. The following year, a local Congregational church rejected the Amenia church's request for affiliation because it had apparently begun following "the Methodist way." In 1797, representatives contacted the local presbytery, formally reorganized as the Amenia Presbyterian Church, and obtained a Presbyterian minister. By 1808, the church was "filled with joy at the revival of the work of God among them." On January 26, 1815, Susan Nye added her signature to those of fourteen other members, signing a "Confession of Faith as revised and agreed to by the church."[15]

Religious ideology melded with Enlightenment ideas about the higher education of females. Some educators argued that women could play an important role in the new republic by promoting religion and teaching the next generation to be useful members of a democratic society. As Pierce explained to her students at Litchfield, "A free government like ours can only be supported by the virtue of its citizens. . . . It is indispensable to the existence of a republic to be moral and religious."[16]

Religious revivals were a common phenomenon in schools during this era, with intense feeling and enthusiasm arising from a revival in town at times enveloping students. Student culture often played an important role. As historian Catherine E. Kelly has pointed out, young women in New England schools with evangelical affiliations sometimes pushed each other toward conversion. Missionary Harriet Atwood Newell later recalled that in 1806, when she was thirteen, "I was sent by my parents to the academy at Bradford. A revival of religion commenced in the neighborhood, which in a short time spread into the school. A large number of the young ladies were anxiously inquiring, what they should do to inherit eternal life." Bradford Academy, Litchfield Female Academy, and other such institutions were important sites of peer association, acculturation, and identity formation, bringing together young women from different regions of the country, offering intimate contact and the opportunity to establish what would become long-standing friendships with others of similar backgrounds. A shared experience of religious revival among the young women at school strengthened these bonds even further by establishing a common evangelical faith and purpose among northerners and southerners and among young women from different Protestant denominations. The same year that Susan Nye headed south to teach, Litchfield Academy student Abigail Bradley wrote to her cousin, "We trust that more than half the school have been made the subjects of unerring grace."[17]

The evangelical impulse at Litchfield had ideological connections with a religious revival that occurred at Yale when Timothy Dwight (1752–1817) was the school's president. Sarah Pierce knew Dwight personally and admired him greatly, and the admiration must have been mutual, since Dwight enrolled his daughter at Litchfield in 1797. A Congregational minister and grandson of the great eighteenth-century theologian Jonathan Edwards, Dwight sought to counter the deism and secularism of French Enlightenment thinkers and their American counterparts such as Paine and Jefferson. A brilliant and charismatic speaker, he preached to the Yale students each Sunday and initiated campus debates in which he defended orthodox religion. A revival of religion began on the campus in 1802, and many students converted. Revivals of religion then rippled outward through New England. Lyman Beecher, a former student of Dwight's at Yale, brought religious revival to Litchfield in 1810, when he moved there with his family. His daughters, Catharine, Mary, and Harriet, enrolled at Litchfield Female Academy, where he taught a weekly religion course and conducted student prayer groups over a fourteen-year period.[18]

The ideas embedded in Dwight's preaching had long-lasting influences on Susan Nye's views about the importance of community service. Dwight emphasized the Christian's responsibility to take action in the world and improve the lot of others through benevolence and education. In 1810, he articulated a blueprint for action in a sermon based on Psalm 41:1: "Blessed is he that considereth the poor." He urged young women to help build the new nation through teaching and benevolent work. He described the work of the female teachers as "the sublime employment." Through teaching, he proclaimed, "the female character assumes its fairest, highest, richest ornaments; and is arrayed with a luster, and loveliness, which leaves beauty, graceful manners, and fine accomplishment, out of sight, and out of remembrance." He stressed the importance of education not only for poor whites but also for free blacks. Having enacted policies of gradual emancipation, northerners were duty-bound to offer free blacks the education and assistance they needed to improve their lives and gain salvation: "To give them liberty, and stop here, is to entail upon them a curse. We are bound to give them, also, knowledge, industry, economy, good habits, moral and religious instruction, and all the means of eternal life." Susan's journals indicate that when she headed south to teach, she sought to conform her actions to these precepts.[19]

THE SECOND GREAT AWAKENING revived the notion of the calling, a task set by God. In contrast to Catholic monasticism, which entailed a renunciation of the world, Protestants regarded the fulfillment of one's duty in worldly affairs as the highest form of moral activity. The diaries and correspondence of Protestant men and women during this era are liberally sprinkled with the terms "improvement" and "usefulness." "Awakened" individuals sought both internal improvement in the sense of heightened spirituality and external improvement as reflected in ministry, benevolent work, and social reform. After the American Revolution, Americans faced the enormous task of building a new country. In many communities, revivals of religion led Americans to connect the notion of the calling with the task of nation building.[20]

Because both women and men could be called to usefulness, the Second Great Awakening gradually expanded American views of women's proper social role. Many preachers encouraged women's involvement in teaching and community service. As Congregational minister Joseph Emerson explained in 1822, a woman's influence "is not confined to her own dwelling." While some women might be called to be wives and mothers, others might be called to be teachers, "members of the church, of the civil community, and of the human family." Such women could serve God and society by working for "pious and benevolent societies that are engaged for the improvement of the world." As these ideas took root, growing numbers of single and married women became involved in social reform, from education to temperance and antislavery.[21]

Women also became more involved in lay ministry. Quakers had acknowledged women's role in ministry since the mid-seventeenth century, but few other Protestant denominations shared this perspective. During the eighteenth century, Presbyterian clergymen believed that women could interact freely with members of their households and church communities, teach their children, and collect alms but strictly forbade them from leading prayer in circles outside their homes. Most colonists expected women to pursue their political, religious, and social interests within the confines of household and family. But social mores changed during the early decades of the Second Great Awakening. When two new female religious societies met to pray together at an 1817 religious revival in Bridgeton, New Jersey, Presbyterian minister Jonathan Freeman wrote approvingly, "It gives great satisfaction to be able to say of professing Christians ... 'behold they pray.'"[22]

Some women of Susan's generation, both whites and free blacks, went further and began to preach at around the same time that Susan taught in Raleigh. Historian Catherine A. Brekus has identified more than one hundred women preachers and exhorters between 1740 and 1845. The Methodist Church was particularly important in facilitating women's preaching, because unlike the Presbyterians, the Methodists did not require their preachers to have formal seminary training. Jarena Lee, a free black woman born in Cape May, New Jersey, in 1783, converted at age twenty-one; four years later, she felt a calling to preach the Gospel. After repeated denials, the African Methodist Episcopal Church granted her request to preach just after 1818. Over the next several decades, she preached to racially mixed audiences in the Northeast, the Mid-Atlantic, and Ohio. Zilpha Elaw, born in Philadelphia around 1790 to a free black family, converted to Methodism and joined a Methodist society in 1808. At an 1817 camp meeting, she experienced an awakening, and two years later she began preaching independently, without financial support, traveling in both free and slave states before moving to England. During an 1814 revival in the Hudson River Valley, Nancy Cram converted Abigail Roberts, who went on to establish several congregations in New England. New Hampshire's Nancy Towle left her home to take up the life of an itinerant preacher in 1821. She took a teaching position to disguise her true intentions from her family and began to preach as an independent. She eventually left teaching and took up the full-time life of an itinerant, traveling from town to town throughout New England, preaching in Baptist and Methodist meetinghouses, boardinghouses, common schoolrooms, and academies.[23]

Not everyone welcomed the idea of women praying or preaching outside the home. Female prayer meetings were still controversial when the Presbyterian Charles Finney conducted revivals in New York in the 1830s. "Within the last few years," wrote Finney in 1835, "female prayer meetings have been extensively opposed in this state. . . . Serious apprehensions were entertained for the safety of Zion, if women should be allowed to get together to pray. And even now, they are not tolerated in some churches." Several historians have argued for the existence of a backlash against women's itinerant preaching. Dee Andrews has shown that as Methodist societies grew during the early decades of the nineteenth century and began to focus on formal incorporation and church building, they came to reflect the gendered power relations of society at large and barred women from formal positions of authority. According to Susan Juster, after the revolution, as the New England Baptists went from a marginal group to a mainstream religious denomination concerned with legitimacy, they abandoned radical egalitarianism and embraced male authority. Other scholars have identified a parallel retrenchment against women's political involvement during the decades following the American Revolution.[24]

Nevertheless, although the names of most women preachers faded into obscurity after the Civil War, some of them published autobiographies that sold to a substantial readership throughout the antebellum era, motivating subsequent generations of young women to undertake missionary work in the South, in the West, and abroad. Although the Methodist and Baptist churches remained patriarchal in structure throughout the antebellum period, the experiences of these early women preachers and the female missionaries who followed them continued to inspire a generation of young readers during later decades.[25]

A young Presbyterian woman such as Susan Nye may have been prohibited from becoming a minister, but she could still take up a life of lay ministry through teaching. During this era, church and state were not separate in common schools and academies; in many ways, the instruction in schools complemented the sermons in churches. The schoolroom itself bore a strong physical resemblance to a church, with the teacher's lectern, like a pulpit, standing at the front of the room and facing orderly rows of wooden benches. As a teacher, Susan could urge her students toward conversion and teach them about the importance of philanthropy and social reform. She could model benevolence by ministering to the poor and unconverted in the local community. For Susan and other women, the work of teaching offered a socially acceptable way into lay ministry. Many early women preachers, including Elaw and Towle, had experience as teachers. Others, like Harriet Atwood Newell and Ann Hasseltine Judson, received their inspiration while they were academy students.

By the mid-1830s, some reformers began to draw parallels between the work of male ministers and that of female teachers. Litchfield alumna Catharine Beecher strongly encouraged women to travel from home and teach on the frontier. The purpose of education, claimed Beecher in her 1835 *Essay on the Education of Female Teachers*, was to promote "a system of right moral and religious education." She argued that as more and more women learned "to understand and value their influence in society, and their peculiar duties," they would "cease to feel that they are educated just to enjoy themselves in future life, and realize the obligations imposed by Heaven to live to do good." In 1836, years after Ipswich Seminary in Massachusetts first began sending graduates out west to teach, Zilpah Grant claimed that female teachers were doing as much to promote the cause of religion and education as most ministers. By midcentury, such women may have remained barred from the pulpit, but they had gained the majority in the nation's common-school classrooms.[26]

The migration of women across the country to teach or engage in missionary work was supported by the rise of new social networks that facilitated the spread of people and ideas. The close bonds that developed within churches and schools created supportive social networks within local communities. Traveling preachers, migratory teachers, and students who attended schools from different regions extended those connections across the United States. The evangelical churches were particularly skilled at forging extensive and far-flung bridging relationships through collaboration with other denominations. A common faith in the Bible, individual conversion, and evangelism allowed Protestant Christians from a fairly wide range of denominations to share resources with each other. As a result, evangelical teachers or ministers traveling far from home could expect to encounter a warm welcome from members of different denominations.[27]

Supported by these sorts of networks, men and women traveled to all regions of the country to convert and educate the population. When he visited the United States in 1831, French political thinker Alexis de Tocqueville concluded that this evangelistic fervor was inextricably linked to patriotism. "I have known of societies formed by the Americans to send out ministers of the gospel into the new western states, to found schools and churches there, lest religion should be suffered to die away in those remote settlements, and the rising states be less fitted to enjoy free institutions than the people from which they emanated," he wrote. He was surprised to meet northerners who had left the comfort of their homes to cross mountain ranges, weather dangerous seas, and traverse deserts to minister to settlements on the frontier: "I met with wealthy New Englanders who abandoned the country in which they were born, in order to lay the foundations of Christianity and of freedom on the banks of the Missouri or in the prairies of Illinois. Thus religious zeal is perpetually stimulated in the United States by the duties of patriotism."[28]

SUSAN HAD RELIGIOUS zeal aplenty, but other factors probably played into her decision to migrate south. She was not the only young adult to leave rural New York during this era. Despite Amenia's relative prosperity, as the Nye children grew up, they moved away from home. A lack of space was one factor. The colonial farmhouses around Amenia were sturdy two-story clapboard structures, not large by today's standards and certainly not roomy enough to comfortably accommodate a family of ten adults. As Susan noted years later when visiting her parents and brother with a teenager and four young children, "We are so crowded and cooped up at home that I find no quiet resting place." The farm families of the Northeast were nuclear in character rather than extended. Unmarried adults normally moved out from under the parental roof, although single women may have remained at home somewhat longer. In the Nye family, only Meletiah, an unmarried son, remained continually at home to help his aging parents.[29]

The pull of economic opportunity also drew young people away. As historians have demonstrated for other areas of rural New York, after the American Revolution, most of the available farming land around Amenia had already been claimed, but the expansion of industry created other forms of employment for young people who wished to stay in the area. After 1793, American ports became centers of trade because of conflicts in Europe, and the freight and earnings of American ships quadrupled. American manufacturing flourished in a protected market after the Embargo of 1807, and when the War of 1812 broke out between the United States and England, American producers suddenly faced a domestic market free of European and British competitors. Textile manufacturers in the Northeast took advantage of their new monopoly, and as the price of cloth nearly doubled during the war, they rapidly formed joint stock companies, built new equipment, expanded their businesses, and hired more workers.[30]

After 1815, the profitability of such enterprises decreased. The Northeast's fledgling economy went from boom to bust, ushering in a period of economic depression in the region that persisted until 1822. The conclusion of the War of 1812 brought European businesses back to American markets. With intense competition from abroad, many American manufacturers shut down some of their factories; others went bankrupt. Large numbers of workers found themselves unemployed. The depression further pressured young people to relieve the financial burden on their parents by earning an independent living. In Dutchess County, as small businesses and manufacturing centers closed their doors, young people had to travel farther from home to find wage work. From 1800 to 1840, Amenia's population declined 27 percent, from 2,978 to 2,179, and one of those who emigrated was Susan Nye.[31]

In late 1814, when Susan learned of an opening in Raleigh Academy's Female Department, opportunities for employment and advancement in academies near Amenia may already have become somewhat scarce. She probably heard of the position from Arabella Bosworth, who had taught in Raleigh Academy for two years. The secretary of the academy's board of trustees described Arabella as "well educated and a perfect mistress of the polite and fashionable accomplishments of Drawing and every kind of ornamental Needle-work." Academy teachers in the early national period were a peripatetic lot. They moved from one school to another in search of positions of greater responsibility or better salaries and standards of living or to enjoy the adventure of life in a different region. Possibly for similar reasons, Arabella resigned her Raleigh position in the fall of 1814 and moved on to teach in Fayetteville. News of the Raleigh Academy opening appeared in the press. An advertisement in the *Raleigh Register* described the position as "a comfortable and permanent situation" for "a Lady well qualified" to teach both the "ornamental" and English branches in the academy's Female Department.[32]

Women teachers were a minority in North Carolina academies when Susan headed south, but their numbers were growing. As table 1 shows, 13 percent of the teachers working in the state from 1800 to 1810 were women, a proportion that rose to 25 percent the following decade and to 38 percent in the 1830s. The expansion of female and coeducational schools in the South created a demand not only for southern female teachers but also for qualified teachers from the North. Between 1800 and 1840, a growing number of North Carolina academies served female students, either on their own or with male students; thereafter, at least half of such schools enrolled females. Women teachers were essential to the success of coeducational schools. Without a respectable woman to take charge of the "Female Department," academies could not attract female students. Female teachers also earned less than male teachers, a fact that made them quite appealing to an academy interested in hiring teachers to superintend the primary departments that enrolled both boys and girls.[33]

TABLE 1. School and Academy Teachers in North Carolina Newspapers and Other Documentary Sources, by Gender and Region of Origin, 1800–1840 (n = 486)

Decade	Total Male	Total Female	Northern Male	Southern Male	Northern Female	Southern Female
1800–1810	69	10	5	64	1	9
(n = 79)	(87%)	(13%)	(7%)	(93%)	(10%)	(90%)
1811–1820	115	38	9	106	6	32
(n = 153)	(75%)	(25%)	(8%)	(92%)	(16%)	(84%)
1821–1830	139	49	13	126	7	42
(n = 188)	(74%)	(26%)	(9%)	(91%)	(14%)	(86%)
1831–1840	102	63	1	101	12	51
(n = 165)	(62%)	(38%)	(>1%)	(99%)	(19%)	(81%)

Note: Some teachers may be represented more than once if they taught during multiple decades.

Sources: *Raleigh Register*, 1800–1840; Coon, *North Carolina Schools and Academies*; Gadski, *History*, 166–68; Ernest Haywood Papers, Files 143–44, Box 3, SHC; Mordecai Family Papers, Files 1–11, Box 1; File 113, Box 8; and File 15, Box 2, SHC; John Steele Papers, Files 67–69, Box 4, SHC.

MOTIVATED BY A SENSE of missionary zeal and economic opportunity, Susan decided to leave her parents' farm and head south after receiving Raleigh Academy's offer of employment. On April 22, she and her parents traveled to Poughkeepsie, where they "called at the Friends' boarding school and obtained a letter of introduction for a family in New York" so that Susan would have a place to stay while waiting for her ship to dock. Poughkeepsie's Nine Partners Boarding School was a Quaker academy established in 1796 whose faculty at the time of the Nyes' visit included Lucretia Mott (1793–1880), though Susan did not mention seeing the famous Quaker evangelist, abolitionist, and women's rights advocate. At the school, Susan "was received with the cordial smile of pleasure," she wrote, "and left them with regret." The Nyes next visited several friends in town to say farewell and dined with Arabella Bosworth's mother. Mrs. Bosworth had planned to travel south to visit her extended family, and Susan had hoped that they would sail together, but she "learned with surprise [that Mrs. Bosworth] was not going to Carolina."[34]

Susan said farewell to her parents, then boarded alone the sloop for New York City. On the morning of April 23, she awoke "safely moored in New York after a passage of 9 hours" and unable to shake off feelings of sadness. "I felt my lonely situation and walking on deck admidst a forest of masts the novel spectacle had scarce a charm for me." During her five nights in

New York City, Susan boarded with the family of a well-known Quaker philanthropist and abolitionist, John Murray. She was kindly received and went with the family to a "Friends meeting" where she "sat for a long time silent but within 2 hours heard 2 discourses[,] one by Mr. M. well calculated to arouse the mind and soften the heart." Several days later, she was delighted to meet her cousin, Jesse Barlow, a soldier stationed at the West Battery Fort. He took her to see the park and streets around City Hall, and they walked along the Battery "amidst grass plots and gravel walks planted or bordered with poplars."[35]

While in the city, she alternated between feelings of astonishment at the streets, buildings, and parks and regret about leaving home. "Manufactures and merchandize of every description took my attention," she wrote. "I gazed upon the elegant buildings and the superb churches with delight but when I passed the park and viewed the new city hall I was half lost in astonishment. Its magnificence exceeds my powers of description and I leave it for better pens than mine to tell its elegance." Yet at times, homesickness overwhelmed her: "I believe I was never more unhappy than I have been since my residence in New York; all the elegance, the taste, the splendor I witness, are no more to me than the pebbles of the stream or the trees of the forest when I think of the home I left or the friends I have forsaken. I walk till I am fatigued and return to my tasteless meals. I think of Amenia and sleep flies!"[36]

On April 28 she resolutely "put on [her] hat and went on board the Clinton, an old sloop bound for Willmington," North Carolina. She was very pleased to discover that Mrs. Bosworth and her daughter, Susan, had changed their plans again and would be traveling to Raleigh. Jesse Barlow came to see her off. "Twas hard to resign my last friend," Susan wrote, and she wept as the ship pulled away from shore. "I wrapped myself in my cloak, and seated on the deck viewed the rolling billows destined to convey me far from my native home, or bury me in their bosom." The sun disappeared behind a mass of dark clouds, and the wind rose. "A great many vessels were near us," she wrote, "all anxiously endeavouring to exceed each other in capacity of sailing—passing over the shoals by the buoys in safety we came to anchor in a cove off Sandy Hook; the sky was completely overcast, the sea was driven into mountains by a severe gale, and the captain and mate deemed it best to come to anchor."[37]

The ship encountered rough seas the following day. Susan and the Bosworths suffered from the "dreadful tossing of the feeble bark as it mounted toward the sky, and again plunged to the bottom." She confessed,

"No one but those who by experience know the distressing sensation of seasickness, can tell how languidly I raised my aching head from my rocking couch and attempted to leave my berth. Weakness and giddiness threw me back, but at length I succeeded and crawling to the window saw the dark blue waves rolling before me. Fits of puking succeeded each other, my stomach, my head! Ah, what distress!" They sailed into sunlight and calm waters the next morning. Susan went up on deck and watched the storm petrels "as they seemed to dance upon the tossing waves, the gulls as they dropped out of sight."[38]

Two days later, the ship approached Cape Hatteras, the most dangerous place on the southern coast. Mariners called it the Graveyard of the Atlantic. An 1806 congressional report on shipwrecks in the area concluded that "hardly a season passes that does not afford the melancholy spectacle of stranded ships, and a great destruction of property is sure to follow; and it is fortunate, indeed, if the friendless mariner escapes with his life."[39]

On May 2, the ship ran into a tempest near the cape. The wind began to rise at six that evening, and it soon reached gale force, nearly sinking the ship. Susan's 873-word entry describing the ordeal is the longest in her entire journal and captures the fear and panic on board:

> The wind had risen to a tremendous hurricane; our feeble bark was no more before its violence than a feather against the tide. My cabin window was carried into the sea, the waves dashed against the ship, and I expected momentarily to be deluged in brine. The candle in the main cabin was extinguished by the wind, and we were involved in pitchy darkness save when the vivid lightning's broad blue flash rolled through our dreary apartment. The tinder refused to kindle, and our situation beggared description. The Captain came down to calculate his reckoning and ordered the cabin boy to renew his efforts for a light, but it was vain. And now while destruction stood facing us full in sight, Cape H's dangerous, deathful shoals on one side, the Gulf stream on the other, in an old, weak and crazy vessel without even a single inch of sail, at the mercy of a terrible hurricane, the Captain could so far forget himself as to call down the heaviest curses on his wretched cabin boy. Oh who would be a cabin boy![40]

The crew scrambled on deck to keep the vessel from foundering. Terrified, a female passenger rushed to Susan's room shrieking that the ship would soon capsize and they would all drown at sea. Susan wrote, "I viewed death as certain or almost certain; the light of morning would probably never break upon me till the eternal world—but fear found no place of entrance into my tranquil bosom, every power of which was now absorbed in contemplating the blessed Redeemer who had never before appeared half so precious. I hugged his righteousness yet closer to my heart and sank to sleep."

But when she woke the next morning, "the wind had subsided to a perfect calm" and the sun shone through scattered clouds. She reported, "My heart was lifted up in thankful praise—the mercy of the Redeemer was my theme." During the previous night's storm, the sailors had caught sight of the Cape Hatteras lighthouse, a sandstone structure erected in 1803 to warn ships off the rocks. "We had obtained a light from the binnacle. The dear light was fastened onto the cabin window—and we had doubled the shoals of Hatteras! Oh enchanting thought!," wrote Susan. "All was peace and joy." The ship was becalmed the following day, but the wind picked up in the evening. "I arose at ten with Mrs. Bosworth to walk on deck. The wind was briskly wafting us over the ocean's waves to a land of strangers. The sky was set with stars; the water seemed studded with brilliants."[41]

After nine days of travel along the coast, through gale-force winds, thunder and lightning, occasional periods of dead calm, and a brush with disaster on the shoals off Cape Hatteras, the ship finally came within sight of North Carolina's smoking tar pits. They reached Wilmington by sailing up the "River Clarendon"—now known as the Cape Fear River—through countryside "low, sandy, and covered with pines, with here and there a scattering plantation." Alligators populated some of the grassy little islands in the river. She had finally arrived in the South.[42]

WILMINGTON PROVIDED SUSAN NYE with her first dose of culture shock. Although she found the inhabitants of the town very friendly and agreeable, the town itself was a "dreary place." It sat on "a confused mass of sandhills, with scarcely a sprig of grass to cover its barren soil, yet shaded by elegant trees, such as Pride of China, Live Oak. Figs, pomegranates flourish likewise. Strawberries were in perfection; the sand was very deep, almost over the tops of our boots—I was never more fatigued walking."[43]

The morning after their arrival, she attended church "at a Methodist meeting house, where the galleries were filled with Africans and half the lower floor." This was her first encounter with a racially mixed southern evangelical congregation. Baptist and Methodist revivals in the South brought small numbers of slaves and freedmen into white pioneer churches near the end of the eighteenth century. The number of slaves worshipping in mixed congregations slowly grew until as many as one-quarter of all slaves were members of mixed congregations on the eve of the Civil War. On the streets, however, Susan was appalled by the condition of the slaves she encountered. Although New York State abolished slavery in 1799, adult slaves were not emancipated until 1827, so Susan would have met both free blacks and slaves when she lived in Dutchess County. According to the 1810 census, slaves represented 2 percent of the population there, and free blacks represented another 2 percent. But she was little prepared for the streets of Wilmington, where 56 percent of the population was enslaved: "Oh, the wretched slaves with which the streets of W. are constantly filled, ragged—almost naked and hungry! What is man?"[44]

From Wilmington, she and her fellow passengers traveled for two days by stagecoach to Fayetteville. They passed through a landscape quite different from the one in which she had grown up, full of "pines and cypresses, from whose branches hung ash-coloured moss often 4 or 5 feet long." At their destination, Mrs. Bosworth reunited with Arabella, now in charge of the Female Department at the Fayetteville Academy. Susan described their meeting as "tender beyond description." In Fayetteville, Susan found the people to be "polite and attentive," offering hospitality "worth remembrance." Nevertheless, she longed to be settled: "I am extremely low spirited and long to get away to a place I may call *my* home."[45]

Finally, after two days in Fayetteville, under the light of a new moon at eight o'clock in the evening, Susan and Mrs. Bosworth took their seats in the stagecoach for the last leg of the journey. From Fayetteville, the road to Raleigh cut through miles of seemingly endless forest, the wheel ruts so deep "one is often thrown from her seat." They reached Raleigh at eleven o'clock the following morning. They called at a hotel, changed their dresses, and met Mrs. Bosworth's nephew, Dr. Beckwith. He invited them to his house. "I dined and went to bed," wrote Susan, "so overcome with fatigue that I could no longer sit up."[46]

News of her arrival quickly spread. Just four hours after she set foot in town, the academy's principal, the Reverend William McPheeters, called to invite her to come to his house to meet his family. Although she and McPheeters had never before met, she wrote, "I believe I was never more happy to see an old friend in my life." As a devout Presbyterian, Susan knew she would receive a warm welcome from a minister of the same denomination even though the town did not yet have an organized Presbyterian church. Several months earlier, she had applied to the South Amenia Presbyterian Church "for a Certificate to be one to form the Church about to be formed in" Raleigh. Such certificates served as documentation that the individual was a member of the church in good standing, assuring a warm welcome from the religious community when he or she took up residence in a new town. By presenting her certificate to McPheeters, she became a member of the town's Presbyterian community. A year later, when McPheeters organized Raleigh's first Presbyterian church, Susan Nye's name appeared among the founding members.[47]

However, when she arrived at the McPheeterses' household, she realized that her visit was neither a simple social call nor a formal welcome from the local Presbyterian minister. "Many of the misses of the academy were summoned," and Susan was "led round and introduced to each one particularly." Retiring by nature and probably exhausted from the journey, she concluded, "I was deeply embarrassed, and though pleased with them, was glad to be alone."[48]

But Susan had little time to rest before assuming her duties at Raleigh Academy. Within two days, she was teaching in the Female Department. Her twenty-seven-word journal entry for May 15 was the briefest to date: "I entered on the duties of my profession. The school has been extremely out of order but gave me no trouble; I trust in God—for assistance."[49]

THE DECISION TO LEAVE FAMILY and friends in New York had not been easy, but Susan Nye had the courage and conviction to undertake the long journey and begin a new life in North Carolina. She headed south for reasons that would have been familiar to many other single women of her era. Teaching appealed to her evangelical sensibilities and gave her a socially acceptable path into lay ministry, and working in the South allowed her to earn an independent living in a region where female teachers were in high demand.

The Second Great Awakening fostered new kinds of social networks that facilitated the migration of young single women across vast geographic distances. Susan Nye's female ancestors had leveraged traditional kinship relations to support their migration over great distances, and in keeping with this tradition, Susan received assistance from her family. Her parents supported her decision and provided transportation, and her cousin Jesse spent time with her in New York and bade her farewell. However, unlike her grandmothers, Susan benefited from two additional sources of support: the "awakened" churches and the alumni of female and coeducational academies. Through Arabella Bosworth, Susan learned of the available position in Raleigh, and she stayed and visited with Arabella before the last leg of the journey. Throughout her voyage, Susan's religious credentials provided her with a ready-made network of supporters and friends, allowing her to feel comfortable and at home with representatives from several different Protestant congregations, including the Quakers in New York, the Methodists in Wilmington, and her fellow Presbyterians in Raleigh.

Susan Nye and other women encountered new opportunities and possibilities during this era. The religious revivals of the early national period united Christians from a variety of denominations through the belief in the need for spiritual rebirth and social reform in American society. In a departure from earlier tradition, the churches encouraged women's involvement in community revival meetings, public prayer, and social activism. Although a social backlash arose against women's public preaching, women found other paths into lay ministry. A woman prohibited from the pulpit could still find outlets for evangelism in teaching and missionary work.

Susan Nye was determined to make a difference in the world and "be useful" in Raleigh. She quickly set her classroom in order and focused on her students' academic and spiritual well-being: "Oh when I think of meeting them at the bar of God how anxious ought I to be to exhort them in faith in Jesus and repentance towards God—oh let me be useful God of mercy I pray."[50]

CHAPTER 2

Teaching and Mission

June 9, 1815—Assembled with 10 girls, members of the Academy, at the
Academy, from whence we marched to the State House in our Sunday
style; the room was crowded with spectators. Mr. M. and myself took a
very retired seat. The females upon whom the honours of the school were
conferred were placed upon a stage elegantly fitted up. Judge Taylor, orator
of the day, was with them. The trustees were furnished with seats directly
in front of the stage. Mr. McPheeters came back and presented the request
of the trustees that I should sit with them. After a moment's reflection,
I came forward, and trembling with unaffected diffidence, took the seat
destined for me next to the president. The report was read by Judge T.
in elegant manner, and I, by degrees was gaining confidence sufficient to
look at the speaker when unluckily the trustees had thought proper to
notice the teachers of the academy, and I of course, was complimented.
My embarrassment was now increased higher than ever. I covered my face
with my handkerchief and would gladly have shrunk to the smallest corner
of the room.

Susan Nye had some trouble adjusting to the culture of Raleigh Academy.
Several weeks after her arrival, she marched her students to the school's
public examinations in the capital's State House, where she was introduced to the men who served on the board of trustees. Her journal entry
about that event describes her embarrassment at the public attention
she received; she trembled "with unaffected diffidence" and hid behind
her handkerchief. The use of the word "unaffected" suggests that she
believed women should be humble and retiring in public. Throughout
Susan's years of schooling and teaching in the North, she may never have
experienced an institution quite like Raleigh Academy, where female
teachers were expected not only to exhibit decorum but also to hold
their own in public conversation with male politicians and the town's
leading men and women.

The task of making generalizations about antebellum female higher
education is like the proverbial story of the blind men trying to describe

an elephant based solely on what they can deduce by touch. Before colleges began to open their doors to women later in the nineteenth century, the highest form of schooling available to females was found in academies, and as historians have noted, academies varied widely among the country's regions. Some offered female students an "ornamental" course of study; others offered the "English branches," including mathematics and the sciences. Many courses of study included a mix of ornamental and English subjects.[1]

Since the 1970s, scholars have generally credited the all-female academies in the Northeast as the places where "the values of women's liberal education prevailed," but recent studies have challenged this portrayal. Some northeastern academies followed the "French school" model of education. French schools, a transatlantic import to the coastal cities of the American colonies, generally offered elite young women a course of study emphasizing the "ornaments": literature, composition, modern languages, embroidery, art, and music. Connecticut's Litchfield Female Academy fit this model until 1814, when the school added science and mathematics to its course of study. Historian Daniel Kilbride has uncovered a thriving antebellum market in French schools in Philadelphia and other large northeastern cities: wealthy southerners often sent their daughters north to receive an education at such schools, where they studied side by side with the daughters of elite northern families.[2]

Until recently, historians have generally depicted female education in the South as predominantly ornamental, designed to prepare young women to become polished young ladies, obedient wives, and loving mothers capable of managing the plantation household. However, Christie Anne Farnham has argued that southern schools shifted away from the traditional French model of education during the first half of the nineteenth century as academies added the English branches to the curriculum. Farnham's research suggests that this transformation was well under way by the time Susan Nye arrived in Raleigh.[3]

This scholarship suggests that young women's higher education was differentiated and continuously evolving in both the North and the South. The variety of institutions available to females during the early antebellum period helps to explain Susan Nye's initial difficulty adjusting to the culture of Raleigh Academy. Although she was from the North, her own education might have been more aligned with the French than with the English model of education. She might have had little experience with public speaking before an audience of men and women, and during previous school examinations, she might never have found herself in the limelight on a public stage comparable to the one in Raleigh's State House.

The arrival of the "awakened" Susan Nye at Raleigh Academy prompts several questions: What did she teach, and what were her duties at the school? How did she understand her evangelical mission in the academy and community? The records of Raleigh Academy, like those of many other schools, exist today almost entirely in the form of newspaper announcements and advertisements. Together with Susan's journal entries, these documents open a window into the evolving education at a coeducational academy in the South, revealing the way Enlightenment ideas from across the Atlantic combined with the ideology of the Second Great Awakening to influence education during the early national period.[4]

RALEIGH HAD BEEN in existence for only a short period when Susan Nye arrived in 1815. The colonial capital had been in New Bern, near the eastern seaboard. After the revolution, delegates to North Carolina's 1788 Constitutional Convention voted to locate a new capital as close as possible to the geographic center of the state and appointed a commission to select a location. In the spring, nine commissioners set out on horseback to find a suitable site. After several days of exploration and deliberation, the commissioners purchased a thousand acres of land in Wake County, laid out a plan for the town, and named the streets and squares. The nearly six acres of the central area around the capital was dubbed Union Square.[5]

By 1794, a brick State House occupied the town center, surrounded by a number of inns, dry goods stores, residences, boardinghouses, and government buildings. A hawk circling lazily overhead would have spied a vast expanse of forest stretching to the horizon in all directions, blanketing gently rolling hills. In the midst of this wilderness lay a small town in a clearing, its streets laid out along a north-south grid, its symmetry a testament to Enlightenment faith in reason and order. When the former British radical and expatriate Joseph Gales arrived in 1799 with his family, they were shocked at the size of the town: "There were not more than 1,000 inhabitants and at least one third were slaves or free colored persons." In 1815, Susan Nye described Raleigh as lying "in an ancient forest having no marks of cultivation."[6]

During the first decade or so of Raleigh's existence, wealthy residents either sent their children out of town for their education or hired private tutors to school them at home. Newspaper advertisements published in 1800 indicate the presence of one venture school that claimed to offer the so-called higher subjects to both male and female students, but the endeavor was very short-lived. To remedy the situation, Joseph Gales, the publisher of the *Raleigh Register*, petitioned the General Assembly "that an Act might be passed incorporating a body of Trustees for the purpose of erecting and establishing a suitable Academy in the city." Forty other residents signed his petition, and in 1801 the State Assembly passed an act incorporating a board of trustees for the purpose of raising funds and establishing the school in Burke Square, several blocks from the state capital building. Raleigh Academy opened in 1804, enrolling males and females in separate departments.[7]

Many of the individuals who established female and coeducational academies in the late eighteenth and early nineteenth centuries drew heavily from British and French ideas, and Gales was no exception. Education reforms spread across the Atlantic through networks of lay educators, religious groups and teaching orders, missionaries, politicians, social commentators, Christian reformers, pamphlet writers, and newspaper publishers.[8] During his years as a printer in Sheffield, England, Gales had promoted a number of radical reforms, including the abolition of the slave trade, universal manhood suffrage, and tax-supported education for the poor. A Unitarian, he had also supported the Sunday school movement and a modernized curriculum for the sons and daughters of middle-class families that included instruction in mathematics, the sciences, the "evidences of Christianity," history, and government.[9]

When he arrived in Raleigh, Gales opened a bookstore next to his print shop, and the titles he advertised at the turn of the century reveal the way British Enlightenment ideology crossed the Atlantic. His store carried John Locke's *Essay on the Human Understanding*, Philip Doddridge's *Sermons on the Religious Education of Children*, and Joseph Priestley's *The Proper Objects of Education in the Present State of the World*. Gales also imported several books on female education, including John Bennett's *Strictures on Female Education*, John Burton's *Lectures on Female Education and Manners*, and Hannah More's *Essays*. All three authors argued that females were capable of rational thought and advocated the study of mathematics and the sciences for young women along with more traditional subjects. According to Gales, books sold well in Raleigh: "The supply of mental aliment had been meager and precarious. At this period, and for many succeeding years, few books of value were re-printed in this country, and our importations found ready and profitable sale." Gales was a Christian liberal with a strong interest in education reforms that included religious instruction, and for this reason he and the other members of Raleigh Academy's board of trustees—a group that included Anglicans, Presbyterians, Methodists, Baptists, and others—found common ground in their plans for the school.[10]

Susan Nye's first introduction to the scope of education at Raleigh Academy occurred during the school's public examinations, which began just two weeks after she took charge of the Female Department. As the preceptress, she was expected not only to attend the full week of examinations on the stage of the State House with other faculty members but also to interrogate her students on the stage in front of a large audience of relatives, trustees, and interested members of the community. Gales, then serving as president of Raleigh Academy's board of trustees, introduced her to the principal speaker, Judge Taylor, and to other notable guests in the audience. Some of North Carolina's most prominent citizens sat on the academy's board of trustees over the years, including several of the capital's original founders. In addition to rival newspaper publisher William Boylan, editor of the Federalist *North Carolina Minerva*, the lawyers, politicians, and civic reformers in the group included Theophilus Hunter, one of Raleigh's founding state commissioners; Henry Seawell, state attorney general; Sherwood Haywood, a former clerk of the State Senate; and former state representatives Nathaniel Jones and William Hinton. In 1811, Governor Benjamin Smith was elected a trustee.[11]

The published examination results indicate that education at the academy was as challenging as that in comparable schools, north or south. Boys could follow a Latin, Greek, or scientific course, and the Male Department also offered navigation and surveying. Girls demonstrated their knowledge of needlework, geography, literature, and arithmetic; in the higher classes, they answered questions about natural philosophy, chemistry, astronomy, and Latin.[12]

As she attended the school examinations over the next few days, Susan must have witnessed the outcome of another educational reform with roots in the British Enlightenment—the performance of the students in the academy's new Lancaster preparatory school. The trustees of Raleigh Academy had always charged a moderate rate of tuition on a sliding scale to accommodate the sons and daughters of middle-class families. In 1814, the trustees went further, implementing free instruction for poor white children. Announced the *Raleigh Register*, "We congratulate our fellow-citizens on the prospect of establishing, in the Preparatory School of our Academy, the highly approved mode of teaching children the first rudiments of Learning, invented by the celebrated *Joseph Lancaster* of London, by which one man can superintend the instruction of any number of scholars from 50 to 1000. . . . When this plan shall be introduced, the children of all such parents in the city and neighbourhood as are unable to pay for their tuition, may be taught without any additional expence, so that this institution will answer all the purposes of a *Free School.*" A school based on Lancaster's plan used student monitors to teach elementary subjects through recitation and supervise younger children in active, competitive, and highly regimented groups. Although Susan's journal never mentions the students in the Lancaster school, the board of trustees expressed satisfaction with their performance at the May examinations. "Though this school has had an existence of a few months only," reported William Hill, secretary of the board, "the Trustees find that children, who, before they entered it, did not know a letter in the book, can now read, write, have some knowledge of figures, and can repeat by heart a number of moral verses. Some, indeed, have attained a considerable knowledge of English Grammar and Geography."[13]

Susan was somewhat unnerved by the public examinations in Raleigh. On the first day, she examined the younger girls in the lower classes of the Female Department, later recalling, "I felt a great deal of embarrassment at the idea of attending and waited till Mr. McPheeters sent for me. The board of Trustees were seated in style when I entered and one of them to whom I had never been introduced, rose and politely bowed. I was embarrassed and withdrew to a retired seat. I examined my own classes, though with difficulty."[14]

On Friday, the female students in the higher classes performed. Susan assembled with her students at the school and then walked two blocks southeast with them "to the State House in our Sunday style." There, "the room was crowded with spectators." The board of trustees sat in a row "directly in front of the stage." At first, Susan hoped to sit somewhere at the back, out of sight, but McPheeters informed her that the trustees wanted her to sit with them. She reluctantly took a seat next to Gales, and when the speaker complimented her before the audience, she trembled and ducked behind her handkerchief. Yet despite her reticence, Susan found herself drawn to the proceedings.[15]

She was fascinated by the "farewell addresses." Young women graduating from academies traditionally composed final speeches, but the occasion might have marked the first time Susan witnessed a young woman stand and speak her own oration before an audience of men and women. Male teachers or trustees often read the speeches composed by female students because many Americans still believed that women should not address mixed public audiences. At Litchfield Female Academy, male instructors or prominent town residents read aloud the students' compositions. But some schools had already begun to break with this tradition by the time Susan arrived in Raleigh. As historian Mary Kelley has shown, one of the earliest known examples of this development occurred at Philadelphia's Young Ladies Academy, where Priscilla Mason read aloud her own composition in 1793.[16]

Most of the graduating female students in Raleigh Academy's Class of 1815 did not read their compositions aloud but had a member of the board of trustees do so. Susan was therefore very interested and impressed when one female student stepped forward to read her own composition on the stage: "The report being finished, the medals and certificates presented, Mr. Glynn read the Misses White and Littlejohn's farewell addresses, and Miss [Eliza] Haywood came forward with her own. She is not beautiful, but she is interesting, and she never appeared more so, than when addressing herself to the trustees, the teachers of the Academy and her companions. It was a composition of merit, considerably [moving]. I was deeply affected with the whole, but when she addressed me particularly, my confusion was completed and I wept behind my handkerchief, sincere, without restraint."[17]

Despite her initial lack of confidence during the June public examinations, Susan soon settled down to the business of teaching and heading the Female Department, which had apparently been without a preceptress since Arabella Bosworth's resignation. "The school has been extremely out of order but gave me no trouble," she wrote.[18]

THE CURRICULUM IN Raleigh Academy's Female Department had begun to evolve long before Susan arrived. McPheeters, who became principal of the school in 1810, was probably responsible for the addition of moral philosophy, Old Testament, and natural theology to the female course of study. By 1811, the school advertised twenty-three subjects in the Female Department, though no student was required to take them all. Most students enrolled in five or six core subjects plus electives such as music, drawing, or embroidery. By the time Arabella Bosworth arrived from New York to teach at the school in 1812, the course of study included scientific subjects she would never have encountered as a student at Litchfield Female Academy.[19]

TABLE 2. Expansion of the Curriculum in the Female Department, Raleigh Academy, 1806–1811

1806	1807	1808	1810	1811
Reading	Reading	Reading	Reading	Reading
Writing	Writing	Writing	Writing	Writing
Arithmetic	Arithmetic	Arithmetic	Arithmetic	Arithmetic
English Grammar	English Grammar	English Grammar	English Grammar	English Grammar
Geography	Geography	Geography	Geography	Geography
Needlework	Needlework	Needlework	Needlework	Needlework
	Painting	Painting	Painting	Painting
	Embroidery	Embroidery	Embroidery	Embroidery
	Belles Lettres	Belles Lettres	Belles Lettres	Belles Lettres
	History	History	History	History
	Natural Philosophy	Natural Philosophy	Natural Philosophy	Natural Philosophy
	Astronomy	Astronomy	Astronomy	Astronomy
		Music	Music	Music
		Drawing	Drawing	Drawing
		French	French	French
			Moral Philosophy	Moral Philosophy
			Rhetoric	Rhetoric
			Composition	Composition
				Old Testament
				Natural Theology
				Chemistry
				Latin
				Tambouring

Source: Data obtained from newspaper advertisements in Coon, *North Carolina Schools and Academies*, 396–97, 409, 420–21.

Joseph Gales probably played a role in introducing the sciences to Raleigh Academy. In England, Gales had published the ideas of reformer Samuel Catlow, who argued that while the children of wealthy aristocrats might derive some benefit from the in-depth study of Latin and Greek, the rising generation among the middle class required a completely different curriculum, including instruction in mathematics and the sciences. When Joseph Gales and his wife, Winifred, arrived in North Carolina, not all of the state's academies offered scientific subjects. During Fayetteville Academy's 1801 public examinations, the young men demonstrated their understanding of "Greek, Latin, Euclid's Elements,

Geography, English Grammar, Arithmetic, Reading, Spelling, Letter Writing, Copy Writing," while the young women displayed their mastery of "Geography, Reading, Spelling, Arithmetic, Writing, Needle work— embroidery, tambour, Dresden, marking." Gales set out to change this state of affairs. He informed readers of the partisan *Raleigh Register* that support for the sciences was a Democratic-Republican Party virtue. In 1805, he published a reprint from the *National Intelligencer* claiming, "We have frequently had occasion to notice the hostility of Federalism to Science and Literature, and the persecuting spirit with which it pursues their ablest promoters."[20]

Consistent with their beliefs, Joseph and Winifred Gales made sure that both their daughters and their sons studied the sciences in Raleigh Academy. In 1807, Thomas Gales received distinction in composition and "evinced, by his ready and unembarrassed answers, his perfect acquaintance with" philosophy and astronomy. Altona Gales, in the fifth class, was examined in astronomy and received distinction in geography, arithmetic, writing, embroidery, and "Blair's Lectures," an elementary text on natural philosophy (physics). In the 1811 fall examinations, Ann-Eliza Gales was examined in mathematics, natural philosophy, and Latin. By the time Susan Nye arrived in May 1815, the course of study included not only the standard subjects of English grammar, geography, and arithmetic but also literature, French, astronomy, chemistry, natural philosophy, moral philosophy, rhetoric, and Latin as an elective. And in the fall of that year, after Susan took charge of the Female Department, "Caroline Gales distinguished herself in natural philosophy, chymistry & Astronomy; also Composition and singing."[21]

During her first year at the academy, Susan taught core subjects such as reading, writing, grammar, literature, arithmetic, astronomy, natural philosophy, and chemistry, while another female teacher taught drawing and painting. A music teacher affiliated with the academy offered instruction either at the school or in students' homes.[22] Susan also brought a new emphasis on religious education to the Female Department. Within a few years of her arrival, female students were studying the New Testament and answering examination questions on the Bible and "Scripture history."[23]

Raleigh Academy's approach to religious instruction was ecumenical, in line with the spirit and requirements of the times. When the board of trustees was selecting the school's first principal, they sought a "well-educated Minister . . . who would be willing to take charge of the

Academy and become Pastor of the city." The trustees offered a salary of $1,000 per year, "$500 as a teacher and $500 for his pastoral services." Those services included conducting ecumenical services in the State House that would accommodate a variety of denominational backgrounds. The academy consequently maintained a nonsectarian but Protestant character. During school examinations, the teachers grilled students on the Bible and tested their knowledge of the catechism, but students and their families could select the content. Students could choose to recite the Westminster, Episcopal, or other catechism, depending on their religious affiliation. As Unitarians living in a community with no established Unitarian church, Joseph and Winifred Gales probably appreciated the chance to select an appropriate text for their children. Roman Catholic legislator William Gaston served on the school's board of trustees in 1822, and it is likely that any Catholic students enrolled at the school could study texts their families approved.[24]

Religion infused several areas of the curriculum. Students recited from Lindley Murray's *English Grammar*, a book that one advertiser recommended for the way it combined "religious and moral improvement with the elements of scientific knowledge." In their grammar lessons, students learned that "youth is the proper season for gaining knowledge, and forming religious habits." They learned that serving their families and communities was important because no life is "pleasing to God that is not useful to man."[25] According to one example in the section on syllogisms in older students' logic textbooks,

> They, who subvert the foundations of morality and religion, ought
>   not to be respected;
> Atheists subvert the foundations of morality and religion;
> Therefore atheists ought not to be respected.[26]

Religion was closely linked with the sciences at Raleigh Academy. With the popularization of natural theology, the study of the natural world became spiritually uplifting. Central to natural theology was the argument of design, in which the mechanism, instrumentality, or design in nature provided evidence of the existence of an intelligent and benevolent Creator. From the start of the eighteenth century, English natural philosophers published books aiming to reveal the wonders of God's creation through the natural sciences, from naturalist John Ray's highly popular *The Wisdom of God in the Creation* (1691) to William Paley's *Natural Theology* (1802). The best known of these authors, Paley argued that the more humans learned to understand and appreciate God's design in nature, the more they would grow in knowledge of God. By 1811, upper-level female students at Raleigh Academy were reading Paley's text.[27]

Many of the ministers who published texts for common schools and academies recommended the study of the natural world for its spiritual benefits. Congregational minister Jedidiah Morse, whose geography text appeared in Raleigh Academy's course of study, claimed that students should learn astronomical geography because it "furnishes the young Pupil with such a general knowledge of the heavenly bodies, as will facilitate his acquaintance with Geography, and elevate and enlarge his views of the wisdom, power, and greatness of the CREATOR." Murray's *English Grammar* textbooks, which Raleigh Academy students read when Susan taught there, echoed this view. In a section titled "Happy Effects of Contemplating the Works of Nature," Murray wrote, "With the Divine works we are in every place surrounded. We can cast our eyes nowhere, without discerning the hand of Him who formed them." Like many of her contemporaries, Susan Nye believed that the study of science could increase one's awareness of God. Years later, while she and her sister pulled flax on the family farm, she recalled, "It was the same field where I had in early youth had (while studying a work on astronomy) a remarkable sense of the divine omnipresence."[28]

British authors specifically targeting females as well as males wrote most of the scientific texts that appeared in female departments and schools before 1820. One popular text was James Ferguson's *An Easy Introduction to Astronomy for Young Gentlemen and Ladies*. Ferguson (1710–76), a Scottish astronomer and instrument maker, wrote his book as a dialogue between a brother and sister. It first appeared on the American market in 1805 and joined Raleigh Academy's course of study in 1811, along with two other popular British imports, Blair's *A Grammar of Natural and Experimental Philosophy* and *A Grammar of the Principles and Practice of Chemistry*. The latter included "experiments . . . especially adapted to the purposes of instruction."[29]

During this period, it was not unusual for instructors to demonstrate science experiments before their classes. This practice echoed the popular scientific lectures that drew large audiences of men and women in cities. When Benjamin Rush developed a chemistry course for young women based largely on the application of chemistry to household economics, he also demonstrated his experiments before an appreciative but largely passive female audience.[30]

Susan Nye's students broke with this tradition in the fall of 1815. Within six months of her arrival, the young women in the Female Department demonstrated chemistry experiments before a large audience at the State House during the November public examinations. Gales's brief mention of this event in the *Raleigh Register* ("The experiments made by the Students in Chemistry did honor to Miss Nye") constitutes the earliest known record of public science experiments demonstrated by young women in the United States.[31]

Such public demonstrations illustrate an important shift in the way Americans viewed the appropriate scope of women's education. Recent scholarship has emphasized the significance of young women's growing literacy skills during this era, documenting the way women's education prepared them to "write themselves into being" in their diaries and maintain important friendships and social ties through written correspondence. This scholarship has revealed the way growing numbers of middle-class American women gained access to the higher forms of literacy schooling that had long been available to the daughters of elite families in French schools. Still, the practice of teaching women to read and write was not at all controversial in the early national period. As historian Catherine A. Brekus has pointed out, a tradition of publishing evangelical female narratives originated in the American colonies during the First Great Awakening. In contrast, the notion of allowing females to participate in science was a much more recent development. The young women's public display of science illustrates how the radicalism of the British Enlightenment unfolded in both regions of the country and suggests that Susan Nye, who was so interested in the display of public speaking during the female examinations six months earlier, soon began to come out of her shell and influence education at Raleigh Academy.[32]

When Susan's students demonstrated chemistry experiments, they probably used a conversational format to explain the underlying concepts. Chemistry textbooks written specifically for young women began to appear on the American market in large numbers after the turn of the century. One of the most popular imports from Great Britain was *Conversations on Chemistry*, by Jane Marcet, who wrote each of her books as a dialogue between "Mrs. B," a refined lady with scientific interests, and her two young pupils, Caroline and Emily. Over the course of these conversations, Mrs. B illustrates a variety of scientific concepts through experiment and demonstration. In the 1809 edition, Caroline asks whether sulfurous acid can be decomposed and reduced to sulfur. "Yes," Mrs. B responds, "if this gas be heated in contact with charcoal, the oxygen of the acid will combine with it and the pure sulphur be regenerated." After explaining that sulfurous acid is readily absorbed in water, Mrs. B offers to show the young ladies an experiment: "I can show you its effect in destroying colours, by taking out any iron mould, or vegetable stain—I think I see a spot on your gown, Emily, on which we may try the experiment." Emily expresses some understandable reluctance: "It is the stain of mulberries; but I shall be almost afraid of exposing my gown to the experiment, after seeing the effect the sulphuric acid produced on that of Caroline." Marcet's books were very popular in America, spawning dozens of imitators, including Blair's chemistry textbook, which female students studied at Raleigh Academy.[33]

In addition to the sciences, Raleigh Academy's female students began to make inroads into other traditionally male subjects. The academy began offering Latin as an elective in 1811, and by 1819, it appeared in the official course of study, taught by Georgia native Lavinia Richardson, a recent academy graduate. During the eighteenth century, educators believed that the study of Latin and Greek provided a rigorous intellectual training. Schools in both the North and the South gradually began to include Latin in the course of study available to female students after the turn of the century, but the practice was somewhat controversial in some areas. Although a small number of northern schools open to females began to include the classics in their advertised courses of study, it is difficult to know how many female students actually enrolled in Latin during this period. The 1828–30 enrollment records of two Massachusetts schools, Wesleyan Academy and the Sheldon English and Classical School, reveal that whereas around 35 percent of male students enrolled in Latin, only 1 percent of female students enrolled in the subject. Historians often point to Mount Holyoke Female Seminary in Massachusetts as offering young women Latin and other advanced subjects, but records indicate that although the school offered Latin as an elective in 1837, community resistance prevented its inclusion among required subjects for another decade. In North Carolina, female schools increasingly advertised Latin in their courses of study after 1810, but by 1830, only one in five schools had taken this step. Viewed in this context, the Female Department in Raleigh Academy appears to have offered an unusually radical curriculum.[34]

From its inception, Raleigh Academy offered arithmetic in its Female Department. Scholars generally believe few colonial Americans taught arithmetic to girls. According to Mary Beth Norton, documentary evidence suggests that during the revolutionary period, women typically could not assess the value of their property or testify precisely about the state of their family finances, whereas men could do so in detail. Several prominent Americans began to publicly urge the addition of arithmetic to the curriculum of female education during the early national period. Benjamin Franklin, Benjamin Rush, and Noah Webster argued that Americans could benefit from training girls in arithmetic and bookkeeping so that young women could assist their families in business. Educators argued that the study of arithmetic improved mental discipline. By the first decade of the nineteenth century, arithmetic commonly appeared among the subjects listed in the published courses of study for girls' schools and female departments.[35]

Surviving cipher books provide a glimpse into the kinds of arithmetic female students learned in the early national period. In 1781, when North Carolina was occupied by British forces, young Martha Ryan doodled in the margins of her cipher book, drawing pictures of warships and inserting patriotic phrases such as "Liberty or Death." Martha and her sister, Elisabeth, studied bookkeeping and the "Rule of Three," a useful algorithm for establishing the relative values of commodities. After learning the simple operations of basic arithmetic, Martha did exercises in simple and compound interest, discount, profit and loss, tare and fret, barter, and related subjects. In the page on "Single Fellowship," she solved a problem: "Four persons make a joint stock for 12 months. D put in 164£, E 206£, F 199£ & G 312£, and when they settled their accounts, they found they had lost 232£. I demand what part of the loss each person must sustain?" She also learned how to calculate rates of exchange to barter barrels of pitch for gallons of rum or barrels of corn for gallons of molasses. Such lessons constituted "useful knowledge," skills that would enable the girl to take care of the family accounts and engage in successful barter and trade. The published results of school examinations reveal that when Susan Nye taught in Raleigh Academy, she introduced these kinds of arithmetic problems to her students along with some bookkeeping.[36]

During Susan's tenure, the Female Department added more new subjects to the course of study, including mathematics. Contemporaries defined "arithmetic" as the "operations performed by various modes of adding, subtracting, multiplying, or dividing." "Mathematics," however, included such advanced topics as algebra, geometry, trigonometry, and calculus. In 1820, the young women in Raleigh Academy's senior class were examined on geometry for the first time.[37]

Page from Martha Ryan's cipher book, 1781. Courtesy of the Southern Historical Collection, Wilson Library, University of North Carolina at Chapel Hill.

Whereas the notion of teaching arithmetic to girls received relatively wide support after the revolution, the idea that girls should learn mathematics was highly controversial. Educator Almira Hart Lincoln Phelps noted that even Hannah More, in her famous *Strictures on Education* (1799), "did not dare to speak of instructing women in the higher branches of mathematics." According to one critic, opening the doors of mathematics to girls "was attempting to make them move in a sphere, for which Nature never gave them talents, nor Providence designed them." Not only did many contemporaries view females as intellectually incapable of mastering such subjects as algebra or geometry, higher mathematics had long been associated with such male vocations as navigation and surveying. "GEOMETRY. The sound of this word in reference to females, is very terrific," noted one educator in 1828. "Parents startle at it as though it possessed some talismanic power of converting their delicate daughters into tempest-beaten rovers of the deep, and sun-burnt surveyors of the forest."[38]

Some male educators, including Timothy Dwight, had taught young women mathematics in coeducational schools in the late eighteenth century, but nineteenth-century educators generally credited Emma Willard with having initiated the movement to introduce the subject in female schools. She started teaching math with the idea of "effecting an important change in education by the introduction of a grade of schools for women, higher than any heretofore known." After opening her first school for girls in Middlebury, Connecticut, in 1807, she began to teach herself geometry. In 1818, she moved to Waterford, New York, where she opened a girls' school and shocked the local community by offering geometry. The successful public examination of her first pupil in the subject caused a great deal of excitement, although several of those in attendance claimed that the young woman's accomplishment resulted entirely from feats of memory, "for no woman ever did, or could, understand geometry." Next, Willard began to study algebra. Step by step, she learned higher mathematics and then proceeded to teach it to her students. According to a contemporary, "In this independent manner she learned and afterwards taught her students, one class at a time, through Euclid, including trigonometry . . . algebra, conic sections, and Enfield's Institutes of Natural Philosophy." In the spring of 1821, she left Waterford and moved to Troy, New York, where she established a female seminary and began to train teachers. Word of her work soon spread. According to Catharine Beecher, when she and her sister Mary established a school for young ladies in Hartford, Connecticut, in 1823, "I heard that Mrs. Willard and one or two others were teaching the higher branches, but I knew nothing of their methods." The Beecher sisters were quick to follow suit. In 1824, a newspaper advertisement for their school announced that among the books to be used were Day's *Algebra* and Euclid's *Elements of Geometry*.[39]

Whether or not Catharine Beecher knew of Susan Nye, she was one of the few women teaching geometry to females at the time. There is no way to know whether Susan taught the geometry lessons introduced at Raleigh Academy in 1820 or whether she was influenced by Willard's example, but her published course of study demonstrates that she was certainly teaching geometry by 1823 when she moved to Augusta, Georgia, to establish her own female school.[40]

Susan was highly regarded as a teacher in Raleigh. Six months after her arrival, at the conclusion of the fall term, Joseph Gales pronounced his opinion: "Nothing can possibly exceed the zeal of this accomplished instructress." Five years later, the secretary of the board of trustees reported that among "the teachers in the Female Department will be Miss Nye (whose talents as a Teacher are probably unrivalled)."[41]

DURING HER FIRST four months in Raleigh, Susan often struggled to reconcile her dual roles as a teacher in the academy classroom and a gentlewoman expected to participate in Raleigh society. Her duties as head of the Female Department often required her to socialize and exchange pleasantries with some of the state's foremost citizens. She was startled by social and cultural differences. During the eighteenth century, New York women traditionally confined their political interests within the walls of home and family, but Susan's journal suggests that the citizens of North Carolina's state capital expected a female academy teacher to express her political opinions in mixed company. A month after arriving in Raleigh, she wrote, "Mr. McP[heeters] with a goodness peculiar to himself, came for me and accompanied me to Mrs. C. I believed I was never more embarrassed than when attempting to speak my political sentiments—I could positively think of nothing to say."[42]

She was also unfamiliar with the elegance and fashion of southern high society. After attending a wedding party during her first summer in town, she wrote, "The vitiated style of dress, oh surely, the ladies have forgotten that even dress was necessary, or at least that *they* have anything to conceal. Their backs and bosoms were all uncovered." The following morning she paid her compliments to the bride and her mother and was reassured to find "the ladies more decent in morning dresses than in the evening ones."[43]

She also sometimes struggled to navigate the cultural divide between evangelical and secular society. Raleigh residents frequently joined others for meals on Sundays, a custom frowned on in the Presbyterian churches. "I do not like this dining abroad on Sabbath days," Susan wrote shortly after arriving in town. She was frequently invited to join carriage rides, attend formal social events, and dine in the homes of local citizens and patrons of the school. Tempting as these opportunities were, she worried that she might become corrupted by material pleasures: "Oh style, I must not indulge in attending to thy demand!" she wrote after a day of socializing. "How much better would this day have passed had I visited the poor, or the wretched!" Two weeks later, she wrote, "Invited out to dine twice today, but desire to avoid temptation, and prefer a plain dinner at home to an elegant one abroad." Still, sometimes she gave in, and she clearly enjoyed not only the people but also some of the dishes she encountered: "Dined at Judge Potter's, was introduced to Major Hinton; called at Mr. M.; ate some most excellent pears." She concluded, "Surely these Carolinians are the most attentive and hospitable people in the world."[44]

At times, Susan was lonely and missed her Amenia friends and family. At other times, she doubted herself. After six weeks in Raleigh, she wrote, "I find a great many very poor people, and I wish, but in vain, to instruct them in the way of salvation. They receive me with pleasure, invite me into their hovels, and listen with attention, but ah, I fear that I am not sufficiently anxious for the salvation of their immortal souls." Nevertheless, she genuinely enjoyed many of the people she met. During her first few months in Raleigh, she not only developed close relationships with her students but also made many personal friends among the townspeople, and these friendships would endure.[45]

During her years in Raleigh, Susan understood that her duty as a teacher extended far beyond the academic curriculum. Her position as head of the Female Department required her not only to teach and oversee school examinations but also to provide moral and spiritual guidance to her pupils. Still, Susan's vision of her proper sphere of influence extended much further. Her evangelism carried her far beyond the walls of the schoolroom and the confines of her home, bringing her into some of the town's poorest neighborhoods. In fact, her journal suggests that she did not view academic classroom instruction as her most significant work. During her first few months in Raleigh, she wrote relatively little about the day-to-day business of schoolroom teaching. An analysis of the frequency of words appearing in her journal during her first three months at Raleigh Academy illustrates this focus. Although the published course of study indicates the subjects she taught when she arrived in Raleigh, her journal contains no mention of grammar, English, geography, needlework, arithmetic, moral philosophy, chemistry, or any other science. Instead, her journal is filled with reflections on faith, brief descriptions of social visits and events, and anecdotes about some of her charitable work and ministry. During later years, when she taught in Augusta, Georgia, and in Salisbury and Charlotte, North Carolina, her journal entries maintained much of this emphasis.

From her arrival at Raleigh Academy, she expressed concern for her students' salvation. When one of her pupils became ill during the summer of 1815, Susan was "deeply moved for her soul" and "attended prayer with her." Several weeks later, Susan wrote about having spent "great earnestness in prayer for this benighted land and for my dear pupils particularly. Lord, if academy (16) attended (20) believe (12)

breakfasted (13) called (30) dined (13) dinner (11)

evening (23) family (14) fear (14) felt (28) god (33)

heart (40) heaven (11) home (31) house (21) ill (11)

introduced (24) judge (24) live (12) man (11) meeting (22)

mind (11) morning (22) poor (16) prayer (33)

presented (14)

pride (11) returned (16) room (14) sin (12) spirit (11) state (15)

surely (12) tea (14) think (12) took (17) walked (13)

woman (11) world (11)

Tag cloud displaying the top forty words appearing in Susan Nye Hutchison's journal entries, May 12–August 13, 1815. Constructed from a transcription of Susan Nye Hutchison's journal entries from her first three months at Raleigh Academy, using freeware available at http://tagcrowd.com. Frequently appearing names and titles such as "Mr." or "Miss" are not included.

I am not faithful, oh make me so." She and her students regularly went to religious services: "Attended with my girls of the Academy as usual of the Sabbath morning," she wrote. "Felt great anxiety for their immortal souls. Oh, when I think of meeting them at the bar of God, how anxious ought I to be to exhort them to faith in Jesus and repentance toward God—Oh, let me be useful, God of mercy, I pray."[46]

She drew some of her inspiration from the lives of other young evangelical women. In particular, she and many other Americans were impressed by Harriet Atwood Newell (1793–1812). Shortly after arriving in Raleigh, Susan read aloud from Newell's memoirs while visiting one afternoon with several women: "I read Mrs. Newel till we were all deeply affected. Would to heaven we were equally pious!" Three years younger than Susan, Harriet Atwood had attended Bradford Academy in Massachusetts before she met and married Samuel Newell at age eighteen. They were among the first American missionaries to India, where Harriet and Ann Hasseltine Judson were charged to "teach these women, to whom your husbands can have little or no access. . . . Teach them that they are not an inferior race of creatures. . . . Teach them that they have immortal souls." In 1812, a pregnant Harriet became ill, and both she and her unborn baby died. Two years later, her memoirs appeared in print, becoming the second-best-selling book in the United States behind only the Bible.[47]

Newell's memoirs, along with other published narratives of pious women, inspired young women to evangelism and benevolent work outside the home. During the late eighteenth century, many religious journals and periodicals had counseled women to pursue the virtues of piety, submissiveness, and domesticity and to exercise their influence in the privacy of the household, protected from the temptations, violence, and wickedness of the outside world. This prescriptive literature frequently depicted the home as a woman's proper place of action. "Domestic life is to woman the proper sphere," explained Hannah More in her popular 1799 treatise on women's education. However, other kinds of prescriptive messages assumed prominence during the Second Great Awakening. In the Presbyterian Church, all members were encouraged to volunteer for charitable work on Sabbath days. After the service, committed Christians were supposed to spend time reading, meditating, repeating sermons, praying, singing hymns, and "visiting the sick, relieving the poor, and in performing such like duties of piety, charity, and mercy."[48]

In Raleigh, Susan's evangelism and benevolent activity unfolded in public places far beyond the schoolroom walls, and she did not restrict this work to Sundays. Just after the close of the school examinations in the summer of 1815, she "made several calls . . . but none so feeling as one to a poor deranged man next door to Mr. M[cPheeters] who with his wife and children have been turned out of their hovel, and are without any other shelter than a few boards Mrs. Wells herself placed over his bed. Oh wretched man! I talked to him upon religion. He seemed to hear me with attention and even willingness; wished me to read and stay with him." She worked to set aside her own pleasure and "seek the glory of God and the general good." After spending some time on Sunday reading to a Mrs. Spikes, Susan wrote, "Oh, let me follow the example of my Lord and Saviour and make the poor my companions!"[49]

Susan talked and prayed with slaves and free blacks on the streets of Raleigh as well as ministered to poor whites. She soon realized that black Christians could surpass her in faith and spiritual knowledge and that she could find herself on the receiving end of ministry and prayer. Returning from prayer one weekday morning, she wrote, "I called on a poor black woman whose piety I fellowshipped with joy—Oh, that I may be useful!" Two weeks later, she "conversed with a poor negro, who lame and old, nightly limps past our house, with a basket in one hand, a cane in the other while a bunch of sticks, gathered in the woods, weighs down his venerable grey head. He seemed so grateful for my inquiries after the state of his soul, that it really gave me pleasure. His profession is Presbyterianism." Impressed with his piety, she confessed, "Oh, his soul may be whiter than mine."[50] That phrase not only acknowledges racial difference but also refers to Psalm 51:7, in which King David pleads with the Lord to forgive his sins: "Purge me with hyssop, and I shall be clean; wash me, and I shall be whiter than snow."

Not only her teaching but also her ministry to the poor and infirm in Raleigh made an impression in the town. Within two months of Susan's arrival, a woman asked her to visit a brothel and save the woman's daughter from a life of prostitution:

After dinner, being dull and sleepy, I took up my bonnet and went out for a walk and entering a small house where poverty reigned over his votaries with [u]ndisputed sway, I took up the bible and read to them. They were truly attentive and grateful. After having finished my lecture, I bade them "good-bye" and was about leaving them, when a poor wretched woman begged me to go and see her daughter, a poor abandoned girl at the next house. My heart revolted at the thought, for it was a house of well-known infamy, but I could not refuse the petition, so followed and in silent reflection. I took a seat close at the door, for some how I had a dreadful disgust [of] the people and could scarcely help looking to see whether they would not attempt some violence—The poor lost girl for some time refused to say any thing to me, but at last I proposed attending prayer with them, when she appeared deeply affected, her mother wrung her hands and some times appeared to be almost in despair. "Oh," said she, "I am sometimes afraid to go to sleep lest I wake in hell"; and again she said it appeared as if heaven would set even her very grave on fire. God knows my heart. Oh may he pity and forgive all that he sees amiss! . . . God is able to cleanse away all sin.[51]

Susan's visit to the brothel entailed some risk. As women sought influence beyond the private sphere of the home, they moved into civic spaces where they faced both new opportunities and social constraints. Community members particularly scrutinized teachers' lives out of school. Teachers' high visibility as moral agents required them to use great tact and diplomacy when interacting with others in public. Susan could read and pray with free blacks and slaves without facing criticism; however, a visit to a brothel could spark malicious gossip that might damage a young woman's reputation. After hearing about the encounter, Susan's landlady reacted in a way that sparked Susan's anxiety: "I felt fearful lest my conduct might be misconstrued by a serious world," she wrote. "Mrs. C[radep] increased this fear by some remarks."[52]

Susan need not have worried: Raleigh's religious community embraced her. Traditional social mores that operated to restrict women's public behavior were countered by new models of behavior exemplified by Harriet Newell and other evangelical women. The Protestant churches created an important social network for young women like Susan Nye. As historian Nancy Beadie has pointed out, the evangelicalism of the Second Great Awakening reconstructed society on its own terms. For free men and women, membership in the church was based not on social class, connections, gender, or race but on a public profession of faith. This membership transcended geography, conferring access to a social network of moral peers. Although she had left family and friends back in New York, Susan's religious credentials guaranteed her a new network of friends and support. This social network was not restricted to the men and women of individual churches. In Raleigh, Susan joined with women from other denominations in organizing the Raleigh Female Benevolent Society and the Female Tract Society.[53]

During the Second Great Awakening, Protestant social networks crossed denominational lines. Many preachers and reformers realized the benefits of pooling resources to collaborate. Lyman Beecher argued that if the denominations worked together to support the work of their voluntary agencies, the chance of success would increase. The social bridges that developed among Protestant reformers facilitated the creation of evangelical institutions such as the American Bible Society, which was established in 1816 and included Presbyterians, Congregationalists, Methodists, Episcopalians, Baptists, Quakers, Moravians, and Dutch Reformed congregations. The same sort of collaborative enterprise created national organizations devoted to evangelism, among them the American Sunday School Society (1824) and the American Tract Society (1825). During her tour of the United States, English novelist Frances

Trollope discerned the collaborative nature of the revival movement in the way itinerant preachers timed their entry into various communities. Preachers from varying denominations "enter all the cities, towns, and villages of the Union in succession. . . . They are lodged in the houses of their respective followers, and every evening that is not spent in the churches and meeting-houses, is devoted to what would be called parties by others, but which they designate as prayer-meetings. Here they eat, drink, pray, sing, hear confessions, and make converts." Susan Nye hoped for a revival of religion in Raleigh. A month after her arrival, she attended a Sunday prayer meeting and "had great desires for the salvation of the whole congregation"; to this end, she prayed "for a heart more perfectly devoted to God."[54]

In Raleigh, collaboration among the Protestant denominations was well under way. From the day it opened, the State House served the use of any clergyman seeking a congregation. For example, the Methodist bishop, Francis Asbury, reported that when he preached there on March 6, 1800, "notwithstanding the day was very cold and snowy we had many people come to hear." In 1811, the Methodists conducted such a successful revival in town that when Bishop Asbury preached, two thousand people flocked to hear him—almost double Raleigh's entire population—raising the roof with songs, cries, and shouts. The following year, a Baptist congregation organized in town. Ministers from the Presbyterian, Methodist, and Baptist denominations took turns preaching during the same services in the State House, and representatives from all three religious groups conducted Raleigh Academy's prayer meetings in the Methodist meetinghouse, sometimes alternating roles during the service. Collaboration arose from pragmatic concerns as well as from ecumenical ideology. Given a small pool of prospective students hailing from different denominations, it made sense to share resources, thus meeting the religious needs of as many academy pupils as possible. In later decades, when well-established Presbyterian, Baptist, and Methodist congregations competed for believers, relations at times became less cordial.[55]

Although she was a Presbyterian, Susan enjoyed worshipping with members of other denominations. During the summer of 1815, when Raleigh's Presbyterians still lacked a church building, she alternated attendance at the Baptist and Methodist meetinghouses. She had "a very good meeting" at the Methodist meetinghouse on July 4, heard "a good practical sermon" at the Baptist meeting on July 16, and worried about the state of her soul after worshipping the next two weeks with the Methodists. Although she confessed that she sometimes felt inclined to worship only with fellow Presbyterians, she wanted "to have communion with all societies of professing Christians, and to live as though I was a citizen of the world, as well as of Amenia." In January of the following year, McPheeters organized Raleigh's first Presbyterian church, and Susan was among its founding members. Nevertheless, she continued to worship with Christians of other denominations.[56]

Susan Nye educated hundreds of young southern women during her eight years in Raleigh. During this period, Raleigh Academy influenced her approach to education, and she, in turn, influenced the school, bringing a new emphasis on religious instruction to the Female Department. She had taught students from other states and developed friendships with some of their families. Through such connections, she learned of an opportunity to establish a female school in Augusta, Georgia, a town with an established Presbyterian Church community. At the age of thirty-three, she had the experience and resources to establish an independent venture, and she was ready to strike out on her own. Her younger sister, Amanda, had joined her in Raleigh by 1817, and the two women headed south in June 1823 with the full support of Raleigh's Presbyterian community. Susan wrote, "I left Raleigh—being commended by the prayers of the people of God."[57]

Augusta had developed into a bustling commercial center well before the revolution. During the colonial era, trappers had brought skins to trade; by the 1820s, farmers hauled bales of cotton to be shipped downriver and sold in the European and northern markets. The city's streets were broad, shaded with Pride of India trees and lined with banks, commercial buildings, churches, schools, and a large cotton exchange. The only thing missing was a female school offering the level of higher education that young women could find at Raleigh Academy. Before Susan's school opened, Augusta parents seeking an advanced education for their daughters would have considered sending them away to boarding school or hiring governesses or tutors at home. During this period, wealthy southern parents still sent their daughters to northern cities to attend elite schools offering a traditional French style of education.[58]

Susan Nye's school offered southern parents another option: an academically rigorous female school based on the model at Raleigh Academy. It was not a French school, although French, painting, and embroidery were available as electives—for a price, as a September 1823 announcement detailed:

MISS NYE Begs leave to inform her friends and the public in general, that her second quarter will commence the first of October, at the SCHOOL ROOM employed during last winter, by MRS. WARNE, on Washington Street. As she is desirous to adopt, as soon as practicable, a system of instruction similar to the one, so successfully pursued in the Raleigh Academy, N.C. she takes the liberty to announce her terms of admission under a similar classification.

Minor Class—Spelling, Reading, Writing,	$6.50
Julian Class—Arithmetic; . . . Grammar	8.50
Cornelian Class—Etymological & Syntactical Parsing, Geography	10.50
Decimore Class—History & Composition	12.50
Trophomore Class—Astronomy Mythology and Rhetoric	15.00
Alphenor Class—Natural Philosophy and Chemistry	15.00
Delphenor Class—Logic & Moral Philosophy, with the element of Geometry	15.00

To which one Dollar will be added for firewood to the rates of each class, during the winter quarters. Payment will be expected in advance. The French language, Painting in water colours; on Velvet and Satin—Embroidery and Sheneil work, a separate charge of five dollars each. Private Lessons in the French or in any other branch taught in this Institution, will be given if required. The friends of the pupils are invited to visit the school at the weekly Friday Evening Reports and at the monthly Examinations.[59]

Susan faced some competition, but no other female school claimed to offer such an extensive array of subjects. Augusta schools enrolled a diverse range of white students, male and female. A Lancastrian school, subsidized with state funds, provided a rudimentary education for the children of the poor. B. B. Hopkins offered a "Select School for Young Ladies," in which "children will be *systematically* and *accurately* instructed in all the *solid* and *useful* branches of a well regulated female education." In the fall of 1824, Julia Hayden opened a school for elementary children. But Susan's school offered the most rigorous course of study.[60]

SUSAN'S MOVE TO Augusta exemplifies the way British Enlightenment ideas about the importance of higher education for women spread throughout the country during the Second Great Awakening. The influence of these ideas is evident in the evolving, increasingly rigorous course of study offered by the Female Department of Raleigh Academy. For some women, including Susan Nye and Lavinia Richardson, who became a teacher after having been Susan's student, education had occupational as well as religious and intellectual value. Fewer women may have sought teaching positions in the South than in the North during this period, but when Susan and some of her former pupils left Raleigh to teach elsewhere, they carried the English model of female education to other regions of the South.[61]

The ecumenical and interdenominational nature of the Second Great Awakening provided the glue that bound together diverse communities of Americans in the young republic. The collaboration among Protestant groups enabled reformers to pool their resources during a period when resources were still relatively scarce, facilitating the spread of religious conviction and benevolent enterprise. Young female converts like Susan Nye were an important part of this phenomenon as they left their homes to teach, attended to students' spiritual progress in the schoolroom, and modeled the importance of benevolent work in communities across the country.

During the later decades of the nineteenth century, the ability of the major Protestant denominations to amass the social and financial capital required to establish academies and colleges on a sound economic footing helped higher education become more established across the country. However, even during earlier periods, the evangelical churches had a vested interest in recruiting qualified and like-minded teachers to provide ideological continuity from the pulpit to the schoolroom. Susan's statement that her departure from Raleigh was "commended by the prayers of the people of God" suggests that she received support and encouragement for her move to Augusta from the connections she had made through the Presbyterian Church. This phrase also suggests an evangelical dimension to Susan's work as a teacher, since evangelicals used this phrase to bless missionaries' travels and prospects.[62]

Susan's journal entries from her time in Raleigh suggest that some of her greatest struggles arose from her efforts to live as an awakened Christian. The demands were great. As Presbyterian preacher Charles Finney proclaimed, "You must live a holy life and consecrate all to God—your time, talents, influence—all you have, and all you are, to be his entirely." Susan was often all too aware of her own shortcomings: "Oh, how full of wickedness is the human heart," she despaired one Sunday. "Not even a single action of mine looks like holiness."[63] She often had difficulty reconciling what she perceived as her Christian duty with some of the more sophisticated displays of southern culture she encountered. And as she discovered in Raleigh and in Georgia, it was sometimes difficult to reconcile her faith with the harsh realities of slavery.

CHAPTER 3
Slavery and Emancipation

July 29, 1815—Awakened this morning by the screeching of a female
slave who was fleeing from the whip of an enraged master. Oh I never
witnessed such a scene. Father of mercies guard my heart and keep me
from the seductions of evil—Oh how callous are the hearts of this people!
Surely they can have little hope of mercy when they show none. I will not,
I cannot tell what I felt when the poor girl, whose screeches this morning
awakened me, passed the breakfast room, her neck torn and bloody,
her eye swollen. Oh, day of retributive justice! I live it is said with
one of the best of masters.

Here and there, woven through Susan Nye's journal during her first months
in Raleigh, are references to slaves. Most of these brief entries are about her
prayer and conversation with men and women in town or observations of
slaves and free blacks at worship, but in late July, she recounted an instance
of slave brutality in the household where she boarded. She was appalled.

Given Susan's occasional expressions of shock and discomfort with
slaveholding, her decision to continue working in the South presents an
interesting puzzle. Her experience contrasts with what historians know
about the relatively short tenure of most northern teachers in antebellum
southern schools. Many students from Mount Holyoke Female Seminary
in Massachusetts went south to teach, but in contrast to those who went
west and remained there for a relatively long period, most of the south-
bound teachers returned north within three years. Historian Christie
Anne Farnham has concluded that tensions over slavery played a role in
this phenomenon. Susan Nye was not immune to these tensions, yet she
remained a southern teacher for thirty years.[1]

Most historians have focused on the writings of prominent politicians, ministers, and social reformers to understand antebellum attitudes
toward slavery, an approach that often overlooks teachers and schools. To
a great extent, this emphasis results from the sources available in historical archives. After all, the papers of well-known individuals are far more
likely to have been preserved than the papers of ordinary schoolteachers.

Nevertheless, teachers played an important role in shaping the cultural values and beliefs of the young students in their care, as the many southerners who came to know Susan Nye as a teacher understood. During her long career in the South, she taught hundreds of young women. After her death, one Presbyterian newspaper claimed, "Many of the mothers and grandmothers of North Carolina were educated by her, and had something of her own character impressed upon them."[2]

Susan sought to awaken her students to God and their duty to society, but what did she believe was a free woman's duty to democratic society in light of the actual cruelties of slavery? How did she reconcile her church's views on slavery with her role as an educator in the South? She never addressed such questions in her journal, but Raleigh Academy's published course of study indicates that she taught her female students about slavery and emancipation. She encountered prescriptive messages about slavery not only in the Presbyterian Church but also in the moral philosophy textbooks she used in the classroom. The free and enslaved people she encountered and the events unfolding around her shaped Susan's perspective. Piecing together the social context in which she lived reveals some of the perennial tensions she experienced between the Enlightenment ideals embedded in Christian moral philosophy and the problem of deferred emancipation.

ONE OF THE most notorious instances of slave brutality occurred several weeks after Susan's arrival in Raleigh, on the Fourth of July 1815. That morning, she met early with the Reverend William McPheeters and attended prayer at the Methodist meetinghouse. The worship ceremony was ecumenical, conducted by both Methodist and Baptist ministers. After the service, Susan was invited to dine at three places: "in the family way at Mr. Shaw's, and at Mr. McP, at a public dinner at the White Cottage, and at Mr. Bond's." Afterward, she went to the State House, where she "saw a great crowd of people; heard a fine reader read the Declaration of [Independence], and was presented with a bunch of flowers."[3]

While Susan and other citizens of Raleigh listened to the orator read the words of Thomas Jefferson—"that all men are created equal, that they are endowed by their Creator with certain unalienable Rights, that among these are Life, Liberty and the pursuit of Happiness"—John R. Cooke and William Heflin, both of whom had been drinking heavily, came upon a missing slave named Stephen near the outskirts of town. Using whips, sticks, and a noose, they flogged him and then dragged him along the road, forcing him to keep up with their trotting horses. John Davis joined the group, and the three began to interrogate Stephen, asking if he were a runaway slave. When Stephen failed to respond, Davis suggested they take him to a "certain log" and torture the truth out of him. The three men left Raleigh at two o'clock in the afternoon, dragging Stephen along behind their horses at a swift pace. After seventeen miles, they stopped, tied him lengthwise to a fallen log, and beat him nearly senseless. Then they roused him and forced him to run behind their horses a distance of eight miles to the farm of Samuel Bailey, Stephen's owner.

As Cooke, Heflin, and Davis ran the exhausted slave through the woods to Bailey's farm, the residents of Raleigh continued to celebrate the holiday. After the oration at the State House, Susan spent the rest of the day "very agreeably" at the home of a female friend. There, she met a Mr. Hooper, a teacher at the University of North Carolina, and Edward B. Freeman, a young man from Sandwich, Connecticut. She was especially pleased to meet another northerner, whom she "almost claimed as cousin." Later that afternoon or early evening, they "took a long walk up into the woods (back of the Academy) whose wild and diversified appearance, does honor to the sandy plains of North Carolina."[4]

Susan probably returned to her rooms by dark, well before Cooke, Davis, and Heflin arrived at Samuel Bailey's farm with their captive. When Bailey emerged from his home and recognized his slave, he had the men haul Stephen to a nearby log. Then they laid him over it and flogged him to death.[5]

There is no evidence that Susan witnessed this event, but she was probably aware of it soon after it occurred; on July 6 she wrote, "Felt after I retired to my room great earnestness in prayer for this benighted land and for my dear pupils particularly. Lord, if I am not faithful, oh make me so."[6]

Susan certainly knew of the incident by October, when Cooke, Davis, and Heflin were brought to trial on the charge of murder. Local newspapers reported the story, and northern periodicals followed in November, bringing national notoriety to Raleigh. *American Magazine* reported, "In the course of the Trial, such scenes of wanton and brutal inhumanity were disclosed, as would almost exceed belief, in this part of the United States. Such savage sport as these monsters made of the life of a human being, would disgrace the veriest savages on earth." Only Cooke was convicted of the crime, and he was sentenced to death. On October 20, 1815, he was escorted to Fayetteville Street to be hanged. According to *American Magazine*, "He was actually brought out for execution, and made to cry with fear, when a pardon from the Governor set the culprit free!" Governor William Miller had received numerous petitions on Cooke's behalf: as the editor of the *Raleigh Star* explained, "Many thought it hard to hang Cooke, when it was believed Davis and Heflin were equally guilty, and his brother Joe Cooke, almost equally so. Some thought, as this was the first instance in which a white man had ever been convicted for killing a Negro, that it would be impolitic to hang him so unexpectedly. And others believed it would be wrong in all respects, to hang a white man for killing a Negro."[7]

The *Star's* editor claimed that most of North Carolina's citizens had no objections to Cooke's pardon: "But whatever might have been the motives of his Excellency, we hear no dissatisfaction expressed by any at this act of clemency." Nevertheless, some residents were deeply shocked by what had transpired. One reader wrote to the editor, deploring the governor's actions:

> You say no complaints are made at the exercise of this act of clemency. I know not what public opinion is, as I mix but little with the world. Many may dislike to be restricted in the amusement of whipping Negroes to death. From the testimony on the trial, it seemed to have been a delightful recreation to Davis, Cooke, Heflin & Co. to flog a poor exhausted Negro; two of them quarreled for the privilege, and permission to flog was even a stipulated reward for apprehending him. I can only answer for myself and some of my neighbours. We consider what you call *clemency* as an encouragement to murder. . . . What has been the effect in this instance?—Why sir, just the other day, almost in the neighbourhood of your city, a man hunting, found a Negro in the woods, and without knowing who he was, or asking to know, and without any provocation, he shot him down dead as he would a deer![8]

IN KEEPING WITH the official position of the national Presbyterian Church, Susan believed that as slaveholders converted to Christianity, such episodes of brutality would disappear. The church urged all members to treat slaves with humanity and benevolence while preparing them for gradual emancipation. Church leaders were optimistic. After taking stock of the number of revivals and new congregations in 1817, the General Assembly of the Presbyterian Church proclaimed, "Public Morals are decidedly better than they were some time back, throughout the Church. . . . [I]n those states where slavery unhappily prevails, the negroes are treated with more attention than heretofore. . . . [I]ncreasing exertions are made to promote their comfort, and correct their vices, which are the natural result of their state of bondage." The notion of benevolent Christian slaveholding allowed Christians to reconcile their faith with the concept of gradual emancipation.[9]

As a professed Presbyterian and a New Yorker, Susan was committed to a policy of gradual emancipation. In 1787, the Presbyterian Synods of New York and Philadelphia passed a resolution recommending that all members of their communion "give those persons who are at present held in servitude such good education as may prepare them for the better enjoyment of freedom." The synods also urged slaveholders to prepare their slaves for eventual emancipation and citizenship: "Grant them sufficient time and sufficient means of procuring by industry their own liberty at a moderate rate; that they may thereby be brought into society with those habits of industry that may render them useful citizens—and, finally, they recommend it to all the people under their care to use the most prudent measures, consistent with the interest and the state of civil society in the parts where they live, to procure, eventually, the final abolition of slavery in America." The Methodist and Freewill Baptist churches adopted similar resolutions.[10]

In 1818, just three years after Susan arrived in Raleigh, the General Assembly of the Presbyterian Church adopted an even stronger resolution on slavery, unanimously endorsed by ministers from both the North and the South: "We consider the voluntary enslaving of one part of the human race by another as a gross violation of the most precious and sacred rights of human nature, as utterly inconsistent with the law of God which requires us to love our neighbour as ourselves, and as totally irreconcilable with the spirit and principles of the gospel of Christ, which enjoin that 'all things whatsoever ye would that men should do to you, do ye even so to them.'" This resolution, which remained in force until the division of the Church twenty years thereafter, became known as the 1818 Expression of Views.[11]

In response to the antislavery stance of the major Protestant denominations and the ideas embedded in the Declaration of Independence, slave liberations in the South reached unprecedented levels during the early postrevolutionary era. Virginians freed about fifteen thousand slaves between 1782 and 1808, and liberations accounted for nearly 60 percent of the growth in the state's free black population during that period. Based on an analysis of the Methodist Church's efforts to convince members to free their slaves in Brunswick County, Virginia, historian Art Budros has concluded that religious ideology motivated masters to decide to liberate their slaves, but economic and social factors influenced their decisions regarding when those manumissions were written.[12]

Despite an initial wave of enthusiasm for emancipation, the manumission of slaves tapered off after 1810. As the population of free blacks increased, whites became fearful of social unrest. Economic self-interest also played a role. By delaying the liberation of slaves, owners continued to reap income from slave labor throughout their lifetimes, and because the price of slaves continuously rose, masters had strong financial incentives to hold on to their property for as long as possible. Parents were often reluctant to relinquish a form of wealth that might benefit their heirs. In some families, the decision to free slaves pitted the slaveholder against his offspring who contested manumission decisions in the courts. As one Methodist woman explained when Virginia preacher William Ormond urged her to write a will freeing her slaves, their liberation would depend entirely on whether or not she bore children. In disgust, Ormond later confided to his journal, "Lord keep the Women in a state of sterility if this is their scheme."[13]

Both Methodists and Baptists promoted manumission as a Christian duty during the decades after the revolution, but by 1784, the Methodists had given up attempts to emulate the Quakers and bar slaveholders from fellowship. When he rode through Virginia in the spring of 1785, preacher Francis Asbury noted in his journal, "I found the minds of the people greatly agitated with our rules against slavery, and a proposed petition to the general assembly for the emancipation of the blacks." By the turn of the century, some preachers worried that attacks on slavery would drive away members and prospective converts and urged their brethren to refrain from portraying slaveholding as a sin. Although he still urged emancipation, even Asbury seemed prepared to soften his public stance against slavery if doing so would encourage slave owners to allow their slaves to hear the Gospel. In 1809, he wrote, "We are defrauded of great numbers by the pains that are taken to keep the blacks from us; their masters are afraid of the influence of our principles. Would not an *amelioration* in the condition and treatment of slaves have produced more practical good to the poor Africans, than any attempt at their *emancipation*? . . . Now their masters will not let them come to hear us. What is the personal liberty of the African which he may abuse, to the salvation of his soul; how may it be compared?"[14]

Early nineteenth-century northerners and southerners generally concurred on a strategy of gradual emancipation, but the meaning of the term was open to interpretation. Some northern abolitionists viewed it as a progressive strategy that would culminate in the integration of black citizens into American society. As historian Paul J. Polgar notes, members of the early abolition societies, including New York's Manumission Society, argued that gradual emancipation laws would not only allow former slaves time to transition to republican citizens but also allow antislavery activists time to persuade skeptical whites to set aside their prejudices and allow blacks equal participation in a democratic society. According to Julie Winch, many leaders of the free black community agreed with this strategy of emancipation. For slaveholders in the New England and mid-Atlantic states, gradual emancipation represented a conservative compromise between slaveholders' property rights and enslaved persons' natural rights to life, liberty, and the pursuit of happiness. Southern slaveholders also accepted the idea of gradual emancipation, not only because some may have agreed with these arguments but also because the policy deferred the thorny problem of emancipation to the future.[15]

When Susan Nye lived in Raleigh, southern clergymen regularly defended slaveholding with some embarrassment and liberally sprinkled their writings with such formulaic phrases as "I am no advocate for slavery" and "The Bible does not by any means *Justify* slavery." Some slaveholders expressed hope that something could be done to alleviate its consequences. Such feelings made possible the movement to establish colonies for African Americans outside the United States.[16]

In 1819, a branch of the American Colonization Society (ACS) was established in Raleigh, with Joseph Gales serving as its secretary. The ACS advocated gradual emancipation through manumission, followed by emigration to Liberia. Supporters viewed this plan as a compromise solution to the problem of slavery: "It seems to be the middle ground, upon which the several interests throughout the country, in relation to slavery, can meet and act together." Gales remained a member of the Raleigh ACS until 1833, when he retired, moved to Washington, D.C., and joined the national organization, holding the position of treasurer until 1839.[17]

By the 1820s, the meaning of the terms "gradual emancipation" and "abolition" had changed significantly in American discourse. In both the North and the South, gradual emancipation no longer necessarily entailed a strategic outcome in which both whites and freed slaves would live together as citizens. The gradual emancipation promoted by the ACS bore little resemblance to the progressive strategy of the early republican abolitionists. Ministers endorsed the colonization of Africa as a means of bringing Christian faith to the unconverted, but many free blacks saw colonization as a racist strategy designed to remove black people from white society. The early abolitionists had viewed gradualism as a necessary tactic to prepare prejudiced whites and slaves for the full participation of free blacks in American society. In contrast, many members of the ACS saw danger in allowing large numbers of free blacks to live among whites.[18]

THROUGHOUT THE ANTEBELLUM period, young Americans encountered evolving ideas about slavery and emancipation, not only in sermons and newspapers but also in schoolbooks. The courses of study in the higher grades of antebellum common schools, academies, and colleges often included moral philosophy, and texts in that subject commonly included sections on slavery.

Susan Nye taught her students about slavery using the Reverend William Paley's *Principles of Moral and Political Philosophy*. Published in England in 1785, more than two decades before the abolition of the slave trade in the United States, Paley's book became the most popular moral philosophy text in America before 1830, and Susan used it for more than two decades. Understanding Paley is thus critical to understanding her perspective on emancipation.[19]

William Paley (1743–1805) argued that the practice of keeping human beings perpetually in slavery went against the laws of nature and that the slave trade was inexcusable because of its cruelty. Throughout the eighteenth century, some advocates had argued for the continuation of slavery in the Americas on grounds of economic necessity. Others had turned to the Bible to find support for the institution. Paley dismissed both rationalizations: "But *necessity* is pretended; the name under which every enormity is attempted to be justified. And after all, what is the necessity? It has never been proved that the land could not be cultivated there, as it is here, by hired servants. It is said that it could not be cultivated with quite the same conveniency and cheapness, as by the labour of slaves: by which means, a pound of sugar, which the planter now sells for sixpence, could not be afforded under sixpence halfpenny—and this is the *necessity!*"[20]

Paley acknowledged that "slavery was part of the civil constitution of most countries when Christianity appeared; yet no passage is to be found in the Christian scriptures, by which it is condemned or prohibited." Nevertheless, past practice did not justify slavery: "But does it follow, from the silence of Scripture concerning them, that all the civil institutions which then prevailed, were right? Or that the bad should not be exchanged for better?" He argued that the spread of Christianity had eventually banished

Greek and Roman slavery and that the advance of Christianity in the modern world would "banish what remains of this odious institution."[21]

Although Paley portrayed slavery as against the laws of nature, he also believed that full emancipation could be carried out only "by provisions of law, and under the protection of civil government." He justified the continuance of slavery using arguments related to national and state security: "The discharging of slaves from all obligation to obey their masters; which is the consequence of pronouncing slavery to be unlawful, would have no better effect, than to let loose one half of mankind upon the other." His argument—that slaveholders, like citizens of the pre-Christian Roman Empire, would gradually abandon slavery over generations as they converted to Christianity—removed responsibility for emancipation from the shoulders of the current generation. Christians could turn their energies to converting the slaves and teaching them habits of industry and obedience, leaving the hard problems of emancipation for another day. This line of thinking absolved slave owners from the need to liberate their slaves.[22]

One reason Paley's text was so popular in American schoolrooms is that it so well represented the prevailing anxiety of the age. For example, although Jefferson wrote that he hoped to see the end of slavery, he also feared that whites and freed slaves could never live together in peace. Freed slaves, full of resentment and anger over their past treatment, might seek retribution against their former masters, with a bloody race war the result. "Unhappily it is a case for which both parties require long and difficult preparation," he wrote in 1815. Multiple editions of Paley's argument about gradual emancipation found their way into hundreds of American academy and college classrooms during the early national period, contributing to a national discourse regarding slavery. Common school students between the ages of fourteen and sixteen recited lessons from Paley's text, which was used in the courses of study at Columbia College, the College of Philadelphia (now the University of Pennsylvania), Yale, and Harvard, among many others.[23]

Young women as well as men studied Paley's text. Prominent female educator Emma Willard assigned the book in 1814, when she opened a boarding school for females in Middlebury, Vermont, and she continued to assign Paley's text when she established New York's Troy Female Seminary seven years later: "My studies are Paley's *Moral Philosophy*[,] Kames *Elements of Criticism* and Botany. I do not attend to Music," Troy student Mary Ann Cole informed her cousin in 1821. Describing the ordeal of Troy's 1833 school examinations, Chloe Cole reported, "I came up five times once in

French, twice in Euclid, and twice in Paley." As Sarah Pierce reminded the graduating class of Litchfield Female Academy in 1818, "To improve those general principles of morality upon which all ought to act you have studied Paley's *Moral Philosophy* and I trust that you will find in the knowledge it has given you of your duty and the motives for its performance it has not been an unnecessary or useless part of your education." Harriet Beecher Stowe recalled hearing the older pupils at Litchfield Academy recite passages from Paley's text: "I listened with eager ears to historical criticisms and discussions, or to recitations in such works as 'Paley's Moral Philosophy' ... all full of most awakening suggestions to my thoughts." Susan Nye likely also studied Paley.[24]

Editions of Paley's book also were used at North Carolina's educational institutions before 1830. Gales began importing Paley's text from England in 1800, and by 1811, it was listed among the books studied in the Female Department of Raleigh Academy. Female students at Warrenton Academy read Paley in 1813, young men encountered the book at New Bern Academy in 1823 and at the Roanoke Institute in 1829, and when Susan Nye Hutchison was head of Salisbury Female Academy in 1836, her course of study included the text.[25]

For forty years, the American editions' treatment of slavery remained unchanged, but in 1828 a new adaptation of Paley's text softened the criticism of slaveholding. Bethel Judd, rector of St. James Church in New London, Connecticut, edited this version, which was reprinted in numerous editions on the U.S. market. As he explained in his preface, although Paley's *Moral Philosophy* was "one of the most useful works in the English language," it had been authored by an Englishman and thus contained "many things contrary to the constitution, laws, and usages of this country." Judd inserted some of his own language into the section on slavery to bolster the argument against immediate emancipation and introduce the concept of humane or benevolent slaveholding, and he added recitation questions to the appendix so that teachers could examine their pupils using the traditional method of question and response.[26] A recitation based on Judd's book would have had the teacher read each question, with the students answering in unison by reciting directly from the text:

Q: What is slavery?
    R: Slavery is an obligation to labour for the benefit of the master, without the contract or consent of the servant.
Q: What is said of the humane master?

R: The humane master, who knows and feels the evils of slavery, must suffer deeply with the view of that which he has no power to cure, and but little to meliorate.

Q: What is said of sudden emancipation?

R: Sudden emancipation will ruin the slaves, as well as their masters.

Q: Who is not to be blamed?

R: I do not blame the humane master who holds his slaves in bondage, that he cannot emancipate with safety to the community.

Q: Who is to be blamed?

R: I blame him who stole them from their country, and the man who encourages this inhuman traffic.

Q: In what manner should the emancipation of slaves be carried on?

R: The emancipation of slaves should be gradual, and carried on under the provisions of civil law, and under the protection of civil government.

Q: What has produced some effect?

R: Christianity has produced some effect, and this effect is constantly increasing.

Q: What slavery and tyranny has declined before the power of Christianity?

R: Greek and Roman slavery, and since these, the feudal tyranny, has declined before the power of Christianity.

Q: What good effects are seen from the influence of religion?

R: As the knowledge of religion advances in the world, it will banish what remains of this odious institution.[27]

During the 1830s, a regional divide appeared in the way moral philosophy textbooks treated the topic of slavery, and Paley's *Moral Philosophy* gradually lost ground to other texts. In the North, an edition of Paley's text for the Boston common schools was reprinted up until the 1850s, but Francis Wayland's *The Elements of Moral Science*, which carried a stronger argument against slavery and racial discrimination, came to dominate the market. The first book published specifically for use in southern academies and colleges appeared in 1837 and was authored by Jasper Adams, president of the College of Charleston, South Carolina. Rather than characterize slavery as against the laws of nature or a social evil, Adams provided biblical support for slavery, describing slaves as "servants born in the house, or bought with the money of their master" and explaining, "The greatest part of the servants mentioned in the Scriptures were of this third class." His text included no mention of any possibility of emancipation: "The relation of servants of this class to their masters, subsists for life."[28]

By the 1850s, academies and colleges in the South had begun to replace northern textbooks with proslavery books authored by southerners, some of which argued that God sanctioned slavery. As Richard Henderson Rivers put it in his *Elements of Moral Philosophy*, "Slavery is not a sin; . . . it was established originally by the Divine Being, for wise, just, and benevolent purposes; . . . it was directly sanctioned by Christ and his apostles, and is not, therefore, the sum of all villanies."[29]

OF COURSE, ENSLAVED black Christians had an entirely different perspective. Susan Nye talked and prayed with slaves and free blacks on the streets in Raleigh, but only her account of these conversations has survived. The thoughts of the Christian slaves who spoke with her—whether about salvation, happiness, or freedom—have been lost. Although it is an imperfect proxy, the surviving narrative of Lunsford Lane provides some insight into this missing point of view.

Born in 1803, Lane was twelve years old when Susan arrived to teach at Raleigh Academy. As a slave, he was the possession of Sherwood Haywood, a former clerk of the State Senate, plantation owner, and founding member of the academy's board of trustees. As a young man, he became determined to purchase his freedom and initiated a number of entrepreneurial business activities to earn money toward his goal. He later became famous for publishing a slave narrative that included descriptions of his life in Raleigh and of his difficulties in obtaining his family's freedom. Lane's narrative illustrates his reaction to contemporary justifications for slavery, the nature of covert resistance among slaves, and the vast divide between enslaved and free Christians on the issue of slavery and emancipation.

Susan knew the Haywood family well, since several Haywood daughters attended the academy during her time there. Like Susan, some Haywood women were members of the Raleigh Female Benevolent Society and the Raleigh Female Tract Society, and Susan occasionally attended prayer meetings at the Haywood home. Because of these relationships, Susan probably encountered Lane during social events at the Haywood home, where he worked, though she never mentioned him in her journal. Both Lunsford and Susan were professing Christians—he a Baptist, she a

Presbyterian—and they listened to some of the same sermons preached in the State House by McPheeters. Despite such connections, they inhabited very different worlds.[30]

Raleigh's whites, slaves, and free blacks worshipped together in the State House, in the Methodist meetinghouse, and in the Baptist church, where worshippers commonly brought tallow candles to evening services. On one occasion, when Susan attended worship there, "a warm and animated preacher, Mr. Daniel, gave us a sermon with which the audience seemed much delighted." She reported, "The room was crowded with black and white" and the "candles began to glimmer in their sockets."[31]

But Christian blacks and whites were separate and not equal in racially mixed congregations. Lane sat in a segregated back row or second-floor gallery when he heard McPheeters preach one Sunday on "the superiority of American freedom over the despotism of Europe." After thanking God for the privileges Americans enjoyed as a result of their free institutions, McPheeters made a statement that Lane would long remember: it was "impossible to enslave an intelligent people." McPheeters was referring not to the enslavement of Africans but to the previous "enslavement" of Americans under tyrannical British rule; however, his words had a different meaning to the young man. According to William Hawkins, who befriended Lane in his later years and wrote a biography of his life, the former slave thought deeply about this sermon and discussed it with other blacks, and the more they considered McPheeters's words, "the more determined they became that they would be free."[32]

Lane could not attend Raleigh Academy's Lancaster School, which was open to whites only. During his early childhood, he played with the other boys and girls of both races on Haywood's plantation. He later recalled, "I knew no difference between myself and the white children, nor did they seem to know any in turn. Sometimes my master would come out and give a biscuit to me, and another to one of his own white boys, but I did not perceive the difference between us." When he grew old enough to work, however, "I discovered the difference between myself and my master's white children. They began to order me about, and were told to do so by my master and mistress. I found, too, that they had learned to read, while I was not permitted to have a book in my hand. To be in the possession of anything written or printed, was regarded as an offence." Like many slave masters, Sherwood Haywood probably forbade the teaching of his slaves to prevent them from gaining the ability to forge passes and escape. According to historians John Hope Franklin and Loren

Schweninger, when captured, nearly 6 percent of black and 10 percent of mulatto runaway slaves possessed forged papers.[33]

In 1830, North Carolina passed legislation that forbade the teaching of slaves to read and write in response to fears of slave insurrection. Nevertheless, despite similar laws and customs in many slave states, a small percentage of slaves acquired literacy. Advertisements placed in newspapers asking for help in capturing and returning runaway slaves sometimes mentioned the ability to read or write: one 1808 Virginia newspaper advertisement stated, "Ten Dollars Reward—Ran away from the subscriber living at the lower end of Buckingham on the 19th day of this month, a Negro Man named Jack Going. . . . It is very likely he will forge himself a free pass, as he could write and read prior to his elopement." According to W. E. B. Du Bois, "The very feeling of inferiority which slavery forced upon them fathered an intense desire to rise out of their condition by means of education." Du Bois has estimated that around 5 percent of slaves learned to read, while historian Eugene D. Genovese finds that estimate possibly too low. The letters, narratives, and biographies of ex-slaves, travelers, and slaveholders indicate that many communities and plantations had at least one literate slave, enabling news about the outside world to spread relatively rapidly among the slaves.[34]

Genovese concludes that the slaves' efforts to teach each other must have originated with opportunities created by friendly white individuals. White children sometimes taught their black playmates behind the backs of their parents and other adults. Some planters instructed one or two of their slaves either to equip them for work that required literacy or to allow them to read the Bible. Sarah Frew Davidson, a former student of Susan Nye's, started teaching slaves to read on her widowed father's plantation in the 1830s, although doing so was against the law. In her journal, she wrote, "Attended the instruction of our young servants—being much troubled and perplexed (relative to my duty) on this subject—and believing religious instruction cannot be well communicated without some knowledge of letters . . . I commenced learning them to read." Within six weeks, "by their faithful attendance and application," she wrote, "they can now—repeat the Lord's Prayer—His commandments—(and in same degree understand) and also can answer all prominent questions which may be asked on the 1st & 2nd Chapters of Genesis—and the 1st and 2nd chapters of Matthew—and progressing as fast as I can reasonably expect in learning to read."[35]

However, although some whites may have provided occasional covert instruction, most slaves learned from each other. In cases where they received lessons in reading Bible passages, slaves sometimes leveraged that instruction to read more widely and teach others beyond the plantation and Sunday school walls. In villages, towns, and cities, literate slaves and free blacks had greater space and opportunity to teach others. Even on the plantations, some slaves gathered in secret to learn from each other before dawn and well after sunset. White authorities sought to prevent such covert instruction: in 1800, the South Carolina Legislature forbade anyone from providing slaves with "mental instruction," which included not only reading and writing but also arithmetic and memorization. Historian Heather Andrea Williams concludes that this law specifically sought to stop blacks from conducting secret schools.[36]

Lunsford Lane never explained how he learned to read and write beyond saying, "While in the South I succeeded by stealth in learning to read and write a little, and since I have been in the North I have learned more."[37]

The churches were important sources of religious instruction for slaves. When Susan first lived in Raleigh, slaves often worshipped together in independent prayer meetings. After attending an evening prayer meeting one night in August, Susan returned to her lodging and wrote, "As we returned, passed a negro prayer meeting—Oh, may not their souls be whiter than mine. Their singing was delightful. Long after I came into my room, I heard their shouting." Such meetings were outlawed after slave preacher Nat Turner led followers in a bloody uprising in Southampton County, Virginia, just across North Carolina's border, in August 1831. In response, the North Carolina Legislature prohibited all slaves and free blacks from preaching or exhorting in public "or in any manner to officiate as a preacher or teacher in any prayer meeting, or other association for worship, where slaves of different families are collected together." Lane's narrative never mentions any independent black congregations, possibly because he was not permitted to attend such meetings. When he worshipped, he listened to the exhortations of white preachers.[38]

Slave owners and white preachers often collaborated to promote spiritual and moral values that they believed would lend safety and stability to the institution of slavery. During his years in Raleigh, Lane acquired a religious education. However, as in many other cases, the results differed substantially from what his teachers had envisioned. Some slaveholders who considered African Americans little more than beasts of burden inadvertently converted them to a religion that emphasized not only their humanity but also their divinity and equality before God.[39]

Regardless of masters' vested interests in encouraging Christianity among their slaves, the slave community often developed its own interpretations of preachers' lessons. Slaves did not hear prescriptive messages uncritically. According to Lane, familiar sermon topics such as "Servants be obedient to your masters" and "He that knoweth his master's will and doeth it not, shall be beaten with many stripes" comprised most of these public instructions. "The first commandment impressed upon our minds was to obey our masters, and the second was like unto it, namely, to do as much work when they or the overseers were not watching us as when they were." But the audience members understood the motives behind such messages: "There was one very kind hearted Episcopal minister whom I often used to hear; he was very popular with the colored people. But after he had preached a sermon to us in which he argued from the Bible that it was the will of heaven from all eternity we should be slaves, and our masters be our owners, most of us left him; for like some of the faint hearted disciples in early times we said,—'This is a hard saying, who can bear it?'"[40]

Lane encountered several contemporary rationalizations for slavery, including the notion of the good master and the myth of the happy slave. Whites sometimes lulled themselves into believing that slaves—particularly house slaves—were happy. As a house servant who waited on the Haywood family's guests, Lane required appropriate attire. While he was being fitted for a suit, the tailor remarked how superior Lane's life was to that of a field hand, adding, "I suppose, Lane, nothing could induce you to become a free man. You would not take your freedom if it were offered you. You must be a happy man to be allowed to wear such fine clothes as these your master has ordered you."[41]

But Lane and other slaves were far from content with their lot. By the time this conversation took place, he had for years been secretly saving money to buy his freedom. When he was just a child, he explained, "My father gave me a small basket of peaches. I sold them for thirty cents, which was the first money I ever had in my life. . . . The hope that then entered my mind of purchasing at some future time my freedom, made me long for money; and plans for money-making took the principal possession of my thoughts." After he married a woman belonging to another master and they had several children, Lane devised a long-range plan to free himself and his family. He accumulated a substantial amount of money by laboring "at dead of night, after the long weary day's toil for my master was over, till I found I had collected one hundred dollars."[42]

By 1835, he had earned a thousand dollars and had purchased his freedom, but North Carolina authorities refused to recognize his free status. With the help of a friend, he left for New York, where he petitioned for and obtained freed status. Over the next seven years, he struggled to emancipate his family and eventually brought his wife and children north to Boston, where he spoke and wrote about his life in Raleigh.[43]

The narratives of Lunsford Lane and other former slaves undermined the concept of benevolent slaveholding. Although southern state legislatures banned such publications for fear they would spark slave uprisings, word of their contents still circulated. Lane's narrative triggered a defensive reaction from his former owners. Just before the Civil War, Lane received a letter from Lucy Haywood Bryan, who had studied in Raleigh Academy's Female Department in 1820 and 1822 and had remained in touch with her former teacher, Susan Nye. Bryan wrote to Lane with news of the family, adding, "You know we look upon our servants as friends, and not as slaves, and we feel as much for them as if they were children. . . . The abolitionists say a great deal about Southern people; but you know from your own experience, and that of your family, that you never received any but the kindest treatment."[44]

The idea that a Christian slaveholding woman could create a positive and happy environment for her slaves was important not only to Lucy Haywood and other slaveholders but also to Susan Nye and other teachers who promoted this idea by instructing their students to promote the spiritual and physical welfare and happiness of their slaves. Ultimately, it was an impossible task. As more former slaves began to speak in public and publish their stories, some women began to openly challenge the premise of benevolent slaveholding. As the South Carolina abolitionist Angelina Grimké proclaimed in a public speech in Philadelphia in 1838, "I have *never* seen a happy slave."[45]

White evangelicals committed to gradual emancipation often clung to the belief that although slavery was evil, it had brought Africans the beneficial prospect of conversion to Christianity. During her years in the South, Susan Nye sometimes comforted herself with this point of view. "Surely to every Christian, there is something in the thought," she wrote, "that so many of the long neglected race of Ham are brought to know the Savior . . . even though to gain this salvation they are doomed to pass through 'all the ills' that slaves are heir to."[46]

Lunsford Lane rejected such rationalizations. As he recalled, "I, with others, was often told by the minister how good God was in bringing us over to this country from dark and benighted Africa, and permitting us to listen to the sound of the gospel." However, "To me, God also granted temporal freedom, which man without God's consent, had stolen away."[47]

AFTER MORE THAN two decades in the South, Susan Nye probably would have been considered a northern-born southerner by contemporary observers but for the fact that she later publicly identified herself as a northerner. During the 1840s and 1850s, some northern teachers working in the South privately criticized slaveholding society, and sometimes the feeling was mutual. According to Christie Anne Farnham, by the 1850s, northern teachers either accommodated themselves to slavery or left the region.[48]

But Susan's case is not necessarily unusual, given the period in which she taught. Virtually all of the archival evidence of southern hostility toward northern teachers is based on documents from the two decades leading up to the Civil War. In contrast, northerners who came south to teach in the early decades of the century were well integrated into southern culture, not only because slavery still existed in some regions of the North but also because many white Americans in both regions shared similar beliefs about emancipation. While Susan lived in Raleigh and Augusta, the majority of Americans in both the North and the South agreed that the immediate emancipation of southern slaves should be avoided. Sermons and schoolbooks broadcast this message, creating a mainstream political and cultural consensus about gradual emancipation after the American Revolution.[49]

Throughout her time in the South, Susan devoted herself to the task of teaching her students to treat slaves well. She probably viewed this as part of her mission, a perspective triggered or reinforced by one particular incident. On July 29, 1815, several weeks after the murder of the slave Stephen, Susan was awakened by the screams of a female slave being battered by the landlord, Mr. Cradep. The young woman ran through the house, "her neck torn and bloody, her eye swollen," as the enraged man chased her down the hallway, whip in hand. "Oh I never witnessed such a scene," wrote Susan. "Father of mercies guard my heart and keep me from the seductions of evil—Oh how callous are the hearts of this people! Surely they can have little hope of mercy when they show none."[50]

Some of Susan's surprise and outrage arose from her initial impression of the Cradeps as a "good family" with Christian values. She had come to admire the Cradeps very much, describing Mrs. Cradep as "a lovely little woman" and expressing contentment with her boarding arrangement in their household. In her opinion, Mr. Cradep was "one of the best husbands of one of the best wives in America." She frequently joined the family to attend prayer meetings where Mr. Cradep, a lay Baptist minister, preached. She was shocked and appalled to awaken one morning to the sight of this man, furious and armed with a whip, pursuing a battered and bloodied woman through the house: "Oh, day of retributive justice! I live it is said with one of the best of masters."[51]

Susan never sat down and analyzed this incident in the pages of her journal, but perhaps it instilled a long-standing commitment to the notion of benevolent slaveholding. The Declaration of Independence had proclaimed that God had endowed all men with certain rights, including the pursuit of happiness. But how could a slave be happy? As historian James Oakes has pointed out, the happiness of slaves was a serious issue during the early national period, revealing contemporary thinking that was central to political culture. The moral philosophy textbook Susan used at Raleigh Academy taught that the immediate liberation of slaves would bring ruin to society and that slave owners were morally bound to continue holding their slaves until the spread of Christian religion induced civil governments to abolish slavery. The contradiction inherent in this proposition—that although slavery was evil, slaveholding was not—was resolved only by the belief that the benevolent Christian slaveholder could provide an environment in which slaves might find both salvation and happiness.[52]

In later years, Susan struggled with the moral dilemmas inherent in the proposition. On the one hand, she wished to fully belong and accommodate to the southern communities in which she lived; in fact, such accommodation was essential to the successful operation of any entrepreneurial school. But on the other hand, she desired to uphold the traditional antislavery stance of the New York Presbyterian Synod. In later years, this dual identity became more difficult to maintain, and sometimes she warred within herself. Twenty years after she first arrived at Raleigh Academy, Susan returned as a widow, with years of experience under her belt and a sense of independence and agency. At that time, she began to resist the state's slave codes. But as a young, unmarried, and inexperienced teacher, she often felt overwhelmed and powerless. One of the first entries she penned after arriving in North Carolina provides a glimpse of her feelings during her first months in Raleigh: After expressing shock and dismay at the ragged condition of the slaves in Wilmington, she wrote, "What is man? I, but alas, I do not know even mine own heart."[53]

CHAPTER 4

Marriage in Adversity

Dost thou take this man, before God and these witnesses, to be thy husband?
Dost thou promise to love him, honour him, cherish and obey him, in
joy and in sorrow, in health and in sickness, in prosperity and in adversity?
Wilt thou be faithful to him in all things as becometh a good wife, and never
forsake him so long as ye both do live?
—*The Presbyterian Book of Public Prayer, 1857*

Susan and Amanda Nye traveled to Augusta, Georgia, in the summer of
1823, and by October "Miss Nye's School" was open for business. Like well-
known educators Catharine and Mary Beecher, who established Connecticut's Hartford Female Seminary that same year, or New York's Emma
Willard, who had opened Troy Female Seminary only two years earlier,
Susan must have had high hopes of success. Perhaps she had heard of these
women's ventures and dreamed of founding an institution of similar reputation in Georgia. But if this was her dream, it was very short-lived, because
she soon married and gave up her school.[1]

She met Adam Hutchison (1781–1834), a widower with three children,
sometime after joining Augusta's First Presbyterian Church. He began
to court her, and on Christmas Day 1824, she "first solemnly considered
the subject of becoming the wife of Mr. H." He and his brother, William,
had emigrated from Scotland to work as merchants in Georgia, and by the
time Susan arrived, his brother had moved west to Alabama and Adam had
begun to trade on Augusta's Cotton Exchange. He had been "Admitted on
Profession" of faith to Augusta's First Presbyterian Church in 1820, so he
and Susan probably met through the church.[2]

Susan was a mature, intelligent, and independent woman, yet she
ignored a clear warning sign when she married Adam. Just five days after
she first seriously thought about his proposal, some incident caused him
to fly into a rage. Six weeks later, on February 10, 1825, she married him
anyway. Perhaps, as a woman in her thirties, she feared that she would
never have another chance to have a family of her own. Perhaps the prospect of a financially secure life, coupled with a sense of Christian duty

toward Hutchison's motherless children, played a role. Perhaps she convinced herself that she could improve his character. At the end of 1826, she would write of that angry outburst with regret: "Today two years have elapsed since I first saw Mr. H. *angry*, would to God that I could say it was also the last."[3]

During the course of her very difficult marriage, Susan eventually established "Mrs. Adam Hutchison's School" and began teaching to support her family. Most of what historians know about married women who conducted their own schools is based on women who taught very small children in their own dwellings or women who taught in schools owned and operated by their husbands; we know very little about married women—especially those with children of their own—who operated their own schools outside the home, and we know even less about how their communities viewed and responded to their work. Susan's journals thus provide an important perspective on married women's work outside the home in the antebellum South. Her writing also presents a detailed picture of the growing strains on her marriage that eventually impelled her to send two young sons north: her husband's episodes of rage, the collapse of the family finances, the death of a child, and the threat of slave insurrection in Augusta.[4]

MANY WOMEN DREAMED of entering a companionate relationship with a husband upon marriage, but for some wives, this dream remained out of reach. Some family historians use the term "companionate marriage" to describe a new trend in marital relationships that allegedly arose among the middle classes in the eighteenth and nineteenth centuries. Companionate marriage was based on love and mutual respect. After the Revolutionary War, some American writers carried the concept of companionate marriage even further, associating republican virtue with equal partnerships in marriage. Nevertheless, as historian Mary Beth Norton has noted, both conservative notions of married women's subordination and liberal ideas about mutuality in marriage coexisted throughout the early republican period.[5]

Despite the existence of some liberal rhetoric about equal partnership in marriage, marriage cost women their relative independence and economic freedom. The law in Georgia was English common law, inherited from the colonial period and largely unrevised until after the Civil War. Under common law, single women and widows could own and control property, but their married sisters could not. As James Wilson explains,

"The husband and wife become, in law, only one person: the legal existence of the wife is consolidated into that of the husband." Under the law of coverture, husbands took control of all of their wives' assets and future earnings. Married women had no independent economic standing. They could neither sue nor be sued. They could not make contracts or execute valid wills, and they could neither purchase nor emancipate slaves. In return, husbands were responsible for providing for their wives and children.[6]

To varying degrees throughout the early national period, sermons and religious literature emphasized men's authority over women in marriage. "The family will become a little church," explained Congregational minister Joseph Lathrop in 1810. "The husband, under [Christ], is ruler in his own house, and when he governs it according to the laws of Christ, all the members are to be subject to him." According to Methodist leader John Wesley, women had a duty to obey: "The husband's will is a law to his wife, and binds her conscience in all things indifferent. Nor does even this suffice, unless she obey readily, quietly, cheerfully, without brawling, contending, sourness." Presbyterian John Witherspoon, president of the College of New Jersey (now Princeton University), acknowledged the importance of companionability and near equality in marriage, but like all ministers of that era, he concluded that ultimate authority lay with men. In 1808, the *Married Lady's Companion* advised young women to beware of the deference men accorded them in courtship, warning that once the honeymoon was over, husbands would expect submission and obedience from their wives.[7]

Schoolbooks and popular essays sometimes combined conservative messages about marital obedience with more liberal ideas about the intellectual equality of the sexes. William Paley's *Moral and Political Philosophy* explained that while "nature may have made and left the sexes of the human species nearly equal in their faculties, and perfectly so in their rights," equality could not exist in marriage. Without a designated superior, men and women were bound to disagree and engage in competition over every aspect of everyday life. For this reason, the Bible mandated absolute obedience from wives. To clinch his argument, Paley quoted St. Paul: "Let the wife . . . be subject to her own husband in everything." According to historian Nancy Cott, this perspective also permeated contemporary print media, which published essays bearing such titles as "Thoughts on Matrimony," "On the Choice of a Wife," "Character of a Good Husband," and "Reflections on Marriage Unions."[8]

When he visited the United States in the early 1830s, Alexis de Tocqueville saw no evidence of equal partnership in American marriages and used the phrase "distinct spheres of action" to describe what he viewed as the social divide between male and female activity: "In America, more than anywhere else in the world, care has been taken constantly to trace clearly distinct spheres of action for the two sexes, and both are required to keep in step, but along paths that are never the same." He found this distinction particularly evident in the case of married men and women. Although he believed the single American girl to be far more independent and worldly wise than the typical French girl, Tocqueville concluded that the American woman completely sacrificed her independence when she married, subjecting herself to her husband's authority and living in his home "as if it were a cloister."[9]

Historians have questioned the extent to which the "separate spheres" ideology Tocqueville described existed in practice. As Linda K. Kerber has noted, both men and women used the cultural trope of separate spheres to characterize and understand gendered power relations in society, but contemporary rhetoric did not always reflect actual experience. Most Americans lived in rural areas, and among middle- and working-class families, the lines between public and private activity overlapped. Even in small towns and villages, some married women worked outside the home as innkeepers, herbalists, shopkeepers, printers, midwives, textile workers, or teachers. As more women gained education and began to participate in voluntary associations, some married women moved into civic public spaces, and the traditional lines between women's domestic and men's public spheres blurred, requiring renegotiation and redefinition.[10]

Nevertheless, law and tradition gave men the upper hand in marriage. Dreams of a companionate marriage could set women up for disappointment, and the more independent the woman—the more she believed in her right to make decisions for the family—the greater the possibility of conflict with a husband who reserved that right to himself.[11]

SUSAN'S SURVIVING JOURNAL entries resume on October 1, 1826, by which time she was an established resident of Augusta, a wife, a stepmother, and the mother of an infant son, Sylvanus Nye Hutchison, born on December 29, 1825. In these entries, Susan refers to the impact of a long drought on the low level of the Savannah River; she knew that suspension of shipping on the river would hurt her husband's merchant business, but she had no idea how much.

October 1 Sabbath—I spent this holy day at home with my dear Sylvanus. He has been unwell for more than a week with a distressing bowel complaint which possibly my ignorance of all medical matters may have rendered worse. I am ashamed to know so little of a subject in which all are so deeply interested. Sister Amanda and Mr. H were much pleased with Mr. Moderwell's sermon in the morning, it was upon the Pharisee. In the evening Mr. H. read to us Saints Rest.

3—Dr. William Shaw from Raleigh via Charleston came to see us. We were greatly pleased to hear from our old friends.

5—I slept little my teeth and head and arms and ankles all pained me.

6—By the divine mercy I rose somewhat relieved but I was afraid to take the shower bath which until this time I have continued to use.

7—Our quilt was taken off—we had a very heavy rain throughout the whole day. So much water has not fallen at once since our residence on the Hill. It is a melancholy time, the river is lower than it has been for years. Commerce by Steam Boats is at an end consequently prices of all imported articles, at least heavy ones, are much enhanced. Mr. H. has already been a pretty severe sufferer by being obliged to pay an exhorbitant freight.

The Hutchison household of 1826 bore some of the hallmarks of the secluded domestic retreat that some historians have ascribed to the middle-class households of the mid-nineteenth century. Within the privacy of their home, the couple enjoyed a quiet family life. Hannah (born December 14, 1812) and Elizabeth (born May 26, 1817), Adam's daughters from his first marriage, lived with them, while their brother, Robert (born July 14, 1814), attended school in Scotland. Susan's younger sister, Amanda, also resided with the family. In the evenings, Adam frequently read aloud from sermons and religious books such as Richard Baxter's *The Saints' Everlasting Rest* while Susan and Amanda listened, their hands probably busy with needlework. Some scholars have emphasized the centrality of southern women's role as advocates of religion in the antebellum home, but it is clear that in the Hutchisons' marriage, the evangelical head of household took seriously his educative duties. On Sunday afternoons and evenings, Adam's readings paralleled the minister's morning sermons, creating a little church in the home. Susan perceived these Sunday observances as a form of worship: "Another day finds me able to unite with my dear husband and family in domestic worship and domestic comforts."[12]

Her journal for October 1826 is filled with brief notes about the day-to-day rhythm of domestic family life. Ten-month-old Sylvanus was unwell for more than a week, and Susan worried that she knew so little about medical care. Nevertheless, he soon recovered, and she enjoyed watching her husband and son together: "He loves his father better than any other of the household," she confessed. "I am glad of it—it affords me much more pleasure than if I were his favorite!" Sylvanus did not absorb all her attention. She and fourteen-year-old Hannah sometimes went into town to call on friends, and she helped nine-year-old Elizabeth begin a wheelwork bed quilt.[13]

Despite the domestic focus of Susan's journal entries during the first years of her marriage, she was never secluded at home. The Hutchisons' marriage was both private and public, unfolding within full view of the local community. Married life in Augusta was highly sociable. Susan's days were filled with interaction both inside and outside the home. During the first week of January 1827, Mr. Robertson dined at her house and spent the night. Four days later Mrs. Jones, Mrs. Davis, Mrs. Moore, and Miss Cumming stopped by to visit, and two days after that, the Presbyterian pastor and his wife, Mr. and Mrs. Moderwell, stopped in for tea. Susan also went into town to call on friends.[14]

The middle-class circles within which Susan moved resembled those in northern towns and cities. Recent scholarship on the white southern middle class has revealed a culture more closely related to that of the North than has been suggested by earlier studies focusing largely on the experiences of planters and slaves in rural areas. Historian Jonathan Daniel Wells has demonstrated that much like the North, southern towns and cities had thriving middle-class communities composed of merchants, printers, doctors, and teachers. According to Wells, the growth of the periodical press after 1820 helped build a cultural bridge between the two regions, and the emerging southern middle class imbibed northern middle-class ideas about gender roles and social reform. Susan Nye's journal entries reveal the interactions of one woman in the sort of middle-class southern community Wells describes and suggest that the churches played an important role.[15]

The First Presbyterian Church was an important hub of middle-class women's social life in Augusta. Both Susan and Amanda joined the church in November 1825, and they became very engaged in the life of the Presbyterian community. As in most evangelical churches, women predominated in the Augusta congregation: in the two years after the church's 1804 founding, twenty-one of the twenty-nine individuals admitted were women. That proportion persisted, and in 1853, women still comprised 70 percent of members. Just under half of the congregants had been born in Georgia. The community was connected not only with the North but also with England and other European countries. More than a quarter of the members hailed from Ireland or Scotland, while others had come to Augusta from elsewhere in the United States, both above and below the Mason-Dixon line, as well as from the West Indies, France, England, and Germany. It is fair to say that middle-class culture in Augusta, Georgia, developed in the context of multiple influences and connections.[16]

Susan became very good friends with some of Augusta's prominent Presbyterian women, including Elizabeth Jones and her sister, Mary Smelt. Elizabeth Jones was a wealthy slave owner and the widow of Seabold Jones, former mayor and member of the Augusta City Council. She had gained recognition in the national Presbyterian Church when she published the memoirs of her niece, Caroline Smelt, who had died at age seventeen, professing her faith and with "joy unspeakable and full of glory." The memoirs received endorsements from both northern and southern Presbyterian ministers.[17]

Susan and her friends were drawn into church elections, an early form of women's political engagement. Although Augusta's Presbyterians did not permit females to vote in church matters, the women closely followed the December 1827 election of a new pastor and lobbied for their favorite candidate: "Mrs. Smelt and Mrs. Jones spent the evening here," wrote Susan. "Great excitement prevails respecting the election of a pastor. Some expressions dropped by Mrs. S makes me fear she and some others will feel it right to separate from the church in case a certain event takes place." When the Reverend Samuel Kennedy Talmage was elected by "a considerable majority," Susan and her friends were pleased.[18]

Susan also participated in local benevolent and missionary societies, which expanded women's interests and activities beyond the domestic concerns of the household. Adam Hutchison had been "deeply affected" when he read an 1816 memoir, The Power of Faith, by Isabella Graham, who served as a model of Presbyterian female benevolence outside the home as a consequence of her missionary and charitable work in New York in the late eighteenth century. Adam would thus have approved of Susan's activities with the Augusta Benevolent Society and the town's Foreign Mission Society.[19]

Susan and her friends also shared an interest in religious revival. In November 1826, Susan wrote, "Mrs. Smelt and Mrs. Moore called to see us, the former read a most interesting letter from Athens by Mr. Davis, descriptive of the revival now going on in the college and village." The following month, a revival occurred in town, and Susan participated in prayer meetings at the church and in parishioners' homes. Revivals were always highly social events. "Great excitement is now existing among the youth," she wrote. "Many seem to be anxious about eternity." Later that week, she noted, "The anxiety continues, 3 or 4 meetings are held in a day." In January 1827, she hosted a prayer meeting at her house led by the ministers of the church and attended meetings at the homes of other families. In February, "Mr. Talmage preached to a very great audience," moving a dozen people to join the church, including Susan's fourteen-year-old stepdaughter, Hannah. Susan wrote, "My feelings were powerfully acted upon when I saw Hannah standing in the broad aisle in the immediate act of subscribing to the covenant."[20]

Like other southern churches, the First Presbyterian Church of Augusta offered membership to slaves, but only with their masters' approval. According to historian Christine Leigh Heyrman, just after the American Revolution, some slaveholders argued that evangelical churches subverted slavery by allowing slaves to participate in worship with whites. Such concerns prompted white church authorities to reassure slave owners by censuring slaves who attended worship without their masters' permission, and by 1800, requiring such permission was standard procedure. Three slaves joined the First Presbyterian Church when Susan lived in Augusta. According to church records, "Anthony & his wife Cloe, two colored persons belonging to . . . Mr. Sh[amons], handed a certificate of membership from the Church at Liberty County dated 15 Sept. 1826 and requested to be admitted as members of this church." The elders discussed the request and granted it "on condition of the approbation of their master being obtained." Six months later, the church admitted Leah, a slave belonging to Fanny Moore, after Leah was "examined by the Pastor and recommended by her mistress." Leah was one of many visitors to Susan's home.[21]

Susan also attended to the conversion of slaves. When Sylvanus was eleven months old, she began to continue the kind of lay ministry she had begun when she lived in Raleigh, spending some time each Sabbath day reading the Bible and praying with slaves who lived and worked in Augusta. "Today I began to instruct the black people," she wrote on November 12, 1826, "for a little my heart said I will do it next Sabbath but conscience whispered next Sabbath may be too late, so I took a testament, went out, read and prayed with them." She followed closely news of revival conversions in town among slave and free residents, noting on one Sunday, "It has been a solemn day with the black population as well as the white[;] 120 persons of colour are to be immersed."[22]

By the summer of 1827, Susan and Adam had opened their kitchen to an independent black congregation that met once a month at night to worship. Independent congregations offered slaves and free blacks far greater opportunities to participate meaningfully in a Christian community, since they could vote in church affairs, establish benevolent enterprises, and speak freely without white supervision. In June, according to Susan, "The black people held their monthly meeting here and it was near morning before they left the kitchen. I love to hear their worship especially their singing." The members of this small congregation included several hired slaves who worked in Susan's home, including an elderly woman named Grace, and others who gathered at the house after the end of the workday while Susan and her family slept upstairs.[23]

Both Susan and Adam Hutchison appear to have supported the aspirations of slaves to establish their independent forms of worship. As a couple, they shared interests in religion and had many friends in the Presbyterian Church. But over the years, these common interests were not enough to sustain their marriage in the face of growing financial problems and personal tragedy.

Susan's first inkling that something was amiss with the family's finances occurred in October 1826. The river at Augusta was commonly around five feet deep year-round, allowing barges and steamboats to make semiweekly trips to Savannah. Augusta had the largest inland cotton market in the country, and river travel was essential to the cotton trade. However, the water level could fall substantially during dry seasons, making it impossible for the boats to travel on the river. As the *Georgia Courier* explained, "There is a radical defect in the construction of the steamboats which were first built to navigate on the Savannah River. . . . They are too narrow, and consequently sink too deep. If Steamboats were constructed with much greater breadth . . . they could ply at all times on our river." In the autumn of 1826, the river was lower than it had been in years, making it impossible for boats to travel inland to Augusta. As a result, the prices of imported goods rose as merchants rerouted shipments overland. In mid-October Susan noted, "Husband seems distressed that the river is falling." The anticipated November rains never came, and on November 11 she wrote, "The river continues low. Every promise of rain seems delusive." Near the end of the month, Adam came home with some more bad news: "He brought news of the fall of cotton and I had reason to fear that he had been a loser." To economize, they let their hired housekeeper go.[24]

Adam kept Susan in the dark about the full extent of the damage. In mid-December, she wrote optimistically, "Mr. H. is again buying cotton." Unfortunately, his purchases did not result in profitable trades. Within two months, he began to confide a bit more about their financial situation: "Last night his mind was a good deal opened to me on the subject of his business," wrote Susan, "which he considers too fluctuating to depend upon to support a family. He has been purchasing largely in the hope that cotton would rise, now (I have cause to think) he begins to doubt. He however says little, and it is only from circumstances that I draw this conclusion." Adam traveled to Charleston in the hopes of negotiating a more profitable deal for his cotton. When he sent a letter describing his progress, Susan concluded, "I perceive from it that his spirits were desponding when he wrote—I see the cotton threatens him with loss." He returned after nine days but told Susan little about what had occurred. Not until the following week did she begin to learn about the cotton market's volatility. "Towards evening Mr. and Mrs. S[mith] called," she wrote, "and while here informed me of the decline in cotton." A month later, when she and Adam called on the Smiths, Susan learned more: "While sitting there Mr. Smith and Mr. Hutchison spoke upon the low price of cotton." After returning home, Adam "expressed his intention of abandoning the business."[25]

Her husband displayed more outbursts of anger as the bills piled up and his anxiety increased. She believed it was her duty to "talk calmly with my husband on the necessity of his making greater efforts to govern his temper," but she found it difficult to confront him. She confessed one evening, "Fear of giving offense—deterred me and I went to sleep without speaking upon the painful subject." Several days later, Adam took out his anger on the baby. Susan noted that Sylvanus had been so "exceedingly fretful at night, his papa found it necessary to whip him. I fear he will need a great deal of this kind of correction for he discovers marks of high temper." Two days later, a doctor visited and informed Susan that Sylvanus had cut a tooth "earlier than any child he has ever known before." His fussing had resulted from teething, not willful bad temper. Her journal provides no evidence about whether Susan felt any remorse for having allowed her husband to whip a teething baby, but the following day, she recorded only one line: "My nerves seem totally unstrung—I weep as easily as an infant."[26]

Their situation gradually worsened. In mid-April, Adam sold his cotton at a loss. Five days afterward Susan was alarmed to learn that the local banker had dropped by the house: "Mr. Edwards called while we were absent and expressed great anxiety to see husband[,] he is a banker and but for the help of the Lord I should suffer with many fears." In early May, the Hutchisons relinquished their expensive house and moved to a much smaller rental. Susan was pregnant at the time, and on the Fourth of July, she gave birth to Ebenezer Nye Hutchison. Despite their reduced living expenses as a consequence of the move, she worried that they might never emerge from debt. In an anniversary entry she wrote, "Just two years since I first saw our dear children. . . . At that time how little did I foresee all that has since befallen us—losses upon losses."[27]

In the hope of drawing a valuable lot of land, Adam entered the 1827 Georgia Land Lottery. Between 1805 and 1833, the state of Georgia held eight land lotteries to distribute lands taken from the Creek and Cherokee tribes. Through the lottery system, Georgia sold roughly 75 percent of the state's land to around one hundred thousand families and individuals. The 1827 lottery offered twenty-three thousand two-and-a-half-acre lots. Lottery organizers placed slips or tickets representing the lots into boxes along with a number of blanks. All free white males aged twenty-one or older who had resided in the state for at least twelve months were eligible to draw once. Every white male with a wife and one or more underage child, widows with underage children, and families of underage orphans were allowed to draw twice. Susan prayed, "Mr. H. might come home with a blessing." He drew a slip for "a small tract of land," but it was virtually worthless.[28]

One possible solution to the Hutchisons' financial difficulties was for Susan to return to teaching. She had a reputation as an excellent teacher, and the board of trustees of an Augusta academy had already offered her a position. Susan had wanted to take it, but as she wrote in her journal, "this wish so displeased Mr. H. that he never spoke to me or my baby during the whole night and this was followed by another, and more forceful exhibition of violent temper." Adam held on to his anger. Not until two days afterward did Susan write, "Mr. H. begins to answer reasonably the questions I ask," and it was four days before she noted, "Tranquility seems restored." She did not bring up the subject again for nine months: in July 1827, she recorded, "Today for the first time I ventured to speak to him (*husband*) about going to town to open a school. Mrs. Watkins and Mrs. Clarke here—Mrs. Jones came up in the evening." By raising the question on a day when the house had several visitors, Susan may have been seeking to help her husband control his temper and consider the question more rationally. Or perhaps Adam's opposition simply wore away under the pressure of imminent insolvency. At any rate, in August, he changed his mind: "My husband spoke with great feeling of his continued losses and expressed his wish that I should return to town to open a school."[29]

The notion that a married woman might teach outside the home was not controversial at the time. After the Civil War, school boards across the country began to impose restrictions on the employment of married women in public schools, and by 1889, a U.S. Bureau of Education report stated, "We believe that in no State are *married women* employed as *teachers.*" But during the first half of the nineteenth century, restrictions against the employment of married teachers were virtually nonexistent. During the Second Great Awakening, Christian missionary organizations encouraged married couples to teach and evangelize in the American West and abroad. The Board of Popular National Education, an evangelical group that sent teachers west and south to promote a "sound Christian education" starting in 1846, not only employed married women teachers but also sought to retain women in the schools after marriage.[30]

Southern views of a white mother's appropriate social role did not prevent Susan from working outside the home. Based on a survey of women's prescriptive literature, historian V. Lynn Kennedy has concluded that elite southern women and men idealized domesticity and motherhood as a way of reinforcing the hierarchy in marriage and in southern society. But Susan Hutchison's experience in Augusta between 1827 and 1834 suggests that the experience of elite white women did not necessarily apply to the middle and working classes. There is no evidence that Augusta's evangelical community sought to prevent Susan from establishing an educational business in town while she had a baby and toddler at home.[31]

Multiple prescriptive messages regarding the appropriate behavior of men and women circulated throughout the antebellum period. Whether the prescriptive messages in women's magazines had any effect on a particular woman depended on the circles in which she moved and the reading material she enjoyed. Susan Nye Hutchison's journal indicates that she read a range of texts but no popular women's magazines. Instead, she read biographies of male and female missionaries, collections of sermons, histories, and reports of various missionary societies. The Presbyterian men and women with whom she socialized probably read the same sort of material. Published sermons of that era indicate that evangelical Protestants justified married women's work outside the home using biblical texts such as Proverbs 31. This Old Testament passage appeared in hundreds of sermons, books, and magazines, extolling the virtuous wife not only for her piety and benevolence but also for her industry, executive ability, and contribution to the household finances: "She considereth a field, and buyeth it: with the fruit of her hands she planteth a vineyard. . . . She perceiveth that her merchandise is good. . . . She maketh fine linen, and selleth it; and delivereth girdles unto the merchant." The Reverend Henry Hunter, a British writer whose books went through multiple editions in the United States, concluded from this proverb that in creating woman, God aimed to provide "an help meet" for man, one capable of "managing his scanty portion with discretion, and doubling it by participation." In 1819, a sermon reproduced in the *Ladies' Literary Cabinet* pointed out that half of the verses in Proverbs 31 "are taken up in setting forth her *industry*, and the effects of it" and noted that the Bible recommends "good housewifery and honest labour to be admired, in the rich and noble, as well as the poor and obscure among women."[32]

Such messages justified married women's work outside the home. Some American historians have debated the extent to which a "golden age" existed earlier in the colonial period during which married white women were accorded more freedom outside the home and regarded as equal "helpmeets" to men. Extending this argument, others have theorized that women experienced something akin to a social and cultural backlash during the early nineteenth century, as evidenced by rhetoric regarding women's appropriate sphere in the home. But as Susan's case suggests, the concept of the wife as a helpmeet was alive and well within middle-class evangelical circles during the years she lived in Augusta.[33]

Confident of support from her local community, Susan placed an advertisement in local newspapers announcing her intention to establish a female school. The venture opened with three pupils in a house on Broad Street on October 4, 1827.[34]

Several other married or widowed women operated schools in Augusta that fall. The same week the *Georgia Courier* printed Susan's advertisement, it also advertised four other girls' schools: Mrs. H. Blome's school "on Green-street, for the Instruction of young Ladies in the English and French languages, Drawing and Painting, &c."; Mrs. Wharton's new Male and Female Seminary "a few doors above the upper market"; Mrs. O'Driscoll and Miss Canuet's Seminary for Young Ladies in "the house formerly occupied by the Rev. Mr. Shannon"; and Mrs. Guerineau's "boarding and day

> # Mrs. Adam Hutchison's
> # SCHOOL,
>
> WILL be opened on Broad-street, a few doors above Doctor Wrays, at the house formerly occupied by Judge Wilson, on the first Monday of October
>
> Mrs. H. will be happy to give private instructions in Composition, and the higher branches of Education, to young Ladies who desire to devote a portion of their time to mental improvement
>
> Instructions also given in Drawing and Paint-ing, in Plain and Ornamental Needle Work.
>
> Terms of admission made known at the School Room.
>
> Sept. 24   40 tf

Newspaper advertisement for Susan Nye Hutchison's School, *Georgia Courier*, September 24, 1827. Courtesy of the Georgia Newspaper Project, University of Georgia, Athens.

school for young ladies, in Ellis Street." The *Augusta Chronicle and Georgia Advertiser* announced that "Dr. Cleary and Lady" proposed to open a male and female academy based on Johann Pestalozzi's European methods of teaching. Despite this relatively crowded field, two weeks after the opening of Susan's school, the Hutchison family moved back to town, renting a house in a less expensive neighborhood and rehiring a housekeeper.[35]

The Augusta community may have sanctioned Susan's teaching as a married woman, but she soon faced new challenges. During the colonial and early national periods, local communities scrutinized teachers' lives inside and outside of school. A teacher's behavior in church or at a social function could reflect on his or her perceived effectiveness as an educator, and a carelessly scribbled note on a student's paper could prompt criticism of the teacher's penmanship. Shortly after Susan opened her school, her friend Elizabeth Jones "called to see me and told me that people complained of my handwriting." Several days later she added, "Mrs. Jones called in the kindness of her heart to inform me of the unkind remarks made by some of our patrons respecting the school." These sorts of criticisms were not unfamiliar to a veteran teacher; however, Susan soon discovered that her performance as a mother became grist for the gossip mill. Members of the community in Augusta did not hesitate to comment publicly on her child-rearing practices. In October 1829 Susan wrote, "Mrs. Jones called to inform me that some person who had been annoyed by my children in the Church had published some remarks in the paper and that it was said if I would not govern my own children I would not be fit to manage the children of other people."[36]

As the principal of her own school, Susan strove to keep her patrons happy. Like Sarah Pierce, founder of Litchfield Female Academy, she motivated her students with occasional treats for good behavior and "premiums" for academic excellence. She also invited local pastors to visit the school and speak with the pupils. Those who established academies and little venture schools like hers depended completely on their local communities for support, and principals therefore attended keenly to any gossip that might damage their school's reputation and enrollments. In her efforts to please her patrons, Susan sometimes admitted to frustration: "Teaching is a trying employment—the effort you make to satisfy one parent is almost certain to disoblige another." Nevertheless, her efforts slowly paid off, and two years after opening, her school enrolled twenty students.[37]

The revenue from her little school should have helped the Hutchisons' finances, but instead, they sank deeper into debt. Two months after Susan returned to teaching, she wrote, "Today for the second time since our marriage Mr. H. told me he had no money." She considered ways to economize and urged Adam to pursue other lines of work, with little success: "I have been striving to inculcate lessons of industry upon my girls but I fear I do not do it in a good way. I have also been endeavoring to encourage my husband to make an effort to enter the druggists business (and an excellent opportunity seemed to open for this) but here I totally failed."[38]

On January 6, 1828, the Hutchisons dismissed their cook, housemaid, and nurse. Susan recorded in her journal that "all the servants except John went away." John, a young hired slave, worked as their handyman, while Amanda Nye helped her sister fix dinner and care for the children. Three days later, Susan wrote, "Last night Mr. H. spoke more freely than ordinary of his circumstances and observed that none but God could have brought him through the last summer for often it was that he knew not where to get bread."[39]

The tuition revenue provided just enough to scrape by through the spring. With no fixed employment, Adam occasionally helped out in the schoolroom, and on at least one occasion when Susan was too ill to teach, fifteen-year-old Hannah assisted with the younger students. In January, Susan despaired, "Tomorrow our Grocer's bill becomes due—at 2 o'clock we have no money." Fortunately, three families paid their tuition bills that same day, and she noted, "Our painful situation much alleviated." Adam gradually shared the details of their financial predicament, enabling Susan to begin to understand the extent of their problems: "This morning my husband spoke freely of his affairs mentioning without reserve things of which I was quite ignorant—When I think of the amount of our debts and of the inability under which we are placed I could almost think it impossible for us to repay them." She worried that they would not survive on the revenue generated by the school: "Often during this day my heart desponded. . . . [H]ow is it that we shall find a subsistence when our expenses are so great and our income so small?" By the end of February, they were "in debt on every side." On March 31 she wrote, "Our situation becomes more and more trying. We are beginning in some degree to feel the pressure of poverty— our school is dwindling or rather falling to pieces—Today we had neither money nor meat but through mercy we were enabled to borrow of a neighbour a small sum of money."[40]

As Susan sought a way out of her family's predicament, she found her husband "more gloomy than ever" and averse to seeking wage work. She wrote, "He seems to be determined to sit down in supine neglect of every means now in his power." Their friends the Smiths stepped forward and paid the princely sum of eight hundred dollars to settle the Hutchisons' debt—more than two years' worth of Susan's earnings. Susan noted Mr. Smith's generosity and "asked the Lord to enable us to pay him." When she learned of an employment opportunity at the local branch of a regional bank, she urged Adam to apply. He did so reluctantly and set off for Charleston to interview with the bank directors there. "Mr. H left home in a very unhappy frame of mind," noted Susan. In late April, when she learned that her friend Elizabeth Jones entertained no expectation that Adam would get the position, Susan tried to intervene on her husband's behalf by writing to one of the bank directors (also one of her husband's creditors) and invited two of the bank directors to call on her. She received no response.[41]

To Susan's relief and despite the pessimism of her friend, the bank directors eventually offered Adam the position. On May 8, one of the directors called on Susan before Adam returned home to give her the good news in person. But when Adam arrived several days afterward, he was surprised to hear that he had received the offer and did not seem pleased. In fact, "Mr. H. seemed rather dejected than rejoiced—His nerves were unstrung—the idea of entering a new business was far from pleasant to him." Nevertheless, he accepted the job.[42]

Susan continued to teach school while her husband worked in the bank, but their debts never lessened. In the fall of 1828, she was shocked to learn that all her household furniture was headed to the auction block. Adam had mortgaged everything to Mr. Smelt, who had subsequently become bankrupt. In January, she learned that Mr. Smith, their benefactor, had also become bankrupt. She despaired: "I begin to be much concerned about the payment of our rent." Adam wrote to his relatives in Scotland asking for help, but in February he received a response "of a painful nature": although Adam's family had helped to fund Robert's education, such assistance had apparently ceased, and no more was forthcoming.[43]

THE NEXT YEAR brought new anxieties and tragedy to the Hutchison household. In the fall of 1829, Augusta experienced a series of fires. The townspeople initially suspected arson, but talk then turned to the possibility of insurrection among the slaves.

Every community experienced one or more fires a year during the early national period. The ubiquitous presence of candles and cooking fires in wooden structures made conflagrations inevitable. The public was well aware of the danger, and nearly every newspaper issue carried advertisements for fire insurance. Susan recorded three fires in 1827 and one the following year. In 1829, however, she recorded thirteen separate incidents. On February 22 she wrote, "I heard the cry of fire and soon afterward a whole square was in flames. . . . For a while flashes of fire passed over our roof but at length the wind turned." The newspapers reported that thirty tenements were destroyed. And another fire broke out the next day.[44]

Augusta residents probably would not have seen anything suspicious about the February fires if not for the fact that the authorities subsequently discovered evidence of attempted arson. According to the *Augusta Chronicle and Georgia Advertiser*, "On Monday night last an attempt was made to fire the buildings of Maj. McGraw, on the corner of Reynolds and Macintosh Streets. The fire, together with some fodder, paper, cotton, &c. was placed against a pile of small pieces of lightwood, under a shed."[45]

Having realized that more than carelessness might be going on, authorities urged citizens to take "such measures as circumstances may suggest, for the protection of their lives and property and the discovery of the inhuman wretches who are prowling about them." By early March, the paper reported that the town would be patrolled by a volunteer city guard comprising nearly three hundred men. Augusta had long feared slave uprisings. In 1809, residents were alarmed when authorities learned that a North Georgia slave had written to a slave in North Carolina that on April 22, 1810, "we are to fall to work" and "freedom we want and will have." Nine years later, a slave named Mills retaliated for a whipping by burning down his owner's stable, killing twelve horses. Shortly thereafter, a slave named Coco or Coot reportedly developed a plan to break into local stores for guns and ammunition, set fire to the town perimeter, and massacre white residents as they gathered to put out the blaze. Authorities learned of the plot, arrested Coot and several coconspirators, and quickly had them tried, convicted, and publicly executed.[46]

Fear of insurrection became widespread after six more fires broke out during April 1829. Of the largest, Susan wrote, "Today a most awful conflagration occurred in town. . . . The cry of fire aroused us, at first a dark smoke arose but soon the blaze burst out and rising toward heaven swelled and spread till all the southeastern part of the city was one wide conflagration—it continued till near sunset destroying all in its reach except two or three lonely habitations, from 400 to 600 habitations are supposed to have been consumed besides a vast amount of other property—Our own house seemed threatened and we were packed up and ready to be gone." Three days later, after the family had unpacked and begun to relax, came another fire. "Great fear begins to be prevalent that the negroes are about to rise," wrote Susan. Within a matter of days, the *Augusta Chronicle and Georgia Advertiser* came to the same conclusion: "A fire was discovered in the loft of Dr. Anthony's house, on the corner of Greene and Centre streets. . . . It is supposed to have been a premeditated attempt to destroy the building." After another fire broke out in a stable at the rear of a Broad Street store, the newspaper reported, "A coal of fire, which had been apparently wrapped up in some combustible materials, was [found] in the stable. [There] can be no doubt, that we have among us . . . desperate incendiaries, who contemplate the entire destruction of the City."[47]

Adam Hutchison and other white men began to arm themselves. "Oh it is indeed a time of deep anxiety," Susan wrote, "Mr. H busy in loading his gun and pistols in expectation of an alarm of insurrection." On April 11 she reported, "Today the street[s] are full of armed men. 500 stands of arms came from the arsenal and all capable of doing military duty are to be prepared for the evil which I trust in God may never happen—Col. Cumming is Commandant." The excitement and panic continued for the remainder of the month.[48]

By May, Amanda had had enough and was "making haste to be ready to go home." Susan had no money to pay for her sister's trip, so Amanda sought her own teaching position. The following month, a "note came inviting Amanda to teach a small school at the Sand Hills." The situation prompted Susan to consider more ways to save money. "We are not lessening our debts," Susan wrote, "I have resolved—to break up housekeeping"—that is, to move her family into a boardinghouse or hotel.[49]

She also considered taking in boarders. During the early national period, middle- and upper-class families that sent their children to school far from home commonly paid to board them with local families. This family boarding system allowed students the opportunity to attend distant academies while living within a family that held similar values and cultural beliefs. The boarding system offered families in towns with schools an important source of revenue. By the end of the eighteenth century, single women and widows as well as families provided lodging to boarding students. But Adam would not even discuss the possibility: "I feel very anxious to know whether Mr. H will give in to my plan of boarding," she noted in July, "but he will not converse at all on the subject." With no funds available to pay for travel, "Amanda has about relinquished the hope of going home," Susan noted at the end of the month.[50]

Adam's temper worsened. He occasionally flew into rages, not only at home but also at church. In August, Susan wrote, "At night I deemed it [my] duty to converse with Mr. H. on the sin of giving way to anger— he broke out into [the] most ungovernable rage." Two days later, Susan learned "that Mr. Hutchison and Mr. Poe had had some very high words in the Sunday School—Alas—Alas." Before marrying Susan, Adam had been expelled from a church, though it is not known why, and Susan worried that his public displays of bad temper would imperil his standing in the First Presbyterian Church. In September, she spent some time reading over "a parcel of Mr. Hutchison's letters to his former wife," learning "that her trials were just as deep as my own."[51]

Just as the outbreaks of fire finally appeared to have ceased, sixteen-year-old Hannah suddenly became ill on October 6. "Hannah sick all day," wrote Susan. "At dark Hannah was very (to me) abnormally ill— she was in a stupor or sound sleep. . . . I sent for Doctor Wray who advised a wine glass of castor oil." Hannah seemed somewhat better the next day, but by that night, "she said she felt better, but she was not in her right mind—her thirst was intense—complained of great pressure on the breast."[52]

Dr. Wray prescribed wine and brandy, painful mustard plasters, large doses of calomel to induce vomiting, and digitalis, a poison. Such treatments were standard parts of eighteenth-century medical practice but could prove as deadly as the disease. Some writers had already begun to contest some of these traditional remedies—in 1827, an Augusta newspaper had printed an article recommending that persons suffering from illness "avoid all kinds of spirit, wine, ale, and even cider. Dismiss care, but never attempt to drown it with stimulating liquors, unless you would increase the violence of your symptoms sevenfold." Unfortunately, Hannah's doctor did not heed this advice.[53]

On October 16 Susan wrote, "At two o'clock Hannah was worse. I could—hear her labouring for breath—in one half hour she sweetly slept as I trust in the bosom of her Redeemer." The funeral was held the same day: "A good many were present," noted Susan, "the dear child was laid at the side of her mother." Susan had come to love her stepdaughter dearly and was devastated by the girl's death, carefully crafting an epitaph: "As a daughter, a sister and a friend she was tenderly beloved. . . . Let her early death teach parents how soon their earthly hopes may perish and youth how suddenly they may be called to judgment."[54]

After Hannah's death, Adam's behavior became more erratic and his temper more violent. He had buried not only his first wife but also five of his first seven children. Probably suffering from depression, he began to spend even more money, and Susan "suffered much, very much with a temptation to repine at Mr. H's indulging himself in unnecessary expenses." A few weeks later, she described Adam as "sick and unhappy." Her January 9, 1830, entry consisted of a single line: "A night of trial on account of Mr. H's violent temper."[55]

Less than a month after Hannah's death, the fires resumed in Augusta. On November 6, according to Susan, "About two o'clock an alarm of fire aroused us—we got up [and] found the fire—was only distant two squares being just above Col. Cumming's new stores. Amanda and I packed up and waited to remove as the danger became more imminent—the fire fell thick around us sometimes landing upon our roof—in a little time a gentleman passing under the window informed me that the danger was arrested." Four days later, "a fire was discovered under Mrs. Walker's stable just as it had got under way."[56]

Rumors began to circulate that a slave named Cinda had confessed to arson and implicated another slave, Jenny, who was owned by Elizabeth Jones. On November 12, Susan wrote that Jenny "has confessed she set fire to Mrs. Walker's stable—she was under punishment for her faults and was excited to take this dreadful revenge by Cinda living with Mrs. Arnold who has by her confession established the fact—both are in confinement." The *Georgia Constitutionalist* described Cinda and the "young negro girl" Jenny as "misguided and foolish blacks engaged in a recent attempt to set fire to the city." Jenny was likely between twelve and sixteen years old.[57]

Jenny and Cinda were quickly brought to trial, found guilty, and sentenced to death. The judge scheduled Jenny's execution for December 4 but granted Cinda a six-month delay because she was pregnant.[58] On November 28, Susan noted in her journal, "Went with Mrs. Jones to visit poor Jenny in her cell"—her first recorded visit to a condemned prisoner.[59]

Susan may have had personal motives for visiting and praying with Jenny. Susan was four and a half months pregnant with her third child, and her husband had grown more unpredictable and abusive. She was still grieving over Hannah's death, which had come so unexpectedly that there had been little time to pray with the young woman and help her prepare for the afterlife. Susan was desperately trying to gain more control over her own life and make sense of the tragedies that had befallen her. Perhaps on some level, she identified with the imprisoned and pregnant Cinda and with Jenny, who was about the same age as Hannah. Although Susan had not known that Hannah's death was imminent, Jenny's was a foregone conclusion. In this case, there was time to prepare and pray, time to save this one young woman.

Susan probably visited Jenny again before her December 4 execution. She wrote two journal entries that day, the first in present tense: "Jenny is as calm as it is possible for a living thing to be. She desires death." For Christians of that era the phrase "desires death" indicated that someone was looking forward to the afterlife, sure of his or her place in heaven. Susan likely wrote this entry after visiting Jenny in the morning. After walking with Adam to the jail to witness Jenny's execution, Susan returned home and wrote, "Poor Jenny was today launched into eternity—on the gallows she prayed after the Reverend Mr. Sinclair and spoke in a collected and impressive manner to the spectators."[60]

There is no evidence that Susan grasped the political implications of Jenny's hanging, which marked the first time an Augusta slave convicted of arson received a death sentence. Convicted arsonists previously received whippings and jail time, but during the weeks leading up to Jenny's trial, the Georgia Legislature passed new laws designed to deter slave insurrection. Henceforth, acts of arson "committed by a slave or free person of colour, shall be punished with death." With this and similar measures, the Georgia Legislature and its counterparts elsewhere in the South began to bolster their control over slavery.[61]

Susan's journal is also silent about a question that would persist in Augusta long after the hanging: were Jenny and Cinda guilty? Georgia governor George Gilmer believed that slaves had deliberately set the fires, but some contemporaries believed that the women were innocent. According to James Stuart, a Scotsman who visited Augusta four months after Jenny's death, "The fire was believed to be the work of incendiaries among the people of colour. One slave, a female, was convicted, executed, dissected, and exposed, but she died denying the crime. Another, now with child, is sentenced to be executed in June, but she still denies her guilt. I fear these unhappy creatures are convicted on what we should consider very insufficient evidence." When Cinda was executed three months later, rumors circulated that she had died proclaiming her innocence. To counter these reports, the *Augusta Chronicle and Georgia Advertiser* announced, "The negro woman, *Cinda*, convicted in November last of Arson, was executed on Friday the 6th. . . . As it has been publicly stated that she persisted to the last in asserting her innocence of the crime for which she suffered, it may be proper to state, for the purpose of preventing misapprehension on the subject, that her guilt had been fully developed."[62]

Jenny and Cinda's incarceration and execution did not put an end to the fires in Augusta. Two weeks after their arrest, Macon Academy burned to the ground. Perhaps because authorities believed they had captured the town's two arsonists, the newspaper attributed the fire to a stove accident. In February 1830, a small fire broke out below the wooden floor of the Hutchisons' dining room. Adam was home at the time and ripped up the floorboards to extinguish the fire before it could spread. The Hutchisons believed that the fire had started when a burning coal fell through a crack in the fireplace.[63]

The number of fires in Augusta declined after Jenny and Cinda's executions, but the fear of arson and insurrection remained. In 1831, city leaders prohibited free blacks and slaves from worshipping in independent congregations, part of a regional effort to suppress independent meetings at which blacks might devise schemes of insurrection. Susan described the demise of the independent black congregation that had met in her home for at least four years: "Gracy went to her meeting and on coming away left the Marshalls around the door—to shut up that place of worship," she wrote. "I am grieved because she is so—but the excitement continues through the country and many deem it a needful measure to compel the coloured people to worship with the whites."[64]

PLAGUED WITH FEARS of fire, threats of insurrection, and the deepening fractures in her marriage, Susan penned a will in the pages of her journal in late January 1830. "Feeling exceedingly unwell I find a sense of duty resting on my mind to make a will," she wrote, "so that no doubt may arise in the mind of any of my friends respecting the property I leave to my children which (having never been in my hands) is yet at my disposal." She was probably referring to money she had saved from earlier in her teaching career, assuming that it remained safe at the bank. "I wish it to be equally divided between my children but not until my parents can no longer be benefitted by its use." She continued, "I desire that Amanda may be entrusted with the direction of my children and that they be raised in the country and early taught habits of self denial, industry and economy."[65]

To look after her children's financial well-being, she expressed her "desire that my brother Meletiah may manage their property for them and that they may be taught above all things to love[,] fear and serve God." In addition, she directed Meletiah to teach her children "to reverence their father and to do all in their power to promote his happiness—to love their [half-]brother and [half-]sister and to preserve an inviolable attachment to one another." Beyond that, she left nothing to her husband.[66] Writing a will may have provided Susan a sense of power and control over her affairs, but the document was unenforceable. Although she clearly did not trust Adam to care for her children, she had no legal right to grant custody to her siblings in the event of her death.

After giving birth to her third son, Adam Alexander, on April 19, she made an important decision with long-term consequences: to "send out" her two oldest sons. She and Amanda returned to their parents' New York farm with Susan's three boys and her twelve-year-old stepdaughter, Elizabeth. There is no record to reveal what Adam Hutchison thought of his wife's departure, but he must have consented. There is also no record of where Susan and Amanda obtained the money to travel north. They reached Amenia on June 3 and spent the summer on the Nye family farm. Susan never intended the separation from her husband to be permanent, and on September 1, she, Elizabeth, and baby Adam Alexander began the return journey to Georgia, leaving behind Amanda, her parents, and four-year-old Sylvanus and three-year-old Ebenezer. The trio arrived back in Augusta on September 18.[67]

By the early national period, the custom of "sending children out," or placing them outside the home, usually at adolescence, was well established. Wealthy families sent sons to live with distant families as part of their educational and social training. Daughters who lived in the city often went to the country during the summer for their health, whereas girls who grew up in rural areas boarded with city families to gain some social polish. In such cases, families accepted the premise that other adults could help their adolescent children make the transition from the family home to adult society. Middle-class families sent children out for more pragmatic reasons. Sons left home to board in families where they could learn a trade or profession. Like Amanda Nye, girls often left home to help in the families of older married siblings. For poor families, the sending out of very young children was often an act of desperation, a way to improve family finances by reducing the number of mouths to feed.[68]

By leaving her two young sons in New York, Susan transgressed the idealized vision of motherhood that sometimes appeared in nineteenth-century literature. Many essayists displayed a sentimental reverence for motherhood, extolling the special relationship between a mother and her children and arguing that her influence was essential to their successful development. According to historian V. Lynn Kennedy, this ideology was particularly prevalent among elite white southerners. Nevertheless, Susan's actions were not exceptional—many American women ignored popular sentimentality when making everyday decisions about the care of their children. Despite espousing an ideology that prioritized the mother-child bond, many wealthy southern mothers in practice shared a wide range of caregiving functions with slaves, tutors, governesses, schoolteachers, and family members, including sisters, brothers, mothers, aunts, grandmothers, and fathers.[69]

From a biological perspective, Susan's decision to delegate the upbringing of her sons to her sister and parents was the best choice possible. As sociobiologist Sarah Blaffer Hrdy has shown, research from a wide range of fields, including archaeology, anthropology, primatology, and genetics, has revealed a complex web of caregiving responsibility among humans in all cultures throughout history. This historical evidence indicates that the more contact a child has with multiple caregivers, the more likely the child is to survive and have children of his or her own. It is probably not a coincidence that in contrast to Adam Hutchison, who buried five of the seven children born to his previous wife, Susan would see all of her children live to adulthood.[70]

The decision to leave her two sons in Amanda's care on the family farm could not have been easy. Nevertheless, it accomplished two goals: it eased the Hutchisons' financial burden, and it provided Sylvanus and Ebenezer with a stable, loving home in a family and community whose values she approved. "Sending out" her two eldest children may have reflected a desire to provide her sons an environment free of slavery; it was certainly an acknowledgment that her marriage had not turned out as she had hoped.

SUSAN SOMETIMES STRUGGLED to render the wifely obedience that was her end of the marriage bargain. Some of the limitations and constrictions of married life were inscribed in civil law, others upheld as traditional teachings of the church and schoolbook. She had long lived as a single, independent woman, and she was frustrated by being kept in the dark about financial matters after she married. Legally, she did not have custody of her children, a fact she may not fully have realized when she drew up her will. Nor did she have control over her own money and property. Adam's desire to protect her from bad news and the secrecy with which he shrouded his financial affairs during their first years together suggests the kind of rigid patriarchal relationship Tocqueville portrayed when he characterized American women as living cloistered lives under their husbands' authority.

Nevertheless, Susan's story illustrates the way marital relations could at times be relatively fluid and negotiable during the early national period. She was never blindly subservient to her husband. She made plans for her family's well-being, and she influenced Adam to accept some of them, including her return to teaching, his employment at the bank, and the placement of two young sons on her parents' farm in the North. Throughout the early national period, conservative and liberal ideas about marriage coexisted, not only among different factions in American society but also within individual marriages. Susan and Adam were often companionable, reading together, visiting friends, attending church, and going on walks. Sometimes he acquiesced to her ideas to improve their finances. At other times, however, he demanded obedience and raged against her perceived interference in his affairs.

For the men and women of this era, the reactions and judgments of their communities were among the most important influences on social behavior. The Hutchisons' marriage was both private and public. It was private in the sense that Adam could at times rage at his wife without witnesses within the confines of their house. Those same confines could also host an all-black congregation, at least until such independent congregations were outlawed. But the Hutchisons' marriage was also public, not only because participation in the church community brought a constant stream of visitors to their home, but also because that same evangelical community so closely monitored men and women's behavior. Adam's financial failures, the conduct of the Hutchisons' children in church, and Susan's management of students at her school were grist for gossip and public comment. To retain community support, both men and women had to live and act within the bounds of socially acceptable behavior. Yet in the context of some contemporary prescriptive literature, those boundaries could be surprisingly flexible, allowing a married woman to establish an entrepreneurial school and send two of her children north.

As difficult as it was to live with a man prone to episodes of rage and depression, Susan understood the promise she had made in marrying Adam: "to love him, honour him, cherish and obey him, in joy and in sorrow, in health and in sickness, in prosperity and in adversity." She returned to her home in Augusta, bringing Elizabeth and baby Adam Alexander with her. Later she remembered and marked the anniversary of the day she said good-bye to her two young sons in New York. Three years passed before she saw them again.[71]

CHAPTER 5

Church Discipline and a Separation

July 24, 1831—Mr. Talmage preached a capital discourse—In the evening
I stayed home with Alexander.

July 27—Another severe trial of temper.

August 8—Mr. Jones called to inform me—about a letter sent at 9 oclock
Saturday night to Mr. H from the Church Session desiring him not to
partake of the communion as the indignation of the people against him
on account of his unjust treatment of me had rendered it injurious to the
cause of Religion for him to appear among God's people. After 6 oclock
Mr. Talmage called but Mr. H had left the house before he entered. He
informed me that at the motion of Mr. C[atl]in it was unanimously
resolved by the Session that Mr. H should be suspended—the whole
community both in the church and out of it were excited against
him for his conduct toward me whom all regarded as a faithful
and an injured and persecuted wife.

By the summer of 1831, the entire congregation of the First Presbyterian
Church of Augusta knew about Susan's marital problems. According to a
journal entry Susan wrote on August 8, rumors circulated that she was an
abused wife.

Susan returned to Augusta from New York on September 18, 1830, after
leaving Sylvanus and Ebenezer in Amenia. What happened just afterward
is unknown, because she apparently did not keep a journal for the next
ten months; but it must have been a very difficult period, because when
her writing resumes, her entries describe Adam's suspension from communion in the church.[1]

Within the evangelical churches, the interactions of husband and
wife unfolded in full view of the religious community, and contemporary notions of morality sometimes justified interventions in the private
family. Church oversight of family life had been common during the
colonial period, and to a great extent, the churches of the Second Great
Awakening evidenced continuity with Puritan traditions. Like their
forebears, the church elders in Augusta did not believe that individual

households should be free from outside criticism or interference. In contrast to judges in the civil courts, the elders did not endorse the notion of marital privacy.[2]

In the civil courts, antebellum judges and lawyers commonly used the term "marital unity" to mean privacy within the household. The household sphere was private in the sense that it entailed private property and was not usually subject to public regulation. When a woman married, she became subject to her husband within this private domain.[3] From a legal standpoint, a husband had a great deal of discretion. He could defer to his wife or give her some degree of control over his financial affairs. He could also be cruel and abusive within his home, just as a wife could be lazy or disobedient. The State of Georgia did not make wife beating a criminal offense until 1857. In cases where one suffered from the bad behavior of the other, neither husband nor wife necessarily had grounds for a legal separation in civil court.[4]

Susan Nye Hutchison eventually decided to leave her husband and return to the North. The Hutchisons' case is somewhat unusual because it occurred outside the civil courts and with the support of their Presbyterian church. As one consequence of that support, Susan gained the ability to earn a man's salary teaching common school in the North. It all began with church discipline.

WITHIN THE EVANGELICAL churches, a couple's relationship was subject to evaluation, judgment, censure, and discipline. Church elders sometimes summoned husbands and wives to appear and answer for conflicts within their marriage. During such ecclesiastical "trials," marital and family disputes could be heard and sometimes resolved. As historian Monica Najar has put it, "Church discipline provided an ongoing and immediate lesson in marital expectations."[5]

The goal of church discipline was to induce repentance in the errant individual through confession, temporary separation from communion, or even expulsion. Among nineteenth-century Methodists, itinerant preachers administered church discipline, acting as both judge and jury. In Baptist churches, disciplinary proceedings originated at church conferences, and if the charges were serious, members were requested to appear for trial. By the 1800s, the most serious offenses in the American evangelical churches involved drunkenness, profanity, neglect of worship, violation of the Sabbath, disorderly conduct, slander, theft, forgery, sexual offenses, and violation of marital duties.[6]

In Presbyterian churches, the Session served as the primary administrative and judicial body. The Session, composed of male elders elected for life by the congregation, could try any member except the minister. American Presbyterians used the *Book of Discipline* adopted by the reformed church in Scotland, later revised as the *Constitution of the Presbyterian Church.* According to the 1827 edition, "Church censures are necessary for the reclaiming and gaining of offending brethren; for deterring of others from like offences; for purging out of that leaven which might infect the whole lump . . . and for preventing the wrath of God which might justly fall upon the church, if they should suffer this covenant, and the seals thereof, to be profaned by notorious and obstinate offenders." As the elders of Augusta's First Presbyterian Church explained, "You can never hereafter be as you have been. Transformed you *must* be the servants of the *Lord*. Hereafter the eyes of the world will be on you, and as you conduct yourselves, religion will be honored, or disgraced!"[7]

Most censures in the Presbyterian churches involved cases of intemperance, or drunkenness. Augusta's First Presbyterian Church appointed a committee in 1828 "to converse with Thomas Walker and [Mr.] McCoy, two members of this church who have unhappily been guilty of intemperance, to desire them both in the name of the Session to abstain from coming to the communion table next Sabbath. . . . They are also to be admonished, carefully to avoid in future, the repetition of a crime to injurious to the Church & so fatal to their own souls."[8]

Sabbath violations could lead to suspension from communion, especially if the offender persisted in working or engaged in other undesirable behaviors on the day. The elders in Augusta were particularly worried about rumors that some members attended the theater and dancing parties on Sundays. They resolved to proclaim to the congregation, "Ball Room and Dancing Parties [are] the improper places of resort for members of the Church of Christ—and a desire to admit such practices can scarcely exist in one properly prepared for the solemnities of the Lord."[9]

In addition to disciplining members for drunkenness and neglect of worship, the elders in Augusta occasionally cited individuals for disorderly conduct, slander, profanity, theft, or marital problems. Disorderly conduct covered a range of bad behaviors, from dancing at parties to displaying a foul temper and quarreling in public. The Session minutes are very vague about the details in the case of Mr. Dunn in 1820, but his offenses were serious enough to warrant a suspension: "As the sins confessed were of an awfully aggravated nature, and committed before the members," wrote

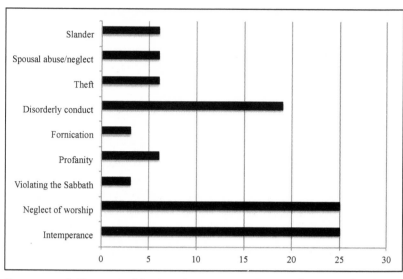

Frequency of offenses cited for disciplinary actions, First Presbyterian Church of Augusta, Georgia, 1808–1837. Data derived from Session Minutes, February 17, 1808–October 16, 1837, First Presbyterian Church of Augusta, Georgia, Records, 1804–1969, Presbyterian Historical Society, Philadelphia.

the elders, "the Session conceive it expedient to recommend Mr. Dunn to abstain from participating in the holy Sacrament of the Lord's Supper, until further and satisfactory evidence of repentance and reformation is given to the Church & the world by well ordered life and conversation."[10]

Some offenses and disciplinary actions in the evangelical churches were gender-specific. All of the members disciplined for intemperance in Augusta were men. Some churches disciplined women for fornication far more often than men, leading some historians to conclude that a common double standard existed in which women were blamed for sexual misconduct. But this pattern is not apparent in all church records. Historian Cynthia Lynn Lyerly has found that among the Methodists, men were also punished in cases where unmarried women became pregnant. Augusta's Presbyterians appear to have followed a similar policy: of 191 sessions recorded in the First Presbyterian Church of Augusta from February 17, 1808, to October 16, 1837, a man named Reveridge was the only member disciplined for fornication.[11]

Overall, the evangelical churches disciplined men far more often than women. In Augusta's First Presbyterian Church, women comprised just over 70 percent of members throughout much of the antebellum period but only

26 percent of the members disciplined by the elders. In other words, the churches intervened far more often in men's behavior than in women's. How did women view the relatively frequent admonitions, censures, and suspensions doled out to the men? To some, it must have been a welcome relief. According to historian Stephanie McCurry, women used the church courts to protect themselves from the "abuses of husbands, brothers, fathers, and other male relatives."[12]

In 1831, church leaders did not yet view Adam Hutchison as a notorious offender. They hoped to set him straight by suspending him from communion and giving him the opportunity to repent and reform his behavior. Nor had Susan Hutchison raised the question of separation. However, over the next two years, the community's opinion of Adam's qualities as a husband changed from bad to worse.[13]

IN THE FALL of 1831, the Hutchisons remained in debt. Nevertheless, desiring to maintain his former standard of living in some respects, Adam spent money he did not have. "I have had a trial of temper in seeing Mr. H with a new pair of boots," wrote Susan. "We are destitute of even one blanket and I do believe Mr. H has twenty pairs of boots now on hand besides shoes in profusion." The following month, "Mr. H expended nearly 20 dollars for stockings." Although she was pregnant with her fourth child, Susan resumed her little school in Augusta to help support the family, but enrollments remained low. "I have only eight pupils," she wrote in November.[14]

Adam hoped that the earnings of his son, Robert, might ease the family's financial troubles. Having finished school in Scotland, seventeen-year-old Robert sailed to the United States and joined the family in Augusta two weeks before Susan gave birth to her fourth son, John Grey, on January 28, 1832. By September, Robert had found employment, which should have been a great relief, since Susan was home with the newborn and could no longer teach, but "Mr. H was much hurt by learning that Robert's employer would only give him 150 dollars per year"—less than the earnings of a female academy teacher. To make matters worse, Robert seemed to have inherited his father's propensity for outbursts of anger. "Robert's temper is a severely afflictive dispensation," noted Susan.[15]

Casting about for a way to bring in more money, Adam Hutchison once again entered the Georgia Land Lottery. "The great State lotteries began their drawing today," Susan noted on October 22. Two days later, Adam informed her that one of their acquaintances had drawn a valuable lot worth eight thousand dollars. "For a moment I wished Mr. H to draw something also, then thought of the poor Indians agony while their lands are thus torn from them."[16]

Despite her sympathy for the Cherokee and Creek tribes forcibly removed from their lands, Susan's desire for financial stability soon trumped her conscience. The next day, her husband told her that one of the elders in their church had drawn a valuable lot. "Again I felt—a strong wish that a blessing should also be given to my husband and again this was succeeded by painful sympathy with the poor Indians," she wrote. She turned to the Bible for guidance and found a story she believed might justify her husband's participation: "I read how God gave the land of Canaan to Israel." Robert scoffed at their hopes of winning anything of worth: "Robert seems to have no expectation that the lot drawn is worth anything but the Lord is able to make it a rich blessing." The following month, Adam informed her that he had drawn another lot of land in northern Georgia's gold region. Gold had been discovered on Cherokee lands several years earlier, and by the summer of 1829 thousands of prospectors flooded the region. Susan was excited about the possibility of finding gold on Adam's lot, but her stepson ridiculed the idea: "When Robert returned I informed him of it but he treated it with derision," she wrote.[17]

During the summer of 1832, Adam Hutchison developed a bad cough, and when it persisted into the fall, Susan confronted the possibility that he was seriously ill. In November, the doctor paid a house call. "Mr. H was alarmingly unwell—his breath was oppressively short," Susan wrote. The doctor prescribed calomel and bleeding. In late December, "Mr. H [was] so unwell that he told me he had for some time been thinking he must inform me that he should be obliged to resign his place in the Bank unless he mended." Two days later, he informed his superiors that unless he recovered, he would have to give up his position. "Our circumstances are gloomy," Susan reported.[18]

As Adam's health deteriorated, both he and Susan fantasized about the possibility of striking it rich in the state lottery. Ever the optimist, Susan was convinced that "the blessed Lord can crown the [lot] with fruitfulness as the widow's oil till all our debts are paid." She thought about all the good she could do with the earnings. She could free Grace, the elderly slave they hired to work in their home. A professing Christian, Grace had participated in the independent black congregation that Susan had hosted in her kitchen, and over the years, the two women had occasionally prayed together. In 1828, as Grace's owner prepared to sell her, she had come to

Susan for help. "Poor old Grace about to be sold came with tears to beg me to purchase her," Susan wrote. "She has been for some time desirous to belong to us and now that she is about to be sold she is very anxious. I also desire to have her live with us but it must be a wonder of mercy if she should be ours." After she was sold, Grace continued to work for hire and eventually came to work for the Hutchisons. Now, thinking about the possibility of lottery winnings, Susan fantasized about helping Grace and others in the community: "I desire to free Gracy and to help Mrs. Abbot and to assist my own family if it be the Lord's will." Adam dreamed of leaving his job: "Mr. H told me that he did not think it would be possible for him to return to the bank and that he desired to get two or three thousand dollars worth of goods and go into the up country—perhaps into the land he had drawn," wrote Susan. But two months later, Susan discovered that they had only twenty-one dollars left in the bank.[19]

Adam sent his resignation to the bank on January 28, 1833, but the directors asked that he procure a substitute rather than resign his position outright. He acceded to this request and then, though still unwell, prepared to travel to Savannah to take care of some financial affairs. He left Augusta on February 21. He wrote to Susan while he was gone but did not convey any news of success in his business dealings. On February 22, the doctor informed Susan that he had become alarmed about her husband's symptoms. Susan never wrote about a specific medical diagnosis, but it is possible that Adam had developed consumption, or pulmonary tuberculosis.[20]

Rumors of Adam's illness spread in town. In March, Susan's friend Mary Smelt stopped by to visit and offered her opinion. "Mrs. Smelt spoke of my husband as if there was no hope of his restoration to health," wrote Susan. "I am aware that from Mr. H's temper many might suppose such an event would be met without much sorrow, but it is not so—I have always hoped that mercy would be poured upon us in the decline of our days according to the sorrows which we had been called to suffer—and I still pray . . . that we may dwell together in undisturbed affection."[21]

Susan wanted to return with the children to New York, but moving back to her parents' farm required Adam's consent. During the antebellum period, both civil and church law recognized the husband's "right of gentle restraint." Because he exercised marital authority over his household, a husband was allowed—by moral coercion, if not by physical force—to regulate his wife's movements. He could prevent her from associating with people or engaging in pursuits he viewed as undesirable. He could forbid her from going to places he disapproved on rational grounds. Adam opposed the idea of moving to New York. That March, while he was in Savannah, she wrote, "I received a kind letter from him but he sets his face against my returning home."[22]

Up to this point, Adam had always exerted patriarchal dominance in their marriage, maintaining his right to veto Susan's actions and making some effort to provide for the family financially. And up to this point, Susan had always submitted to his authority, even when she had misgivings about some of his decisions. But the balance of power in their relationship changed when Adam came back to Augusta after a six-week absence. Shortly after his return, he surprised Susan by asking her to sign a loan on his behalf: "My husband—told me he should wish me probably to join my name with his in a note of 20 dollars for a horse saddle and bridle—I cannot tell how the requirement distressed me." His financial affairs were still in disarray, and his cough had grown worse. She worried that if she refused, "the shock of his feelings should injure his health." Nevertheless, she denied his request: "I would not consent for I saw no way of meeting the engagement." Any hopes she might have had that Robert's earnings would help defray their expenses were soon dashed. Robert resigned his position and, like many young men hoping to strike it rich, packed up his trunk and departed for the gold region in North Georgia.[23]

Susan then took stock of her family's dire financial straits and decided to take matters into her own hands. She would return to teaching to support the family, an idea Mary Smelt had suggested the previous fall. Teaching was attractive in large part because she could earn a relatively large amount of money: a woman teacher in Augusta could charge each student $3.50 per quarter to teach elementary reading and writing; with arithmetic added, this fee could rise to $6.50. Susan was qualified to teach the "higher branches," including moral philosophy, geometry, and chemistry. If a female student wanted a comprehensive course of study, her tuition could reach $15.00 per quarter. If she could enroll a dozen students in a small school, she might thus earn between $168 and $720 per year, possibly enough to support the family and begin paying down some of their debt. However, the Hutchisons would have to relocate because they could no longer afford to pay the rent on a house in town. Adam gave his consent, and Susan began making inquiries in Beach Island, a small community about nine miles from Augusta. In April, she learned that her offer to conduct a school there had been approved and that she could lease a property that would function as both a home and a small school.[24]

In early May, the Hutchisons loaded their belongings into a wagon and made the trip to Beach Island, accompanied by their three children, Grace, and another hired slave, Maria, a young cook who had recently given birth. The wagon lurched ponderously through a "very heavy shower of rain and hail," and they arrived at their new home a bit before dark, all their belongings soaked through. Everyone suffered. "My large terrestrial globe was quite ruined by the hail—my mattresses and bedding were completely drenched with the rain," Susan wrote. Maria's baby was crying. Grace had brought several chickens in a closed basket in hopes of both supplying the family with eggs and selling some to earn money, but the birds suffocated during the trip, eliminating both "her hope of gain from eggs as well as her comfort in supplying Mr. H." After kindling a fire, the Hutchisons hung up the bedding to dry and spent the night on the floor, without table or chairs.[25]

Adam at first seemed to accept his family's changed circumstances. During the move, he was cheerful. Several days later, when Susan's first group of students arrived, he spent the day "busy directing a workman to fit up a bower under some trees in the edge of the wood." But he soon fell sick again. Susan wrote, "He is exceedingly feeble and dejected—his cough is so much worse that if it were right and pract[ical] I would desire to return tomorrow to Augusta, howbeit a sense of duty would keep me here at least for one quarter." Despite his ill health, he went to town and purchased a horse, to her dismay. "I am grieved to see our debts increase when our means are so limited," she wrote. The horse provided him with freedom of movement, and he began to go out on long rides, sometimes spending the day in Augusta and returning only for dinner.[26]

After three weeks in Beach Island, Adam left his family for good. "Mr. Hutchison rose feeble and depressed," noted Susan. "He made ready to remove to town as soon as possible—He could with difficulty mount his horse." He returned to Augusta and took up residence in a hotel, leaving her to run her little school and manage the household alone, coming by to visit her once a week or so. "Mr. H stayed with us till five and then after prayer left us to return to his hotel in Augusta," she wrote after one visit. She began to send him letters. He wrote back, informing her that he expected to return to work at the bank, but he never did so. Her school enrolled thirteen students, and the tuition payments were probably enough to support the household in Beach Island and begin paying off their debts, but now she also had to pay for Adam's horse and his lodging in Augusta.[27]

One month after her husband left, Susan grimly pondered her situation. She felt stranded in the middle of nowhere. She missed her family in New York and her friends and church community in Augusta. "Just ten years since I left Raleigh—Mr. H went off at six. . . . I sat alone with Alexander and had time to meditate on the providence by which I was established here separate from friends, kindred, husband and house of God."[28]

Near the end of June, Adam came to visit, "looking a little better in health, but filled with unholy anger toward me." His visits became less frequent, and he rarely stayed overnight. In July, Susan recorded that he showed up one evening "in a sulky with a horse holding his head more like a cameleopard than any I ever recollect to have seen." In August, "My husband thought of staying all day as it rained but the school proved too annoying to him and he set off while it was drizzling to return to town." She felt abandoned.[29]

Depressed and in a situation she found intolerable, Susan repeatedly pondered returning to Amenia. Could she take the children back to her parents' farm and reunite with Sylvanus and Ebenezer? She might find a teaching position there, and staying with her parents would allow the family to retrench financially. By the end of the summer, Adam finally seemed to relent. In mid-August, she wrote, "In the course of the day I took an opportunity to ask Mr. H on the subject of going on to the North and he told me it was his opinion that I had best go and that Elizabeth might either go with me or remain in Augusta." Having gained Adam's permission to leave, Susan prepared to inform her minister, the Reverend Samuel Kennedy Talmage, of her plans. She did not have enough money to travel north and hoped that the elders might provide some assistance.[30]

ACCORDING TO HISTORIAN Hendrik Hartog, the law recognized a variety of separations between husband and wife during the early national period: (1) judicially ordered separations, (2) separations based on equitable agreements or legal contracts between the spouses, and (3) informal separations, including desertions, abandonments, bigamies, and separations founded on legally unenforceable contracts. Two additional sorts of separations did not exist legally but were not uncommon in antebellum society: (4) cases where the divorce of a couple in one jurisdiction was unrecognized in another, and (5) temporary separations arising for reasons other than marital conflict. Sometimes men and women simply walked away from their marriages. Notices of runaway wives commonly appeared in newspapers when husbands wished to publicly air the couple's problems or inform the community that they would not cover their wives' debts. Historian Mary Beth Sievens has used such sources to explore the way such notices enabled couples to negotiate marital roles, economic support, or property ownership outside of the civil courts. But Susan Hutchison neither sought help from the civil courts nor simply walked away from her marriage. Instead, she turned to her church.[31]

The Presbyterian Church did not tolerate the separation of husbands and wives without justification. Only two cases of marital problems appear in the Session minutes of Augusta's First Presbyterian Church from 1808 to 1837, and both involved separated spouses. In 1833, the elders initiated an investigation of a married woman who had left her husband. The woman had "been accused of conduct highly unbecoming a Christian; in having had an infant child, while living separate from her husband from whom she had been separate for more than [a] month, and is still living separate from him." The elders did not find her guilty of adultery, but they did express concern that she had abandoned her marital duty by separating from her husband without justification. They appointed a committee to meet with her "and require of her such satisfaction as they may deem proper, and [as] her not giving them proper information on the subject, they direct her to abstain from the Communion Table, and report to the session at their next meeting."[32]

The Augusta elders described an unwarranted separation as a "reproach upon the Church." In 1837, the Session investigated a married couple who had separated amicably. The elders concluded, "No sufficient reasons have been assigned which can justify them in the eyes, of either God or man for virtually undoing a relation which of all others should be held the most sacred and inviolable." They resolved "that Mr. and Mrs. Danforth be solemnly admonished for having thus sinfully and publicly violated their marriage vows to the grief and mortification of their brethren and the deep reproach of their Christian profession" and ordered the estranged couple to "recognize each other as *Husband* and *Wife*," move back together, and begin fulfilling their marital duties.[33]

But the church elders supported Susan's decision to leave. In her case, they perceived separation as the morally correct course. Although pastors sometimes preached from the pulpit that wives should live with their husbands' failings and turn the other cheek, a woman still had to put her own salvation first, and she did not have to submit herself and her children to ongoing abuse and exploitation. As one minister explained in a lecture on domestic duties, "Some husbands are unreasonable in their commands; and their orders cannot be obeyed, even should their wives be ever so much disposed to serve them.... It must therefore be kept in mind, that she is to obey in the Lord." Near the end of August, Talmage called to inform her that the congregation would provide the money to enable her to travel to Amenia.[34]

Susan eventually learned the reasoning behind the church's decision. In early October, Talmage visited again to ascertain whether Susan expected to return again to the South: "He said deep feeling was manifested on account of Mr. H treatment to me in regard to requiring of me all I earned to support my family—while he employed his salary to liquidate other debts—Mr. Talmage said the friends feared their bounty should be apportioned to Mr. H benefit—Oh that my God would enable me to return without their aid."[35]

The church saw Adam Hutchison as derelict in his duty as a husband. A husband's primary responsibility in marriage rested in economic support. If he provided reasonably well for his dependents, he fulfilled his duties as a husband, just as a wife fulfilled her duties by providing obedient service. A wife was not justified in leaving her husband as long as he treated her kindly and provided for her to the extent of his ability. If a man lost his fortune, economic retrenchment in the family's standard of living was understandable. But a husband could not reduce his wife's comforts without very good cause, nor could he squander household income on gambling or drinking. Both the civil courts and the churches recognized a wife's right to compel a competent husband to support his family. Ministers frequently quoted the Bible to reinforce this message: "He that provideth not for his own, especially for those of his own household, has denied the faith, and is worse than an infidel." Adam had not only failed to provide for his family financially but had exploited his wife by having her labor in his stead. He had moved out of the marital home and was living independently on his wife's earnings, leaving Susan to assume the duties of head of household, an act that reversed traditional gender roles to an unacceptable degree. In the eyes of the church, Adam's actions went beyond the pale. That he was unwell—perhaps seriously ill—was beside the point.[36]

The church elders were so incensed with Adam that they sought assurances that he would not benefit from any assistance provided to Susan and the children. This was not an entirely unfounded fear. Ever the obedient wife, Susan had for years dutifully turned her earnings over to her husband. If she returned to the South and to her husband, the money provided might wind up back in Adam's hands. Susan regretted her situation: "I feel sad at the prospect of depending upon the assistance of such friends as are so fearful of conferring any kindness upon my sick husband."[37]

As she began to prepare for the trip north, Susan faced one last setback. Although Adam had seemed to acquiesce in the decision and expressed the hope they might one day "yet have a home at the north," he wavered and "expressed a wish that I should comply with the desire of the friends of the Walton family and try to open school again in Augusta." She, however, "did not feel it to be right as by the letter he brought me from home they now expected me this winter and my old parents have their hearts set upon seeing me."[38]

Although she had previously been tractable and obedient to her husband, Susan had developed a growing sense of agency and control over her life, and she now held firm. The next day, she told Adam that she did not believe it was her duty to open a school again in Augusta. "I feared he would be angry," she wrote, "but he was not." Even though Adam told her he had been coughing up a little blood, she persisted with her plan to leave.[39]

Susan began selling her furniture and other household items. Some of the Beach Island churchwomen came to purchase her things. "The young ladies took home most of their books," she noted. "Miss Miller bought of me my little work table which I bought a good while before my marriage—I felt sad at parting with the silent companion of many trials." Although she was grateful for the money raised, she felt very downcast. "I went out and did I think desire to cast myself upon God but I did not feel that comfort I sometimes have done." Talmage brought "90 dollars a gift of the friends of Jesus" to cover the costs of her travel.[40]

The elders of her church officially dismissed her from the congregation, documenting her good standing in the church and thereby enabling her to join a Presbyterian congregation elsewhere. According to the Constitution of the Presbyterian Church, "When any member shall remove from one congregation to another, he shall produce satisfactory testimonials of his church membership and dismission, before he be admitted as a regular member of that church."[41]

Susan and her children rose early on October 23, 1833, and boarded a boat to carry them to Savannah. "I found parting from my poor husband a trial," she wrote, "both of us wept." On the river, the boat's cramped quarters proved a challenge: "I find the care of my little ones very difficult. . . .

Elizabeth tries to aid me but we sit shivering on deck holding them by main strength, or watching them at every step in the narrow confines of the cabin." Four days later, they docked in Savannah and caught a ship bound for New York City.[42]

After three weeks of travel, they arrived in Poughkeepsie, where they spent the night with Arabella Bosworth and her mother before taking the stage to Amenia on November 16. The familiar hills were white with snow. The stage driver let them off at the house where one of Susan's brothers lived, and soon a pair of wagons arrived to convey everyone to the farm. At long last, Susan reported, "By the rich blessing of God I arrived in safety and was permitted to embrace my dear aged parents, my brother and sisters and my dear little children."[43]

IN AMENIA, SUSAN remained Mrs. Adam Hutchison. But who exactly was she as a separated wife? To some extent, a separated woman took on a new identity. She was still a wife, but she had no husband. In divorce, husband and wife became emancipated from each other. In separation, they remained legally bound. From the perspective of the civil courts, a separated wife was still a "femme covert." Her legal status affected a variety of transactions, including her ability to sell or inherit property, borrow money, remarry, and educate and discipline her children. As a wife, Susan had to consult with her husband regarding decisions about the children's lodging, education, religious upbringing, social connections, and employment. She and Adam would have to maintain contact.[44]

Susan knew she could not depend on her husband for any sort of financial assistance. Within two days of arriving in Amenia, she began to set her financial affairs in order. She needed to support her family and begin to pay off their debts. A teaching position was available at the local district schoolhouse, located an easy walk from the farm. She accepted an offer to teach there for $14.00 a month, the average salary for a male teacher in New York's common schools. During the mid-1840s, women teachers usually earned an average wage of $5.50 in the summer months and $6.98 in winter, but respectable women who functioned as heads of household—often widows—could earn the same wages as men. Susan would probably never have received such an offer had she separated from her husband without justification. But because the church in Augusta had dismissed her in good standing, she qualified for respectability not only in the Presbyterian Church but also in the Amenia community. She could earn as much as $168 per year, less than she had earned in Georgia, but as long as she and her children lived on her parents' farm, her overall costs would also be lower.[45]

Now that she was back home and living under the same roof with all four of her sons and her stepdaughter, Susan began to notice things about the farm that she had previously overlooked. The farmhouse, which she remembered from her childhood as quite spacious, now seemed cramped. During her youth, the house had accommodated two adults and eight children, but the eldest sons and daughters had moved away from home, freeing up some space. With five adults and five children now in residence, "we are so crowded and cooped up at home that I find no quiet resting place," she observed. She also noticed that her elderly parents moved with difficulty and her older brother Meletiah seemed feeble and unwell. She was shocked to discover that the family was struggling financially. On the surface, the farm appeared as prosperous as ever, but her brother could not always pay the bills on time. "Today Meletiah settled with Mr. Butts and paid him in full—I was sad when I saw Meletiah so desponding at our circumstances which to any other eye seem comfortable enough."[46]

Not wanting to be a burden, she pitched in to help with the household chores when not occupied with her school. In the fall, she and Amanda wove a rag carpet for their mother. Keeping warm through the bitterly cold winter required another kind of effort. "I always help my little boys to bring in wood and chips for the night," she wrote one night, "a task which tonight I found troublesome and laborious as the snow blew so strongly in my face as to be somewhat suffocating." The crops ripened in the summer, and she and Amanda went into the fields and pulled flax. In August, she sat down at the wheel and began to spin. "I have felt great depression in view of my temporal circumstances," she wrote. "Cincinnatus after his great services done to his country returned again to the labours of the field, 'Seized the rough plough and greatly independent lived.' . . . Shall I suffer a pagan to attain a virtue in which I fall short?" She applied herself to the task: "Full of the idea of equaling the contentment of the Great Roman Dictator I returned to the wheel today after eighteen years disuse, and by close application spun thirty knots."[47]

Elizabeth was not happy on the farm, so Susan began to make inquiries. Elizabeth's aunt offered to have the girl come be her companion in Charleston, South Carolina. "I was truly glad of the letter [from Mrs. Anderson] and so was E[lizabeth]," wrote Susan. "She is tired of the hard labour of a country life." However, the offer was contingent on Adam's written consent, which would be difficult to obtain, since he communicated very infrequently with Susan.[48]

Through the following year Susan taught, continued her farm work, and kept at the wheel, but although she was relieved to be with her family in Amenia, she was wracked by anxiety and guilt. She had "very painful dreams" about her husband and home in Augusta. "I continue to spin," she wrote in mid-August. "My heart is overwhelmed with regret that I left my home as I did nevertheless I did I think desire to do my duty now it seems probable it would have been better if I had remained with my poor sick husband."[49]

Sporadic letters from Adam began to trickle in on February 15, 1834. Susan learned that his health continued to deteriorate, and he had moved farther south in search of improvement, first to Savannah, then to St. Marys, just north of the Florida border. At the end of April, he was back in Savannah, "hopeless of benefit from a southern climate." He told her that he planned to join her in Amenia as soon as the weather permitted and his strength returned. "I am much bowed down with grief about Mr H," Susan wrote. "Sometime I can exercise a comfortable faith, but again I am afraid I shall never again see him."[50]

In early May she wrote, "This morning I got a letter from Mr H dated April 20 Savannah saying that he now saw he had been guilty of the height of injustice toward me and asking my forgiveness. May God forgive me as sincerely as I forgive him." She immediately mailed a reassuring response and prayed, "May the Holy Spirit comfort him."[51]

From that day forward, she began to anticipate his arrival in New York. Near the end of May she wrote, "Today if my husband be able to set off upon his journey northerly I expect he will do so." Four days later, however, there was "still no news from Mr. H." By June 2, she was so certain of his imminent arrival that she dressed herself formally and waited on the landing and front porch to receive him. But the next day another letter arrived. "Oh it was a saddening one!" she wrote. "My poor husband had left Savannah about the fourth of last month in the steam boat Florida for the Sawona Springs on the St. Johns." Rather than heading north to rejoin his family, he had gone to Florida.[52]

Adam spent June and July in Mineral Springs, where he hoped the waters would restore his health. Susan received two more letters from him, the second one dated July 4. After two months without news, Susan wrote to the manager of the establishment where Adam had been staying, "begging information concerning him." She received no response. At the end of September, Robert wrote to inform her that his father "had left Florida for the Up Country of Georgia." On October 4, Susan had a premonition: "No news from Mr. H, three months today since the date of his last letter. Something seems to whisper that letter was his last."[53]

On October 11, she learned that Adam had died. "Today brought the dreaded and dreadful tidings of the departure of my husband," she wrote. She blamed herself: "My grief is that I left my husband—had I been satisfied that God would provide for us without this exertion on my part I should doubtless been near him in his last illness." She received another letter explaining that a trunk full of Adam's belongings was being forwarded "to the north for the benefit of his family." Those belongings consisted of "clothes, bag and cane—the hat was missing."[54]

Two years later, Susan came across some evidence of Adam's last days: "Today I accidentally took up one of the scholars' books and on the cover found a religious paper in which the writer recommending the climate of the Northern part of East Florida and the excellent qualities of the Mineral Springs said there was an old gentleman from Augusta Ga who was reduced to a skeleton by a dreadful cough whom he prayed with. . . . He bid him adieu but just one month after he returned and found him so much better as to go to the springs and he believed or 'hoped' he would be restored—Alas that was my husband."[55]

Susan never recorded the exact date of Adam's death in her journal, nor is the date found in the records of the First Presbyterian Church of Augusta. Sometime afterward, the clerk of the Session thumbed back through the records and located an old entry: "Mr. Adam Hutchison— Admitted on Profession 11 Dec. 1820." To this, he added a brief note in the margin: "Died 1834."[56]

SUSAN'S CASE ILLUSTRATES the ways a woman—even a Christian woman living in the South during the Second Great Awakening—could transgress cultural ideals of marriage and motherhood without triggering denunciation or criticism. She was able to do so because her actions placed the welfare of her children above any other duty, and everyone around her understood those actions. Historians have sometimes emphasized the influence of essayists, ministers, and politicians in shaping gender norms without considering the way biological imperatives could supersede such influences. Susan's decision to send her two eldest sons away to New York to be raised by her sister and parents did not conform to sentimental ideals of motherhood, and her decision to separate from her husband, taking all the children with her, did not conform to popular Christian ideals of family life and wifely obedience. Nevertheless, her desire to protect her children trumped all such conventions. Augusta's Presbyterian community watched as she prioritized her duty to herself and her children over her duty to obey her husband. Her actions earned the respect of the community, and the friendships she had forged in Augusta endured over the following decade.

Susan's story also reveals some of the ways in which the Protestant churches served as important counterpoints to the civil courts. In the civil courts, a wife was a "femme covert" whose legal rights were subsumed by those of her husband, but the ecclesiastical courts saw things very differently. Church elders often encountered cases that led them to distinguish between husband and wife. In the context of church discipline, a married woman's identity could never be fully submerged in the marital relation. Elders at times admitted wives as members of the congregation but did not admit their husbands; husbands could be suspended while their wives remained in good standing. The church courts maintained tradition—they upheld long-standing gender roles and enforced adherence to beliefs and practices that had originated centuries earlier in the Protestant Reformation. But they also considered husbands and wives as individuals before God, creating an arena where women could "begin to challenge the deep legal dependency that left them almost powerless in the secular courts."[57]

To the extent that they maintained traditional gender roles, the churches remained patriarchal, yet the ecclesiastical courts nevertheless provided women with some leverage in negotiating the terms of their relations with men. When Susan wrote, "The whole community both in the church and out of it were excited against [Mr. H.] for his conduct toward me whom all regarded as a faithful and an injured and persecuted wife," the church community to which she referred was largely female. Women often brought rumors and reports of men's misconduct to the attention of the church elders. In Susan's case, as in others during this period, the intervention of the ecclesiastical court into the husband's affairs served the interests of the woman.[58] The church elders' intervention freed Susan from exploitation and abuse and gave her the opportunity to improve her family's financial situation and reunite with her children.

But for several years after Adam's death, Susan's appreciation of her new freedom was overshadowed by sorrow and regret. She repeatedly mulled over the past in the pages of her journal. "I looked for happiness," she wrote; "how bitterly was I disappointed yet I cannot help turning still toward that season in which it seemed that I might have been happy—for I fully believe Mr. H to have been strongly attached to me—why then were we wretched?" She questioned every decision she had ever made: "I feel that I did not pursue a profitable path with respect to his temper—but I have the consciousness that I strove to make him happy."[59]

Gradually, the self-doubt and sorrow subsided, and Susan stopped berating herself for the failure of her marriage and the death of her husband. She never forgot Adam, though. On March 23, 1839, she recorded in her journal, "Today brought me two interesting letters, one from my dear Elizabeth, the other from Amanda Nye—Margaret Susan was unwell— Expresses a wish to have me come & stay and make my home with her as long as I please, and says she is sure Henry will feel just as she does—I have tonight looked at a few of my dear departed husband's letters—Oh God, thou that knowest all things, thou knowest that I loved him."[60]

CHAPTER 6

School Business

> September 2, 1834—Spent much of the day in writing to Robert and to
> Mrs. Smelt. Amanda does not like it that I have spoken to them to look
> out for me a situation. No school seems to offer itself near me. If the Lord
> see good for me to return to the South perhaps he will enable me to do
> better than for a long time past I have been enabled to do.
>
> September 12—I wrote to Dr. McPheeters. Sister Amanda went to spend a
> few days at Sister R's.
>
> October 28—Recd. a letter from Dr. McPheeters informing me of two or
> three situations where I might get a school. Thus in 1834 I receive an
> invitation to revisit NC, to which state I was invited in 1814.

After her husband's death, Susan considered her children's prospects. Her stepdaughter's future seemed to be resolved: after a period of courtship over the summer, Elizabeth had become engaged to Horace Reed, the son of a neighboring family in Amenia. But what would become of Susan's four sons? Most of Dutchess County's male householders were farmers or laborers, with a smattering of carpenters, smiths, and shopkeepers. Her boys had no inheritance, no future hope of land or money. Once they grew up, they would have to leave the farm and earn an independent living.[1]

She had always dreamed of more for her sons than skilled labor or white-collar work. When Ebenezer was six years old, she had confessed, "I have rededicated him to God whom I asked to make him a missionary of the cross." Writing to her sons in 1836, she urged them in this direction: "If you were pious children you could be thinking of learning to teach the poor heathen who never have yet heard about Jesus—How glad would mother be in the last day to see her sons among those happy souls who have been the means of converting the Heathen!" In Susan's mind, no calling was higher than that of a minister or missionary; had she been born a man, she would probably have chosen this path for herself. However, training for the ministry in the Presbyterian Church required a college education. The salary she earned teaching at the local district common school would not be enough.[2]

In September 1834, she started corresponding with friends and acquaintances in Georgia and North Carolina about opportunities to open a school of her own. In October, her wish was granted when William McPheeters, pastor of Raleigh's First Presbyterian Church and her former principal at Raleigh Academy, wrote to tell her of some opportunities in North Carolina. The following month, McPheeters invited her to return to Raleigh and open an independent school there.[3]

Amanda Nye objected to her sister's plan, but Susan pushed ahead. She was a different person from the idealistic young woman who had first headed south in 1815. As a widow, she now had legal custody of her own children and complete control of her own money. Like all women of the time, she could not vote and thus lacked political power, but she was now subordinate to no one in her own household. She could establish a school, hire assistants, and use her profits any way she wished.[4]

Over the next half decade, Susan Nye Hutchison transformed herself from nearly destitute widow in New York to successful North Carolina educator. Traces of female academy founders are rare in historical archives. Much of what we know about the women who established state-chartered incorporated academies is based on a handful of individuals. As historians have pointed out, it was not uncommon for southern women to establish small entrepreneurial schools based on the French school model, but as academies replaced the traditional French schools, their all-male boards of trustees often preferred to hire men—preferably ministers—as principals and to recruit female teachers to work under that masculine authority. Susan's journals and school documents thus offer a relatively rare look into the business world of the female educational entrepreneur.[5]

Between 1834 and 1841, higher education for women expanded in both the North and the South. In North Carolina and other states that provided no financial subsidy to female higher education, schools depended on tuition revenues, the patronage of private families, and endowments from Protestant denominations and other religious groups. During this period, women began to move up the career ladder in venture schools and academies, progressing from teacher's assistant to teacher to preceptress of a female department to principal and head of a female school.[6]

Susan's career in teaching reflects this broader social development in women's work, yet in some ways her experience was exceptional. Her activities as a school founder and principal fell well within the range of acceptable southern social mores, yet some of her private actions ran completely counter to contemporary prescriptive messages about the woman's role in the family. In financial terms, her role as head of her own female school allowed her to become the head of her extended family, supporting not only her own children but also two brothers, a niece, and a cousin.

What did a woman need to succeed in North Carolina's education market? As an experienced teacher and founder of several independent schools in Georgia, Susan knew that success depended on many factors: a strong reputation, supportive relationships with parents, and effective leadership. To ensure her acceptance in southern society, she would have to be diplomatic when discussing slavery and emancipation. To sustain a school over the long term, she would have to build networks of community support, maintain a ruthless focus on the bottom line, and seek out endowment funds. She would also need impeccable credentials.

FEMALE TEACHERS WITH the education, experience, executive ability, social background, and mobility necessary to search out the most lucrative positions available in academies and venture schools could do well in antebellum North Carolina. The expansion of female and coeducational schools in the South created a demand for female teachers. Before 1825, only 13 of North Carolina's 177 academies enrolled young women, but by the 1840s, half of the state's schools admitted female students. At the highest levels of schooling, women's enrollment outstripped men's by midcentury. According to the first report of North Carolina's superintendent for education, published in 1854, "perhaps between 500 and 600" students were enrolled in the state's male colleges, whereas "the number at Female Colleges ... was not less than 1,000." During the 1830s, some North Carolina institutions advertised salaries as high as five hundred dollars for a female academy teacher or principal, figures that matched those paid to male principals of coeducational academies in New York around the same time. If Susan could establish a school and serve as principal, she could earn a salary at the high end of this range.[7]

She knew she would need additional training to establish a successful school in North Carolina. Academies offered certificates to the relatively few students who persisted through the entire course of study to graduate. In 1833, the *American Annals of Education* reported, "The requisites for a certificate have gradually been made more and more definite, and the standard has constantly been rising from year to year." As more prospective teachers sought positions in academies and higher venture schools, those institutions increasingly began to demand that applicants possess such credentials. Any individual hoping to establish a school and serve as principal needed to meet or exceed these qualifications.[8]

TABLE 3. Wages for Academy Teachers Advertised by Eleven Higher Schools in North Carolina Newspapers, 1808–1841

Year	Male Wage	Female Wage
1808	$220	$125
1819	$500	$285
1822*	$1,361	$776
1824	$500–$600	$285–$342
1826*	—	$500
1829	$300–$400	$171–$228
1830*	$800	$456
1830	$300–$500	$171–$285
1837*	$900	$513
1839	—	$500
1841	—	$500

*Wanted a teacher who would also serve as the principal/head of the school.

Source: Kim Tolley, "The Socio-Economic Incentives for Women to Teach in North
Carolina, 1800–1840," paper presented at the American Educational Research
Association, San Diego, 2004. Data obtained from newspaper advertisements in
Coon, *North Carolina Schools and Academies*, 206, 222, 803, 807, 811–15, 818, 820.

To improve her skills, Susan decided to visit Emma Willard's Troy
Female Seminary, founded in 1821 along the lines of Willard's *Plan for
Improving Female Education*, an address she had submitted to the New York
Legislature in 1819. She had requested that public tax money be granted to
female academies and seminaries, not only to provide education to women
but also to train teachers for the state's common schools. Although the
state did not provide funding for Troy Female Seminary, by the mid-1830s,
the school had a national reputation for training outstanding teachers. Not
only did a certificate from Troy help a prospective teacher land a good
position, but the addition of a Troy-trained faculty member increased a
school's marketability. Female schools in North Carolina and Virginia
commonly announced the arrival of a new teacher from Troy as a means
of enhancing prestige. In 1835 Virginia's Mount Pleasant Academy trum-
peted the expansion of its course of study after "having engaged a female
teacher from Troy Seminary, N.Y." In 1837, North Carolina's Scotland Neck
Female Seminary announced the arrival of Eugenia Hanks, whose "qualifications are believed to be of the first order, having finished her education
at Mrs. Willard's celebrated school."[9]

Susan also arranged for her sixteen-year-old stepdaughter, Elizabeth, to travel with her to explore the possibility of training to teach at the academy level. Elizabeth's fiancé, Horace Reed, had fallen ill in late October and had died the following month. With marriage no longer an option in the near term, Elizabeth would need to find a means of supporting herself.

Because teaching had always provided Susan a way to earn a living, she naturally thought of encouraging Elizabeth to enter that field. In the nineteenth century, education replaced real wealth as a form of inheritance for middle-class Americans. Historians agree that as young people became increasingly dependent on a volatile wage economy to earn a living, parents turned to formal schooling to provide their children with the skills, social networks, and credentials necessary to support themselves in uncertain times. This development explains the culture of educational aspiration that took hold in American society. In fact, Susan's long career in teaching—as a single, married, separated, and widowed woman— illustrates the economic importance of education for females.[10]

But Elizabeth had no interest in teaching and had clashed with her stepmother over the subject earlier that spring. Susan began confiding in her journal about the strain in their relationship in April:

> April 14—At night Elizabeth grieved me exceedingly by her obdurate and unyielding conduct—by her disrespectful and profane language—I now sit writing and thinking it over—and am fully persuaded that I feel none but sentiments of kindness toward Elizabeth—May God forgive her for Christ's sake.
> May 4—After Elizabeth's return from church she grieved me by taking a long walk over the river with Charles—This morning I desired never to be angry with E.
> May 9—Capt. Smith called to enquire whether E. wished to take the Pleasant Valley School.
> May 10—Capt. Smith brought word that Elizabeth might receive 12 ½ [dollars per month] and her board at one place but she must keep eight hours a day.
> May 12—Today father and I accompanied Elizabeth to Pleasant Valley to her School—I fear she will not be pleasantly situated, I know not how to act for the best. She cannot submit to the drudgery of housebusiness and I have no means of supporting her without some exertion on her own part—I had much rather she were near me.

May 15—Miss Bennett went home. I sent a letter to E. by Capt. Smith.

May 17—Capt. Smith brought a letter from E. a pleasant kind one.

May 26—Elizabeth is today 17 years old.

June 7—Elizabeth came home. I was glad to see her but grieved to learn that she was not going to return again to her school.

June 17—Brother M[eletiah] and myself accompanied E. to Pleasant Valley.

June 21—I was surprised at the unexpected appearance of E. at Mrs. G. She had given up her situation.

Despite the fact that Elizabeth had twice before abandoned the schoolroom, Susan believed she might entice the girl back into teaching with the prospect of an academy position. Academy teaching offered opportunities for career and social advancement. In rural New York, common school teaching was at the bottom of the ladder with regard to salary and terms of employment, but it was a starting point. After a year or more teaching in a common school, both men and women could acquire the experience and personal connections to move up. The chance to become an academy teacher, the head of a department, or a school principal might have provided an incentive to become a common school teacher in the first place, despite the relatively low wages rural schools paid. For women, few other lines of work offered the possibility of higher positions and salary improvement over time.[11]

In terms of social status, becoming an academy teacher was considered a very respectable way of making of living in the North, and academy teaching held the same appeal for many southern families. Although some historians have claimed that southern parents did not see teaching school as a socially acceptable activity for their daughters, census records indicate that very few southern whites were sufficiently wealthy to leave their daughters an independent fortune or marry them off to comparably wealthy young men. The 1860 census indicated that only 16 percent of adult southerners owned slaves, although historians generally place this figure at between 20 and 25 percent. Most young southern women were the daughters of yeoman farmers or small merchants who may have hired one or more slaves but owned none. Among these middle-class families, teaching was well regarded. Historian Anya Jabour has found that the letters and diaries of southern female academy students reveal a strong attachment to their teachers and a respect for the profession of teaching as "a genteel way of making a living." Similarly, Suzanne Lebsock has found operating an entrepreneurial school to be a significant business for women in antebellum Petersburg, Virginia. Like her counterparts in Petersburg, Susan Nye Hutchison viewed academy teaching as a desirable occupation that her stepdaughter might profitably pursue in the South.[12]

When they arrived in Troy, Susan had two goals in mind: to enroll Elizabeth at the seminary "on scholarship" and to spend some time familiarizing herself with the school's curriculum and teaching methods. She used her evangelical connections to obtain an introduction to Willard. Her first stop was Presbyterian minister Nathan S. S. Beman, to whom she presented her references: "I exhibited my letters from Raleigh and Augusta and was glad to find that Dr. Bemon knew many of the names they contained. The Dr. accompanied me to the Seminary and presented me to the Seminary and presented me to Mrs. W who received me very kindly."[13]

She witnessed firsthand Willard's reputation and influence in placing Troy teachers in schools across the country. After several days of visiting classrooms, the two women had a conversation that Susan found somewhat unsettling. Willard had "received a letter from Raleigh begging her to recommend a teacher and she had done so." Perhaps viewing Susan as a potential rival to one of Troy's students, Willard suggested Susan consider a partnership. That evening, Susan noted the conversation in her journal: "She advised me to enter a partnership with this lady—I wrote to Dr. McPheeters for counsel."[14]

Several days later, Susan again met with Willard. Susan wrote, "I went to the Seminary again thinking to accept of Mrs. W. kind offer to receive Elizabeth for a year or two and afterward employ her as a teacher which Dr. and Mrs. B. told me she had often done—when I saw Mrs. W., I was mortified that I had taken A[manda], for she told me E. was too young and she could not think of employing teachers who had not a turn for teaching—besides she enquired if she were pious and if she had a good temper, so I sadly dropped my veil and departed."[15] The rebuff had no long-lasting ill effects for Elizabeth. Shortly afterward, she found a position as a companion or helper in Charleston, South Carolina, and eventually met and married "an excellent young man."[16]

After leaving Troy, Susan prepared to depart for North Carolina, determined to disregard Willard's advice and establish a school of her own. She felt some anxiety about what lay ahead. "Oh how shall I stand the separation from my parents, children, brothers and sisters now that I have no husband to share with me the ills I may be called to suffer," she wondered near the end of November. Nevertheless, she did not let fear dissuade her. One month later she steeled herself, left her children in Amanda's care, and returned alone to Raleigh.[17]

THOUGH SHE HAD been away from Raleigh for more than a decade, Susan had been one of Raleigh's most admired teachers, and she still garnered the respect and publicity required to attract students. In early January 1835, the *Raleigh Register* announced "to the former friends and patrons of Mrs. Hutchson (formerly Miss Nye) and to the public in general, that she is expected to open an Academy for Young Ladies, in Raleigh, on or about the first Monday of January." The notice reminded readers that she had provided ample proof "of her superior moral and intellectual qualifications, as an Instructress of Young Ladies," adding that she had improved her qualifications by having recently attended "one of the first Female Seminaries in the United States." Moreover, her work at the academy would be "favored with the counsel, experience and general supervision of the Rev. Dr. McPheeters, the well-known Presbyterian minister and former head of the old Raleigh Academy." These were impressive credentials.[18]

Still, she must have realized that sustaining a school in Raleigh would be a challenge. Susan's journal entries for this period have been lost, but surviving documents reveal the state of the town's education market.[19] Since her departure, a number of schools had closed, among them Raleigh Academy, which had collapsed seven years earlier. According to Joseph Gales, the school failed because the wealthiest families withdrew their support, but from its inception, the academy had experienced cash flow problems. In 1828, the trustees announced that they could no longer guarantee salaries but would turn over tuition to the teachers, allowing the institution to run largely like an entrepreneurial school. With no guarantee of financial support, some teachers left for more profitable forms of schooling.[20]

John Chavis's school had also shut down. Chavis, a minister and freeman, had been teaching in Raleigh for over twenty-two years. When he was a slave, his owner sent him to Washington Academy in Lexington, Virginia, and later to Princeton College to be trained as a Presbyterian minister. Eventually his owner freed him, and Chavis came to Raleigh, where he opened a school in 1808. He taught white children by day and free children of color in the evening, yielding to the demands of town leaders that he segregate his students. In 1832, fearful that black ministers might promote insurrection among slaves, the North Carolina Legislature passed an act to prevent any slave or free black from preaching or exhorting in public "or in any manner to officiate as a preacher or teacher in any prayer meeting, or other association for worship, where slaves of different families are collected together." Like all ministers who presided over schools during this period, Chavis led worship during school prayer meetings and preached to his students on the Sabbath. Unable to continue his ministry under the new law, he closed down his school in the spring of 1832, informed the local presbytery, left Raleigh, and never returned.[21]

By the time Susan arrived, schools catering to the children of white families proliferated on every side, competing for students. Timothy E. Dwight, a graduate of Yale, had opened Dwight's Select School in 1827. Nearby competitors included Wake Forest Pleasant Grove Academy and Mr. and Mrs. Berkeley's Literary Scientific Institution for Young Ladies, which claimed to provide females with an education close to the collegiate level. An Episcopal school for boys, offering a classical college preparatory education, received a state charter in 1833, and the North Carolina Diocese purchased land west of Raleigh for the school site. In contrast to the old Raleigh Academy, which had been founded with the objective of educating "at a moderate expense," all the male and female children of the city in rather plain but serviceable wooden frame schoolrooms, the Episcopalians raised imposing stone buildings. Nevertheless, even with support from the church, the Episcopal Boys' School incurred so much debt that its trustees shut it down in 1837. Raleigh was a tough education market; schools struggled to survive.[22]

One of Susan's first steps to distinguish herself from her competitors was to publish a prospectus explaining her views on female education. She opened her school in the vacant building that had once housed Raleigh Academy's Female Department and soon began to write. Susan had for years considered writing for publication. She had expressed a desire to write while living in Augusta, but Adam and Amanda had dissuaded her: "I have for sometime past been much impressed with a disposition to write somewhat for publication but Mr. H. and sister do not encourage me," she noted in 1828. She returned to the idea of writing for publication in the spring of 1834: "I turned my thoughts toward writing," she wrote that March. "I was so eager in the pursuit that I almost believed I could finish a volume as Goldsmith did the Vicar of Wakefield in one week." She started but apparently did not finish that first draft, confessing two weeks later, "I felt more like writing but did not make much progress." The following week she noted, "I have not written one line." Her literary attempts were shelved until she moved to Raleigh, where they took a new direction. To accompany her prospectus, she wrote an essay explaining "Mrs. Hutchison's View of Female Education."[23]

Susan opened by emphasizing her long history in North Carolina and the continuity of her objectives as an educator: "In returning again to the scene of my former labors, I persuade myself that I have little need of the aid of a prospectus, to explain my views of Female Education, to those whose liberal patronage was, for so long a period, the reward of my persevering exertions . . . to [my former pupils] I can appeal with strong confidence; and in their grateful affection I am convinced there will be, while memory lives, a testimony that my object has been to enable my pupils to do their duty, according to the precepts of the holy scriptures, to their families, to society, and to God."[24]

Although her writing was probably influenced by Willard's work at Troy Female Seminary, Susan expressed a distinct point of view. Like Willard, who wrote, "If the female character be raised, it must inevitably raise that of the other sex," Susan argued that females should be educated because their influence had long-range consequences: "The principle we lay down is this: As woman exercises a powerful influence in the domestic circle, and consequently in society, a proper education alone can enable her to exert this influence in the promotion of virtue and happiness." But whereas Willard emphasized primarily the mother's influence over the family, Susan drew from personal experience and broadened her net to include "the mother, the sister, the wife or the daughter," all of whom could leave deep and lasting impressions "over the statesman, the soldier, the divine, the merchant, the farmer, the mechanic."[25]

She believed that no inherent differences existed between the intellectual abilities of men and women. "The unfortunate impression, that the female mind is incapable of laborious study, has doubtless laid the foundation, in this country and in every other, for a system of education calculated in all its operations to produce a regard for superficial accomplishments, rather than for those solid endowments which, like unadulterated gold, retain their luster under all circumstances." Knowing that she could not prove or disprove intellectual equality, she explained, "How far the idea of female inferiority is founded in fact, is not very important; our object is to remove, as far as in our power, the injury this impression has produced upon our sex."[26]

Susan's opinion on this issue resembled that of South Carolina's Sarah Moore Grimké, who published *Letters on the Equality of the Sexes* just three years later. The majority of Americans may not have accepted the idea of women's intellectual equality with men, but the proposition was far from unusual in the South. As Jonathan Daniel Wells has shown in his study of southern women writers and journalists in the antebellum era, southerners expressed a range of opinions regarding whether the differences between men's and women's intellectual abilities were innate or resulted from culture and custom. Historian Anya Jabour has found the same range of opinion in the correspondence between southern female academy students and their relatives. Chartered in 1836, Georgia Female College opened in 1839 with the goal of offering women an education equal to that of men's colleges. The first president, Methodist minister George Foster Pierce, referring to the debates over women's intellectual equality with men, proclaimed, "The differences of aptitudes and exhibition among men and women are not strictly constitutional, but referable mainly to their mental habits. . . . I insist that all the elements of mind are common to both."[27]

Some historians have concluded that although educated women may have embraced the idea of intellectual equality with men, they nevertheless accepted a subordinate social status based on prevailing notions of gender difference. However, Susan's *View of Female Education* does not quite square with this picture. She did not characterize education as valuable solely for its role in preparing females for domestic life. Instead, she emphasized the importance of education "to fit them for any situation in life to which they may hereafter be called." She knew that while some women might be called to marry, others might be called to teaching or other work outside the home. As sociologist Joel Perlmann and economist Robert A. Margo have discovered, census data indicate that outside the larger cities, the proportion of antebellum white women in the labor force was about the same in the Northeast, the Midwest, and the South. Around 29 percent of native-born white southern women worked outside the home by 1860.[28]

Whereas Emma Willard stressed that females needed "not a masculine education" but an education specifically adapted to the "difference of character and duties, to which the softer sex should be formed," Susan argued that young women could excel in a more rigorous course of study by remaining in school longer. She attributed women's lesser attainments to the fact that men studied a smaller number of subjects in greater depth over a longer period. One of Susan's criticisms of female education was that students crammed too many subjects into their course of study. Compared with the male student, the female student "has passed through more than twice the number of studies, with less than half the benefit." Moreover, relatively few young women remained in school long enough to finish the official course of study. Parents commonly pulled their daughters from school before they reached fourteen or sixteen years of age. "While parents have been liberal to their daughters in other respects, they have imposed on them the most injurious restrictions in regard to the very limited time allotted for their education," Susan wrote. "Paying freely for every thing required in a fashionable education, they have, perhaps very naturally expected their daughters to learn every thing; but unhappily for the best interests of those so dear to them, they seem never to have taken into the account, 'how short the time is!' nor to have reflected that the very sciences they have expected their daughters fully to understand before they were fourteen, or at most sixteen years of age, were never required of their sons under eighteen or twenty." Some southerners endorsed this argument. Seven years after Susan returned south, William Carey Richards, a Baptist minister and editor of the *Orion*, a monthly magazine published in Athens, Georgia, published a similar critique of female education: the "estimate which is made of the period necessary to educate a young girl . . . is far, *far* too low."[29]

Unless young women could study subjects in the same depth as young men, how could Americans ever fairly assess women's intellectual capabilities? According to Susan, "One would almost be tempted to conclude that the expectation of anything like equal attainments under advantages so entirely inferior, was something like an acknowledgement of superior talents; or if not, that there is, at least, sufficient ground to plead that a fairer experiment be made before judgment be irreversibly pronounced against the intellectual powers of half the human family." She particularly recommended that young women study "Arithmetic, Algebra, and other branches of the Mathematics, connected with the sublime sciences of Natural Philosophy and Astronomy," along with logic and chemistry.[30]

Of course, religion and moral philosophy would always play a central role at her school: "The school is opened and closed by prayer and reading the Holy Scriptures, and it is hoped that these serious exercises, the constant occurrence of pious precepts and examples, and the able instructions received from the sacred desk, will lead to the formation and establishment of that correctness of deportment and integrity of character, which next to a new heart, is the surest pledge of a virtuous and useful life." The phrase "sacred desk" referred to the pulpit, and "a new heart" denoted the experience of religious conversion and reaffirmation of faith as a Christian. She specified that her female students would read William Paley's *Moral and Political Philosophy*.[31]

Susan's *View of Female Education* was published to promote her new school in Raleigh, but like a growing number of women, she hoped for a broader audience and a far greater degree of influence. Over the following years, she continued to write, developing her ideas on education in addresses delivered to audiences of parents and community members at school examinations and celebrations. "I am so occupied with a little composition that I give it all the time I have to think," she noted in 1837. A year later, she recorded, "I have finished the address and felt glad to hear it commended—It is serious in the conclusion and I hope may not be forgotten."[32]

Her prospectus probably enhanced her reputation among Raleigh families seeking higher education for their daughters, but her students' academic achievements in a rigorous curriculum cemented her financial success. On November 12, 1835, the *Raleigh Star* announced glowingly, "Mrs. Hutchison's qualifications as an Instructress, her zeal, her kindness to her pupils, her untiring diligence, her acquaintance with polite literature . . . all conspire to mark her out as not unworthy [of] the continuance of the respectable patronage which she has already received." That month, she had examined between fifty and sixty students in "Geography, Parsing, Blank Verse, Mythology, Natural Philosophy, Astronomy, Botany, and the French Language." According to the *Raleigh Register*, "Her Examination furnished additional testimonials of ability and indefatigable assiduity on the part of the Teacher, and of docility and industry on the part of the Pupils."[33]

Her school was very profitable. She charged a fairly high tuition: eight dollars per session in the preparatory department, twelve dollars in the "Second Class," and fifteen dollars in the "First," or highest class, with extra fees for Latin, French, Spanish, drawing, music, and other subjects that were probably taught by other instructors. The course of study suggests that Susan's school enrolled students between ages eight and at least sixteen. Assuming that she had between fifty and sixty pupils during the spring and fall sessions each year, she might have earned between eight hundred and eighteen hundred dollars annually, plus whatever profits she made from extra subjects. Out of that amount would have come her expenses—rent on the school building, her room and board, and probably a stipend to McPheeters for ministerial services. She came out ahead. By the end of the first school year, she had accumulated $215 in bank stock—equivalent to a New York academy teacher's annual salary. She wrote to her family members in New York that if they needed "some money I can do so now as soon as I can get a draft."[34]

DESPITE HER SUCCESS, Susan decided to leave Raleigh at the end of the 1835–36 school year. She had received an offer to establish a female academy in Salisbury, about 115 miles to the west. Academy teachers frequently moved from one area to another, sometimes prompted by a desire to obtain a salary increase or a position of higher status. In Susan's case, better accommodations and geographical location may have induced her to move. Salisbury was thirty miles closer to Greensboro, the home of the Caldwell Institute, where she hoped to enroll her sons as they came of age. She may also have wanted a school over which she had total control. Her Raleigh school operated in the building associated with the old academy's Female Department, and although some advertisements described it as an independent institution, newspaper advertisements placed by the male instructors at the new Raleigh Academy sometimes referred to her school as the "Female Department."[35]

Testimonials from former students, friends, and members of North Carolina's Presbyterian community probably helped to smooth her way. Writing to Salisbury's Cowan family, Nancy R. White specifically mentioned Susan's situation as a widow supporting children: "And I do hope, my dear friends, since Mrs. Hutchison has sacrificed so much in leaving her friends and Pupils here, to go among straingers, that you will all use your utmost exertions to increase her School, and to sustain her by your prayers, and that she may be enabled to obtain that support for herself and dear orphans [sic] Children, of which a widowed mother who has no other dependence than her own exertions, stands so much in need."[36]

She moved to Salisbury in January 1836, boarding in the home of Thomas L. Cowan, an aging elder in the Presbyterian Church and a very wealthy merchant. "I pay 8 dollars a month for board," Susan wrote to her children, "I am furnished a school room and indeed a whole house. . . . The people are greatly anxious to have me send for you all here and have you with me but I do not know what to say about it—I am greatly afraid it will not be very healthy here in the summer and besides I am inclined to think I could not teach and attend to the children too." She reassured her sons that she had not forgotten them: "I am so anxious to see you all that I hardly know how to wait—but I hope God will bless me and all of us so that we may meet again."[37]

Susan's Salisbury school educated young women based on the model she had established in Raleigh, and she hired several instructors to assist her: her niece, Sarah Louisa Nye, came from New York to teach the "ornamental subjects," while Susan Hermans, a New York cousin, provided general assistance. Emma J. Baker of Columbia, South Carolina, was engaged to teach music, and Presbyterian minister Stephen Frontis, a former colleague of Susan's from Raleigh Academy, taught French and led prayer meetings. Within a few days, she had more than thirty students. "I have surely cause to be very thankful indeed," she wrote. "So far I think my prospect better than in Raleigh—But I am so busy that I have not an hour to myself—I expect to teach needlework between schools and painting on Saturdays."[38]

She—not a male instructor or minister—was in charge of the school: "The government of the school will be strictly maternal; and it will be conducted on the principles laid down in Mrs. Hutchison's View of Female Education already before the public. The mode of instruction, now practiced by the most extensively useful Schools in our country, will be adopted so far as shall be deemed practicable, and every effort used to promote the improvement of the pupils whether in a moral, personal or mental point of view."[39]

In proclaiming that the school's leadership would be "strictly maternal," Susan referenced the trope of separate spheres to justify having charge of a female academy. As a number of historians have pointed out, although separate spheres was a limiting ideology, it also supported women's autonomy and independence within realms parallel to men's. During her years in Augusta, Susan had participated in all-female benevolent societies organized and led by women but similar in organization and scope to all-male societies. Susan's newspaper advertisement illustrates her attempt to duplicate the phenomenon in the field of higher education.[40]

As news of Susan's financial success spread back home in New York, other northern teachers contacted her to learn about opportunities in the South. During the summer of 1836, while visiting her family in Amenia, she met several prospective teachers drawn by the higher pay offered in southern private schools. "Mr. Chamberlain and his sister were here at tea," she wrote. "Joan and I walked out to look over the fields and felt sad as we thought of the past. Miss Chamberlain wishes to obtain a situation at the south—Miss Hearn also called to see about a similar subject." Among her

New York neighbors, Susan had become a resource for information about the South.[41]

Susan's financial situation had improved, though she remained far from her goal. Sometimes she envied the economic security others enjoyed. After a breakfast with Thomas Swift, a neighbor in Amenia, she wrote, "Mr. Thomas and I had been long separated from our homes—he had been crowned with success and was about to return home to reside with an independence equal to his wishes. I had been beset with trials and was again to take leave of home and children and parents and go far away to earn for all I loved best the means of comfort—our circumstances were vastly different and sometimes I could almost feel envy of the superior happiness of his station."[42]

Still, she had enough money to bring her ten-year-old son, Sylvanus, to North Carolina and enroll him in a Presbyterian academy in 1836. They left Amenia at the end of the summer. Their trip was much more comfortable than Susan's first voyage south in 1815. From New York City, they took a steamboat to Baltimore, where they boarded a train to Washington, D.C. They completed the remainder of the journey by stagecoach. In September, Sylvanus began his studies at Greensboro's Caldwell Institute, an all-male school run by Presbyterian minister Alexander Wilson, a former colleague of Susan's at Raleigh Academy during the 1820s. She arranged for Sylvanus to board with the Wilson family and spend vacations with her in Salisbury.[43]

SUSAN KNEW THAT attracting students required her school's curriculum to be rigorous and up-to-date. She had taught introductory algebra and geometry in Augusta, but by the 1830s, some female schools in North Carolina were offering their students higher levels of algebra and even trigonometry (see table 4).

Seeking to institutionalize a distinctively female curriculum, a few prominent educational reformers, including Catharine Beecher, Emma Willard, and Willard's sister, Almira Hart Lincoln Phelps, advocated a course of study that included the "domestic arts"—the activities of the household. Given the prominence of these individuals, it is not surprising that some historians have taken the rhetoric at face value and assumed that the concept of a domestic curriculum gained widespread acceptance. However, a broader examination of the courses of study at female schools reveals that such was not the case: antebellum female schools in both the North and the South offered increasingly rigorous curricula.[44]

In North Carolina, newspaper advertisements indicate that schools enrolling females added more rigorous subjects over the years, gradually narrowing the gap between the academic level of subjects offered in male and female academies (see table 4). Although newspaper advertisements serve as imperfect proxies for formal courses of study, they reveal which subjects administrators believed would attract the interest of tuition-paying parents. If advertisements did not accurately represent the schools' curricula, parents would have complained and enrolled their children elsewhere.

To keep up with this trend, forty-eight-year-old Susan began studying advanced algebra. Although her primary goal may have been to upgrade her school's curriculum to compete more effectively with other higher schools, she enjoyed the subject. "I find it an absorbing study and my progress in it give me much gratification," she wrote. "I am delighted with algebra." Several days later she grappled with octic equations, which modern-day college students might encounter in an upper-division undergraduate mathematics course: "got into equations of the 8th degree and felt much rejoiced." She also studied mineralogy and brushed up on her knowledge of French and astronomy. "The young ladies are a good deal interested in astronomy and I also," she wrote on a January day in 1837. "I find it much more easy to retain the names of the stars and their situation than I once thought it was."[45]

She worried about her students' performance during their public examinations, which could either increase or decrease a school's reputation and consequently attract students or damage enrollments. Behind the scenes, such public displays could inspire terror not only among nervous students but also among the faculty. On the first day of examinations in July 1837, Susan confessed, "I feel some excitement and some alarm—near two o'clock—I am mortified—My pupils have spoken too low for any use." On the second day, she fretted, "Now I am here oppressed with fear that my classes have not done so well today." Despite her anxiety, the examinations closed with applause before a full house.[46]

As at the old Raleigh Academy, the curriculum in Susan's school was Protestant but nondenominational to draw students from a variety of religious backgrounds yet satisfy parents who desired a moral and religious education for their children. Protestant communities expected the teachers and principals of nonsectarian schools to involve students in church activities without noticeably favoring one denomination over another. Susan was careful to maintain a neutral position, informing parents "to specify what Church they wish their children to attend." She and her

TABLE 4. Percentage of Female Schools and Female Departments in Coeducational Academies Advertising Specific Subjects in North Carolina Newspapers, 1800–1840, by Decade (n = 55)

Subjects	Decades			
	1800–1809	1810–1819	1820–1829	1830–1840
Reading	100	100	100	100
Writing	100	100	100	100
Arithmetic	100	94	100	100
Grammar	100	100	100	100
Geography	70	100	86	100
Spelling	50	44	64	50
Needlework	60	94	86	63
Music	40	67	59	67
Painting	20	94	86	58
Drawing	30	83	64	54
Embroidery	40	78	45	38
History	20	44	55	88
Belles Lettres	10	28	27	8
French	20	2	14	67
Moral Philosophy	0	28	32	50
Latin	0	2	23	50
Astronomy	10	39	64	54
Natural Philosophy	10	33	73	71
Chemistry	0	22	55	58
Botany	0	0	41	38
Math/Geometry/ Algebra	0	1	18	46
Number of schools in sample per decade	10	18	22	24

Source: Tolley, "Significance of the 'French School.'" Data compiled from newspaper advertisements in the *Raleigh Register*, 1800–1840, and Coon, *North Carolina Schools and Academies*.

teachers accompanied students to worship, alternating attendance at the Methodist, Episcopal, Presbyterian, Baptist, and Lutheran churches. This ecumenical stance allowed her to draw a clientele from a wide range of Protestant backgrounds, but it was not motivated solely by economic concerns. "I desire to feel more and more anxiety about bringing souls to Jesus and less and less about bringing them to a particular church," she confided to her journal.[47]

Although the era of great religious revivals had largely come to a close, all of the major Protestant churches increased their efforts to establish schools and colleges. The competition for students sometimes created friction among denominations. In Salisbury, Susan began to notice that both Methodists and Presbyterians tried to recruit recent converts from among her student body. In December 1837, one of her students "was much affected" during a service at the Presbyterian church, so Susan "stopped and got Mr. Frontis to pray with her." After the girl returned to the home where she boarded, Susan was "greatly perplexed" when she "met the persons with whom [the girl] boarded accompanying her to another church." Later that month, a fellow Presbyterian expressed distress about one young woman's "predilection for the Methodists," a sentiment Susan did not understand: "Surely any attempt on the part of strangers to draw her away from the church of her parents is cruel." Over the next several weeks, she thought more deeply about her position on the issue of church membership, and after a service in early January she concluded, "While I was at church I felt that to make an effort to get an individual to join our church was of small consequence. All that was acceptable was to persuade one to serve God—I perceived that if it was only to get one into our Church it would be but selfishness—which would be offensive in the divine sight."[48]

She sometimes had to use great tact and diplomacy to please parents of different denominations. Her extensive connections within the Presbyterian Church sparked concern among local Methodists, and in 1840 she was shocked when she received a hostile anonymous letter. "I received . . . an anonymous production threatening me with the ruin of my school or it great diminution on account of my having kept young ladies from going up to the altar to be prayed for in the Methodist Church—& a great deal more to the same effect—I was astounded & overwhelmed." She immediately wrote to the local Methodist minister "disclaiming any attempt in any shape to hinder the girls." The minister read both the anonymous letter and Susan's response to his congregation the next Sunday, with Susan present to address concerns and answer questions, thereby solving the problem.[49]

SUSAN BEGAN TO develop plans to establish her school on a more secure financial footing. She was well aware of the economic benefits formal sponsorship could offer a female school. A financial collapse, later dubbed the Panic of 1837, ushered in the most prolonged depression in the antebellum period, affecting both North and South. Many schools lowered the price of tuition "to meet the changes of times and the expectations of the Public," as Raleigh's Episcopal School announced. The Mount Pleasant Academy informed the public that it offered "as reasonable terms as the high prices of the times will possibly justify." Susan's school had difficulty staying afloat, but she managed to remain in business without reducing tuition.[50]

In the summer of 1837, she approached several of Salisbury's leading men and women about the possibility of participating in a subscription fund to endow her school and establish it as a state-chartered institution supported by a board of trustees. With students in tow, she first stopped to see Mary Steele, widow of former U.S. representative John Steele:

> June 12, 1837—Miss Cowan, Miss Sidden and Dr. Burns went
> out with me—After school Miss Allison and I went out to
> Mrs. Steele's and I presented her a subscription for a female
> Academy—I had been maturing the plan—Mrs. S. subscribed
> 5 dollars and her grand daughters together the same—Mr. Giles
> liberally and kindly offered a more noble example—he gave
> 50 dollars—Col. Long pressed me to stay to tea. He wishes me
> to engage to board at one place with all my girls and he will
> provide for us—Mr. Cowan, Mr. Brown and Col. Lemley neither
> subscribed but they will do it in their own time—½ past nine the
> day is past—I am excited and unfit for sleep.

One of her contacts was Maxwell Chambers, a wealthy businessman who was also negotiating with the founders and trustees of Davidson College, an all-male institution with endowment support from several Presbyterian synods: "I called on a number of the first citizens and had the pleasure to find that that Mssrs Chambers and Fisher took an interest (especially the former) in the object of my visit." Chambers ultimately decided that his money should go to Davidson, but others whom Susan contacted made cash donations on the spot or offered different kinds of support. Stephen Frontis, who had served as a commissioner of Davidson College, gave encouragement and advice.[51]

Susan apparently did not ask her local Presbyterian synod for help. Men trained at southern colleges often chose to combine the ministry with teaching, and unlike women, they could easily tap the resources of the church and influence local and regional sessions and synods to help with the establishment of academies and colleges such as Davidson.[52]

She likely calculated that none of the Presbyterian synods would incorporate and endow an all-female higher school headed by a woman, and she was correct—none of North Carolina's synods established an all-female academy or college before the Civil War. By 1857, the country had sixty active Presbyterian academies, all of them with male ministers at the helm. In North Carolina, these academies included the Caldwell Institute in Greensboro, where Susan enrolled her sons, and Donaldson Academy in Fayetteville, both established around 1833. The Methodists did much more to support female education, chartering the Georgia Female College in Macon and Greensboro Female College in North Carolina in the late 1830s. But Methodist men, like their counterparts in the other evangelical churches, were not necessarily open to the concept of female leadership in higher education: these colleges were helmed by male ministers.[53]

The drive to place men in school leadership positions arose primarily from economic and theological concerns, but gender also played a role. Presbyterians held traditional views about women's subordinate position in church and society, yet their churches were increasingly filled with female members, and women usually had less money than men to contribute. According to Peter J. Wallace, writers in the late 1830s argued that whereas Presbyterian ministers in Scotland and Northern Ireland were well regarded and highly paid, their American counterparts were rapidly falling behind men in the professions of medicine and law in terms of both salary and social status. By 1860, only 30 percent of southern Presbyterian churches (just over half if joint pastorates are included) paid their ministers an annual salary of five hundred dollars or more. In contrast, some North Carolina schools offered female principals a salary of five hundred dollars between 1837 and 1840, while male principals could earn nearly twice that amount (see table 3). One solution was for ministers to operate schools on the side. A married minister was in the best position for this kind of work, because the wife could teach the core subjects and take care of the daily management of the school while the husband supervised students' religious instruction and taught the occasional class in Latin or Greek. Wallace claims that on theological grounds, the practice of placing ministers in charge of schools also appealed to Presbyterian leaders who wished to see the church pull back from ecumenical collaboration with the other Protestant churches and develop a distinctive brand of missionary work and education. Motivated by this mix of economic and theological interests, Presbyterians began to discuss establishing church-affiliated elementary schools and academies. Beginning in 1838, Presbyterian newspapers printed articles about parochial education in Scotland and the benefits of establishing schools with orthodox and qualified teachers in every American parish. One editor reminded readers of the days when ministers ran all of the South's schools, claiming that "the great secret of the Scotch character [is] *that the church assumes and controls the education of her children from infancy to manhood.*"[54]

Given this environment, a woman seeking support to incorporate her own school had to tread a careful line among her fellow Presbyterians. Prominent northern women such as Willard and Mary Lyon of Mount Holyoke Female Seminary in Massachusetts served as heads of their own institutions, but neither was affiliated with a specific Protestant denomination. Susan Nye Hutchison followed the same course.

Her efforts to incorporate her school succeeded. In December 1837 Susan wrote, "The gentlemen had a meeting relative to the Academy last night and tonight also." By the end of the year, Susan was so optimistic that she told Maxwell Chambers's wife, née Catherine B. Troy, that she hoped to name the new academy the Chambers and Troy Institute after its benefactors, suggesting that Susan hoped to offer college-level programs. According to Susan, Mrs. Chambers was very pleased with this idea. Susan's male friends and supporters petitioned the state legislature, and although Susan won the battle for incorporation, she lost the prospect of heading an institute. In 1838, the North Carolina State Assembly chartered Salisbury Female Academy.[55]

Unfortunately, obtaining a state charter for her school did not solve Susan's financial problems, since the state did not provide any form of financial subsidies to female academies. In October 1838, Susan brought her second son, Ebenezer, to North Carolina and enrolled him at the Caldwell Institute along with Sylvanus. Both boys boarded with the Wilson family when school was in session and stayed with Susan during the monthlong Christmas break and over the summer. Bringing her sons south was a long-term goal, but the financial costs were almost more than she could bear: "My dread is that I shall not be able to support myself niece and children—yet I have engaged to advance two hundred to brother & I borrowed twenty five of Cousin Jesse."[56]

Susan never recorded exactly how much money she raised from her supporters, but she still worried about revenue and enrollment. Some of the families that boarded pupils during the school year had raised the price of board, and she feared that this jump would dissuade families from sending their children to her school. Her fears were realized when the school opened for business in mid-October: "I closed the week with only 16 scholars," she wrote. "My necessities require sixty." The following month, she decided to petition the state.[57]

AS THEY BECAME more involved in charitable work and social reform, women began to encourage each other to petition state legislatures. Through such petitions, also called "memorials," women demonstrated an increasing desire to influence policymaking and develop a political identity of their own.[58]

Not all Presbyterians supported women's growing involvement in petitioning secular government. In 1837, the *Watchman of the South*, a Presbyterian newspaper, reprinted an essay titled "The Appropriate Sphere of Woman," informing readers that women belonged in the home and that they had no business "sitting in judgment and acting upon the affairs of church and state." Prominent educator Catharine Beecher agreed, writing in her 1837 *Essay on Slavery and Abolitionism* that the proper sphere of action for women was the domestic circle, where they could influence men through moral suasion: "It is Christianity that has given to woman her true place in society." According to Beecher, "In this country, petitions to congress, in reference to the official duties of legislators, seem, IN ALL CASES, to fall entirely without the sphere of female duty." Beecher may have represented mainstream opinion about women's proper sphere, but as Susan Nye Hutchison's actions make clear, evangelical Christian women—even Beecher's fellow Presbyterians—could and did disagree on a number of social issues, including this one.[59]

On November 12, 1838, Susan wrote in her journal, "I began to write my Memorial on the subject of Education." She intended to submit it to the North Carolina Legislature, and her timing suggests that she had been following political developments in the state. As she worked on her document, members of North Carolina's Whig Party prepared a bill on education to submit for a vote at the upcoming January legislative session. The Whigs advocated state funding for education. As a result of the Distribution of the Surplus Act of 1835, North Carolina had received $1,433,757.39 in federal surplus funds the following year. According to historians Hugh Talmage Lefler and Albert Ray Newsome, the expenditure of these funds quickly became a partisan issue: Whigs wanted to use it for public education and other improvements, but Democrats, interested in reducing both taxes and government spending, wanted to use it to pay down the state's debt and fund the government's operating expenses.[60]

Susan may have received encouragement from fellow educators and friends. In Salisbury, she had begun to attend teachers' meetings and correspond with faculty in other schools about education. In 1837 she noted, "Yesterday Mr. Davis and Miss Harding from Cheraw Academy on their way to Fayetteville Tennessee called and spent an hour at our school—I was at first rather embarrassed but I was in the sequel much pleased—If teachers cultivate each other's society more particularly it would be likely to promote more union of effort in the business of education." Several days later, she "attended teacher's meeting at Mr. Horah's." She had also begun to correspond with Mary Edward Jones, operator of a long-standing female academy in Pittsboro. In late summer 1838, just weeks before she began work on her petition, she and her children had stopped in Washington, D.C., to visit with Joseph and Winifred Gales on their way back from New York. Joseph Gales had for years followed North Carolina political developments closely and had published numerous articles and editorials in support of a tax-supported public school system, making the *Raleigh Register* the voice of school reform in the state.[61]

How would the state implement a system of public schools? What sorts of schools would receive funding? Would the legislature consider allocating some money toward the higher education of women? These questions remained unanswered when Susan drafted her petition. She spent six weeks writing and rewriting. "I have written a portion of the day but I am not pleased," she wrote in mid-November. On December 5 she noted, "I wrote all day—the Memorial is finished but I am going to try it over again." She submitted the final version December 20: "I have put my memorial in the office. I sent with it several letters."[62]

Susan was the first woman to submit a memorial to the North Carolina Assembly on behalf of female education. Although the North Carolina *Senate Journal* mentions her memorial, the full text was not printed, and her drafts have not survived. Nevertheless, her journal entries provide some clues about what she wrote. In late December 1838 she wrote, "I begin to feel some anxiety about my memorial more especially as Mrs. Jones sent me a Report upon Education in which was embodied many of my sentiments."[63] Three reports related to female higher education circulated widely at this time. Foremost were those of Catharine Beecher and Horace Mann. Beecher's *Essay on the Education of Female Teachers* was first published by the American Lyceum in 1835 and was subsequently reprinted in newspapers and magazines. In 1838, Massachusetts Whig Horace Mann, the new superintendent of the state's common schools, issued his first report on public education, and newspapers and journals across the country published excerpts. A year earlier, John W. Picket, schoolbook author, magazine editor, and corresponding secretary of the Incorporated Society of Teachers, published "Female Education" in the *Western Academician and Journal of Education and Science*. All three authors recommended a rigorous course of study for females, but Beecher and Mann emphasized the importance of state funding for academies and seminaries so that trained female teachers would be available to staff the new common schools spreading across the country, a benefit Emma Willard had demonstrated at Troy Female Seminary.[64]

Given the content of these reports, Susan's familiarity with Troy, and the common school legislation pending in North Carolina, it is likely that she petitioned the legislature for state funding for female higher education. When Susan drafted her memorial, demand for female academy teachers in North Carolina was already high, and it would grow further when a system of state-supported common schools was established. State-sponsored support for female academies capable of training middle-class women to teach in the new common schools would help meet this demand.[65]

Although many of the wealthy families who sent their daughters to Susan's school expected them only to acquire some polish before settling down with appropriate young men, Susan knew that some of these girls eventually would have to earn their own livings. One such young woman was Miss Sedden, to whom Susan provided free room and board for all of 1837 as her guardian, Mr. Wightman of Augusta, Georgia, teetered on the brink of bankruptcy. Among Susan's former pupils from Raleigh Academy who had become teachers were Elizabeth Haywood, who ran a private school with "twenty seven scholars" in 1835, and Sarah Frew Davidson, who began to teach music after her father, plantation owner William Davidson, a former state senator and U.S. representative, encountered financial difficulties. Women who married ministers often taught school: Susan described former student Ann Solimon as "once a sweet pupil—now a useful teacher the wife of Revd Mr. Rankin." With some funding from the state to provide more financial stability and take in more "scholarship" students who could not otherwise afford the tuition, Susan could establish her academy as a training center for teachers along the lines of Troy Female Seminary. The establishment of public elementary schools in the state would also benefit her school by increasing the demand for her graduates.[66]

Just five days after Susan submitted the document, William W. Cherry, a member of the General Assembly and author of the public school bill before the legislature, "presented the memorial of Susan D. Nye Hutchison on the subject of Female Education; which was, on his motion, ordered to be referred to the Committee on Education." On January 5, 1839, however, Susan recorded, "By a letter from Dr. M[c]Pheeters, I learn that my Memorial was too long to be read before the house."[67]

Two days later, the Whig-dominated General Assembly, with nearly unanimous support from the Democrats, adopted a plan that largely gave the Whigs what they wanted, with a large share of the money going to the cause of common schools. The legislature voted to submit the school question to popular vote in August. A vote in favor would result in a county tax levy of one dollar for each two dollars distributed from the State Literary Fund. The *Raleigh Register* urged voters to support the measure. All but seven of the state's sixty-eight counties voted to ratify the plan, and the common school system began operation in 1840.[68]

The problem that Susan had tried to solve with her petition persisted, however. Once North Carolina established a rudimentary system of common schools, demand for certified teachers grew. By 1854, the demand was so great that North Carolina's state superintendent of education recommended that half of the state's common school positions be filled with women, many of whom were then teaching part time or only at the primary level. But qualified female teachers remained in short supply. As Delia W. Jones pointed out in an 1858 essay on female education, few North Carolina institutions offered middle- and working-class women an education sufficiently rigorous and practical to equip them for teaching. Academies and other higher schools were generally short-lived. Usually located in towns or upscale neighborhoods and charging high rates of tuition, these institutions often enrolled "daughters of wealthy parents, reared amid luxury and fashions [who] would disdain the calling of a teacher." Jones argued that the state needed to establish and sustain schools that would "make her daughters sensible, intelligent women, and her teachers, the best," designed particularly for those "most suitable to become teachers in Common Schools." Susan would have agreed with this argument. In fact, it was nearly identical to the case Willard had made to the New York Legislature in 1819.[69]

AS A HIGHER private school, Susan's institution never received any public funds, and she eventually reached a financial crossroads. Her enrollments declined, and her expenses rose. She had little money for extras. When her oldest two sons visited that spring, she noticed with concern that Sylvanus's clothes were old and worn: "I was greatly ashamed when I saw the poor tattered garments in which my dear child had stood before the trustees of the Caldwell Institute—a poor widow's son he must indeed have shown himself to be." Had Susan been unmarried, like Mount Holyoke's Mary Lyon, or married but childless, like Emma Willard, her income would have been more than adequate for her needs. But sending her sons to the Caldwell Institute cost money, and she had also sent funds north to her brothers Shubal and Meletiah.[70]

As she cast about for a solution to her financial problems, she drew on the social capital she had accumulated during her years in the South. Her success resulted from her reputation as a teacher and the many collegial relationships and long-standing friendships she had developed. She must have reached out to this social network, because in the spring of 1839, she received an invitation to establish a school in Lincolnton, North Carolina, and another to open a school in Augusta, Georgia. In July, she also received "a letter of invitation to the Charlotte Academy." Her friends advised her to accept the invitation to Charlotte. "They do not see that our school here will support my children," Susan wrote.[71]

Charlotte Female Academy was a well-established and incorporated institution with a board of trustees, so she would not have to start a new school from scratch. She had friends, former pupils, and acquaintances living there, and several former Raleigh Academy pupils from Charlotte had presented her with a beautiful medal two years earlier in recognition of her service. The town also had an extensive Presbyterian community that would welcome her with open arms. In 1837, the Concord Presbytery had opened Davidson College outside of town, and Susan was friends with the school's president, the Reverend Robert H. Morrison, and his wife, Mary Graham Morrison. Even before the college had opened, they had made her an attractive proposition: "Mr. and Mrs. Morrison are very desirous that I should teach somewhere in the neighborhood of the college, where I could have my own dear children educated while I educated theirs." This arrangement would secure a college education for her sons.[72]

Moreover, as a Presbyterian institution, Davidson College could attend to her sons' religious education. Susan had never abandoned the hope that one day her children might serve as ministers or missionaries. In the spring of 1837, she read with pleasure news of Sylvanus's academic achievement at Caldwell Institute, and she hoped he was making progress in religion as well. "Mr. W[ilson] speaks most encouragingly of Sylvanus and says his immediate teacher gives a most favorable account of his progress in study—his fondness for books—and his general conduct—I desire renewedly to dedicate him to the service of God." Full of optimism, two weeks later she prayed, "May God preserve my boy to be a Missionary yet to Heathen lands."[73]

Encouraged by the possibilities in Charlotte, she accepted the invitation, said her good-byes to friends and supporters in Salisbury, and took Sylvanus and Ebenezer back to New York at the end of the summer. They returned south in October, bringing Susan's third son, Adam Alexander, and her sister Amanda with them. She was unable to enroll Adam Alexander in an all-male academy because he suffered from epileptic seizures and exhibited some mental impairment, so he lived with her and she hired a slave, Ned, to care for him during school hours.[74]

On October 16, 1839, Susan recorded in her journal, "Opened school and came to the Academy (almost without furniture) to reside—we borrowed furniture and commenced housekeeping—I desired help of God." Former pupils and friends pitched in: "Saturday a good number of people here today—Several ladies have sent us articles of food as vegetables, honey &c &c." They had "great difficulty in getting milk & butter," and so at some point Susan purchased a cow for the school.[75]

During her first year as principal of Charlotte Female Academy, she was acutely aware of the competition from larger schools. Her faculty was small, consisting of Amanda, herself, and her former pupil Sarah Frew Davidson, who taught music. During the first year, enrollments remained higher than at Salisbury but lower than she had hoped. Although she made ends meet, she worried constantly about finances. In the fall of 1840, she heard a rumor that some of her students had enrolled in the Reverend Elias Marks's Female Collegiate Institute in South Carolina: "Mrs. Rea . . . returned bringing news that the Misses Cloud & Hemphill were going to Dr. Marks—I felt a shock," she confessed. The rumor was not entirely true, since the Hemphill sisters returned to Charlotte Female Academy just three weeks later, but Susan remained very sensitive to any suggestion that a student might prefer another school.[76]

Although Charlotte Female Academy had little or no endowment, the school thrived under Susan's leadership. Her reputation drew students not only from North Carolina but also from other states. In May 1840, "two gentlemen knocked at the door—It was Dr. Dunlop and Esq. Mills—the brother of Doctor Mills of Beach Island [Georgia], they came to bring me two pupils one of whom was Miss Mills . . . grand niece of Mrs. Burney & Mrs. Starzenecker and cousin to Miss Nesbitt and their mother to whom I feel so much obliged for kindness exhibited in 1833—I agreed to take Miss Mills as a boarder and scholar and Miss Neely as a scholar." The following October, she noted, "School re-opened—We have four boarders—In all I believe about 24 pupils."[77]

By the end of the year, she looked to the future with hope: "I desire to praise God for his mercy has indeed been great toward us[;] we began the year without any one piece of furniture and now after supporting my children I have a house comfortably filled with humble furniture." Fifteen-year-old Sylvanus had completed school at the Caldwell Institute, taken a paying job in Charlotte, and begun contributing to the family finances. On September 6, 1840, she reflected, "Just six years today since the death of my husband—I have surely great cause of gratitude that I have been enabled to take care of my fatherless ones thus far." Susan and Amanda found that although they were far from rich, they had enough money to purchase a couple of carpets. "We have begun a new year," Susan wrote on January 1, 1841, "I pray God bring us through it with his blessing."[78]

ALTHOUGH SUSAN WAS nearly penniless when she returned south in January 1835 and often fretted about money in her journal entries, she was far from poor when she penned her last surviving entry on New Year's Day 1841. She had changed dramatically from the retiring young teacher who had arrived in North Carolina in 1815 and hid behind her handkerchief when subjected to public scrutiny. She had become a confident leader unafraid of meeting face-to-face with prominent men and women to solicit support for female higher education and willing to petition the State Assembly. Although she faced significant constraints, she took advantage of every opportunity available to the women of her time.

Her success resulted from the social networks she developed through church and school, her skill as an educational entrepreneur, and her unfettered status as a widow. She had learned to respond quickly to changing economic conditions and had proved herself highly adaptable, willing to leave unpromising situations in favor of better opportunities elsewhere. Because she had no husband, she had control of her own money, her children's education, and her place of residence. In financial terms, her career allowed her to become the linchpin of her extended family. She had provided employment for a niece, a cousin, and her sister Amanda, and she kept her brothers Shubal and Meletiah financially afloat.

There were limits to how far a woman could go, however. Women's teaching of very small children had been accepted for generations, and during the early decades of the nineteenth century, women who could teach and serve as heads of female departments became essential to the successful operation of coeducational and female schools. But as the major Protestant denominations began to compete with one another to recruit converts and establish distinctive academies and colleges, church leaders sought men to fill leadership positions. Male ministers competed with women for principalships, and in incorporated schools with denominational affiliations, women lost out. In the fall of 1845, Susan left Charlotte and moved twenty-seven miles northeast to the town of Concord, where she took charge of Concord Female Academy. Charlotte Female Academy's board of trustees replaced her with Cyrus Johnson, a Presbyterian minister. This change in leadership probably pleased members of the local Presbyterian community who wished to promote their church in their academies and lower schools. Denominational leaders had begun to consider ways to increase their influence in education, and a proposal to establish schools under Presbyterian leadership galvanized the 1846 General Assembly of the predominantly southern "Old School" Presbyterian Church. Within a year, thirty-nine schools had opened.[79]

The trustees also took care to point out that Susan's replacement was a southerner, announcing, "Mr. Johnson is favorably known in the upper districts of South Carolina, as well as in this state."[80] It was a sign of the times. The national Presbyterian Church had divided over the issue of slavery. Northern teachers had to tread a careful line. Any teacher at a southern school who persisted in believing that slavery was evil had to either maintain a discreet silence or leave.

CHAPTER 7

"But Still Slavery Is a Great Evil"

Ladies: It is not that I lay claim to any portion of the wisdom given to that
favored mother in Israel, whose counsel saved the chosen people from the
horrors of a civil war.

—Susan Nye Hutchison, 1836

Living in Raleigh in the fall of 1835, Susan Nye Hutchison wrote, "But
still slavery is a great evil . . . *an evil* deplored by citizens of the Southern
States generally as well as by those of the Northern." She was not alone
in believing that most southerners shared her views on slavery, but the
ground on which she stood was shifting. During the 1830s, southern politicians and clergymen increasingly expressed opposition to this moral
philosophy. In 1829, South Carolina governor Stephen Decatur Miller
announced, "Slavery is not a national evil; on the contrary, it is a national
benefit." South Carolina legislator Charles Cotesworth Pinckney proclaimed that slavery was "no greater nor more unusual evil than befalls
the poor in general" and that it was "tolerated by Christian dispensation."
In the summer of 1835, Jesse Wilson told North Carolina's state constitutional convention in Raleigh that "he heard almost every body saying,
that slavery was a great evil! Now he believed it was no such thing—he
thought it a great blessing, in the South." By 1836, arguments over slavery
among Presbyterians threatened to divide the church.[1]

To believe that slavery was evil was to be "antislavery," a term that
evolved to encompass different perspectives. During the first three decades
of the nineteenth century, those who identified with the term generally
supported gradual emancipation. With the exception of Vermont, which
had abolished slavery in its constitution, and Massachusetts, where
slaves were freed as a result of a 1783 Supreme Judicial Court ruling, all
the northeastern states enacted policies of gradual emancipation, and in
Pennsylvania and New York, such policies provided some form of com-
pensation to slaveholders. Opponents of slavery hoped that the southern
states would follow suit, but none passed similar legislation. By the late
1820s, free black activists in the North had begun to demand the immediate

abolition of slavery without recompense to slaveholders, and during the early part of the next decade, some whites who had supported gradual emancipation—including William Lloyd Garrison, who launched *The Liberator* in 1831—began to back immediate abolition. After the 1833 establishment of the American Anti-Slavery Society, the term "antislavery" increasingly referred to the new, more radical abolitionists.[2]

As southern leaders reacted against the abolition movement in the North, they coalesced around a proslavery ideology that emphasized the hierarchal and reciprocal duties of masters and slaves. Teachers who held antislavery beliefs in later decades—whether emancipationist or abolitionist—either remained silent on the subject or saw their school enrollments disappear. When Connecticut's Mary Young Cheyney spoke out against slavery at Warrenton Female Academy in North Carolina, enrollments declined so much the school went out of business.[3]

How did Susan balance her emancipationist beliefs about slavery with her drive to succeed as an academy educator in an increasingly proslavery South? She took up her pen to write for publication during this period, joining a handful of women who publicly expressed their opinions on political issues in journals, pamphlets, and newspapers addressed to a mixed audience of men and women. To increase the odds of publication in mainstream religious media and avoid attracting censure, she used several writing strategies common to the women of her time. Historians have previously been unaware of her two published writings, probably because one essay misspelled her name as "Hutchinson" and because the other appeared in a southern Presbyterian newspaper, the *Charleston Observer*.[4]

The division of the Presbyterian Church has rarely figured as a major event in histories of slavery, yet as Susan feared, that division foreshadowed the Civil War. Together, Susan's published essays and journal entries provide glimpses of her thoughts about the abolition movement, southern benevolence, the division of her church, and the moral dilemmas of slavery. The tension between her long-held beliefs about gradual emancipation and the actual practice of slaveholding created a moral quandary during her later years. She eventually risked her career and began secretly to teach slaves to read.

SUSAN HAD BEEN teaching in Raleigh for a little over a year when the American Anti-Slavery Society in New York began a massive mail campaign in the summer of 1835. With funding from wealthy northerners, the society sent thousands of abolitionist pamphlets, tracts, and newspapers through the Post Office Department to the southern states during the summer of 1835. The society sought to convince southerners "of the sinfulness of slavery, and of the duty and safety of its immediate abolition." Members were confident that the campaign would gain followers in every region of the country because "the doctrine reaches conscience." They could not have been more wrong.[5]

Through August, September, and October, cities across the South reacted with outrage. People staged public protests and held town hall meetings, while newspapers printed angry editorials. More than 150 anti-abolition meetings took place across the South during the fall of 1835. Southerners viewed the mailing as a deliberate attempt to provoke slave insurrection. The *Charleston Observer* characterized the mailings as "recent attempts, under the guise of philanthropy, to interfere with our domestic institutions" by provoking insurrection or revolt. The editor warned northern publishers "that their Southern patronage is cut off at once, if even suspected to be in the interest of the Abolitionists." On December 22, Virginia's John Jones told his colleagues in the U.S. Congress that northern abolitionists had used the public mail "to rouse and inflame the passions of the slaves against their masters, to urge them on to deeds of death, and to involve them in all the horrors of a servile war."[6]

Susan read the *Observer* and must have been shocked by the southern reaction to the abolition movement. Protests over abolition came on the heels of the Nullification Crisis that arose in response to the federal tariffs of 1828 and 1832. During this period, South Carolina opponents of the tariffs had argued that a state could nullify federal law, and some nullification advocates had raised the specter of secession from the union. In November 1835, Susan composed a three-page essay addressed to the women of the Massachusetts Anti-Slavery Society in which she compared the agitation over abolition to the *simoon*, Arabia's hot, violent, sand-laden wind: "Nullification was indeed a hurricane which might have prostrated much that was venerated and valued, but Abolition is the Simoon whose very touch is death!" Her essay appeared in the American Colonization Society's *African Repository and Colonial Journal* in May 1836.[7]

Susan thus became one of the first women in the country to publish an essay on slavery and abolition in a mainstream journal and possibly the first who was living in the South at the time. The first northerner known to have published an antislavery essay was Maria Stewart, a free black evangelical whose 1833 lectures at Boston's African Meeting Hall are believed to have made her the first American woman to speak publicly against slavery.

Stewart's "Religion and the Pure Principles of Morality" appeared in the "Ladies Department" section of *The Liberator* in 1831. Lydia Maria Child of Massachusetts, author of *The Mother's Book*, a popular instructional text on child rearing, published *An Appeal in Favor of That Class of Americans Called Africans* in 1833. Three years later, the Grimké sisters, Quakers from South Carolina who had moved north and become active in the abolition movement, published antislavery essays: Sarah M. Grimké's *An Epistle to the Clergy of the Southern States* and Angelina Emily Grimké's *An Appeal to the Christian Women of the South*. Catharine Beecher—an emancipationist like her famous father, Lyman—responded with an 1837 counterargument, *An Essay on Slavery and Abolitionism*, triggering a critical rejoinder from Angelina Grimké the following year. Women's voices thus became part of the public debates over abolition.[8]

Like the writings of Angelina Grimké and Catharine Beecher, Susan's essay took the form of an address to other women, an approach that probably helped her achieve publication. Within her family circle, her church congregation, or her schoolroom or in female-only settings, a woman could certainly try to persuade others of the moral rightness of a particular cause. But any woman who wanted to express her opinions on slavery and abolition in a mainstream journal with a large male readership, like the *African Repository and Colonial Journal*, increased her chances of publication by adopting a humble and self-denying feminine voice and couching her words as if she were writing to a female audience.[9]

Susan addressed her remarks to the "Ladies of the Abolition Society of Massachusetts," suggesting that she knew about the activities of Boston's Female Anti-Slavery Society, which included both white and black women. A near-riot erupted when the group invited the British abolitionist George Thompson to give a public lecture in October 1835. During a series of lectures in the United States the previous year, he had highlighted the role of Americans in perpetuating slavery, a message that infuriated both slavery's supporters and moderates committed to gradual emancipation. Critics denounced the Female Anti-Slavery Society when it advertised Thompson's 1835 lecture, castigating the society for acting "with undue publicity." The editor of the *Boston Gazette* proclaimed that if Thompson appeared on October 21, "he will be roughly treated by the emissaries of Judge Lynch. If he will drive our citizens to acts of violence, let the blame be on his own head!" As the paper predicted, a mob of four or five thousand attacked the gathering: as the women joined their president in prayer, the rabble seized William Lloyd Garrison, who had arrived to give an address at the meeting, and beat him severely. Boston's mayor convinced the women to leave and the crowd to disperse, and Garrison narrowly escaped with his life.[10]

The Boston newspapers censured the Female Anti-Slavery Society for sowing discord between the North and the South. In the words of the *Boston Mercantile Journal*, "Holding meetings for the purpose of publicly discussing the merits of slavery, and the propriety of taking measures for abolishing it forthwith, at the same time denouncing the conduct of their fellow-citizens of the South, is fraught with evil. . . . It lays the foundation for an unnatural and bitter feeling of hostility, between the citizens of the slaveholding states, and the non-slaveholding states, which may produce the most serious consequences to the Republic. Nor is this all—their conduct tends directly to the disturbance of the public peace." Critics accused the women of leaving the "proper sphere, the domestic fire-side." Unbowed, the women of the society continued their efforts.[11]

Susan published her essay in an attempt to prevent regional divisions from worsening among Christians. She opened with a reference to a biblical story that illustrated the importance of understanding and reconciliation in averting civil war:

> Ladies: It is not that I lay claim to any portion of the wisdom given
> to that favored mother in Israel, whose counsel saved the chosen
> people from the horrors of a civil war . . . but it is that I recollect,
> an earlier, happier period in the history of Israel. . . . I recollect that
> with these upright men who feared the Lord, it was only necessary
> their accused brethren proved their motives just, and instantly the
> generous fire of fraternal love glowed again. . . . It is, that I believe the
> enlightened Christians of our own happy land, will be, at least, as just
> and generous. . . . May we not hope that they, like the pious tribes at
> Shiloh, will bless God, and no longer think of going to war with their
> brethren, when they shall hear they have acted uprightly?[12]

She viewed herself as a peacemaker: "Could you Ladies, see the strong fraternal bond which has hitherto bound us together, (the happiest people upon the face of the earth,) severing slowly and indeed reluctantly, but surely, before the withering touch of Abolition, you would, I am sure, draw back with trembling, lest you should be found spreading a contagion which threatens to destroy the most cherished, the most sacred interests of our beloved country."[13]

She sought to reassure northern abolitionists that southerners had "acted uprightly" by treating slaves with compassion, basing her qualification to assess the state of slavery in southern society on her long residence in the region: "A native of the North, more than twenty years have elapsed since I have resided in the Southern States, and during that period I have had very extensive opportunities of becoming acquainted, more or less, in all the Atlantic Slaveholding States." She continued, "As a people, I have uniformly found them generous and benevolent, affable and affectionate, high-minded indeed, but warmhearted, and more than all, sincere. To all these traits of character, hundreds of our northern brethren could attest, yes hundreds, who, by the Providence of God, have had their lots cast among them, under circumstances of sickness, bereavement and misfortune." She believed that a large majority of southerners did not fit the picture of the sadistic slave owner described in abolition literature: "During the long period of my residence at the South, I have resided in the neighbourhood of five individuals, whom public report stigmatizes as hard masters and mistresses. Three of them had been prosecuted and confined for their inhumanity, and all of them were uniformly held up to view, as objects of public indignation and abhorrence. . . . But would it be right or just to charge upon a whole people the disapproved misconduct of a few?"[14]

Susan characterized slavery as "a great evil" that "calls loudly for the exercise of that religion which is first pure, then peaceable, easy to be entreated, and full of good fruits." She assured her readers that "great numbers" of slaves "in the judgment of charity have been converted, and are according to their station of life, respectable and useful members of the various churches to which they belong." For Susan, the conversion of slaves was the most important part of a policy of delayed emancipation. Like all evangelicals, she believed that conversion brought the gift of eternal life in heaven. She claimed that good work could result from the missionary efforts of the American Colonization Society because freed slaves "who were willing to return to the land of their fathers" could be instrumental in bringing Christianity and civilization to Africa.[15]

Following the arguments in Paley's *Moral and Political Philosophy*, which remained part of her school's course of study, Susan argued that anarchy and violence would result from immediate emancipation: slavery, she believed, "is so closely interwoven into the very texture of society, that it is impossible (by human agency) to remove it suddenly, or violently, without producing a complete disorganization. A state of anarchy must ensue which a reflecting mind may much more easily conceive than describe." Susan was not merely parroting Paley. Given her experiences in Augusta, Georgia, Susan had good reason to believe that freed slaves might take revenge on their former masters or that whites might resort to violence. "And who in the event of such a catastrophe would suffer?" she asked. Those who would suffer most, she argued, were those "who have had no agency whatever in bringing into bondage the slaves who are under their authority, and who have, by the laws of their respective states, no opportunity of giving them their freedom. And the whole community would suffer with them—there could be neither security of property nor personal safety."[16]

Abolitionist efforts, Susan argued, were creating a division in the country, "a wall of adamant between themselves and their own brethren." Reminding readers of the recent nullification crisis, which "threatened by one dreadful disruption the dismemberment of our illustrious Union," she contended that the current crisis over abolition went even deeper, portending irrevocable divisions among churches and families. Susan closed by stating that she had never been a slave owner and that although she was now living in the South, she considered herself a northerner: "My orphan children have a northern home, and (though for the present separated from me) I feel their home to be mine."[17]

Susan's article resembles Catharine Beecher's *Essay on Slavery and Abolitionism*, published one year later. Both Susan and the far-better-known Beecher expressed their opinions on issues that went well beyond the classroom walls—slavery, abolition, and women's proper role in society. Beecher argued that although many Americans opposed slavery, they could not accept the abolitionists' methods of agitation and denunciation. She claimed that continued attacks against slavery would only inflame the South, worsen slaves' condition, and destroy the possibility that slavery could gradually be ended through moral suasion. However, unlike Beecher, who paradoxically claimed that a woman's place was in the home and that a female who took a public stance on a political question or who submitted a petition to the government was "out of her appropriate sphere," Susan did not question women's right to agitate publicly for abolition.[18]

The portrait of benevolent southern slavery Susan presented to readers not only is inconsistent with her fears about the eruption of violence but also stands in stark contrast to some of the journal entries she wrote in 1815. When she first arrived in North Carolina, she had been shocked by the ragged condition of slaves on the streets of Wilmington and appalled by the physical abuse of bondspeople.[19]

What had changed? Her philosophical perspective remained the same—on the issue of slavery, she held fast to Paley's view that slavery was evil but would be gradually overturned by the spread of the Christian religion. She had taught hundreds of young southern women this lesson, and she trusted that it had taken hold. While this may have been simply wishful thinking, it is possible she did observe a cultural shift in the way southerners discussed the treatment of slaves. Historians have provided some evidence to support this idea. For example, Eugene Genovese and Elizabeth Fox-Genovese have argued that the correspondence and diaries of southern white men and women show an increasing commitment to the notion of benevolent slaveholding in response to sermons that sought to promote a Christian conscience among the slaveholding class. Southerners gradually developed a cultural stereotype of the "good mistress," a benevolent Christian woman who treated her slaves with decency and humanity, attending carefully to their happiness and well-being. Although historians have largely credited male ministers with facilitating this transformation, Susan Nye Hutchison and other teachers also played an important role. Nevertheless, sermons and schoolroom messages about benevolent slaveholding did nothing to resolve the moral problem of slavery, and in any case, prescriptive messages never coincided particularly well with the actual behavior of men and women. Susan's essay acknowledged the continuing presence of cruel slave owners. In fact, less than three years later, she expressed more cynical views about slaveholding.[20]

Susan had never intended to promote an ideology of benevolent slaveholding that would justify the permanent establishment of slavery. She consistently argued that slavery was evil, not a blessing. Nevertheless, she never openly challenged the institution of slavery during her years in the South. She was very grateful for the opportunities she had been given in North Carolina. "Where is the individual, I would ask, whom health or pleasure has called to travel through these States, who has not experienced the warmth and kindness of southern hospitality. And where is he whose profession or employment has fixed him here, who has not experienced the sincerity of southern friendship? . . . Such individuals are not to be found." She spoke from experience.[21]

Although Susan's position on abolition is very conservative by modern standards, her characterization of slavery as "a great evil" marked her as a liberal among her contemporaries in the South. By the time her essay appeared in print, some southerners had begun to advance arguments that justified permanent slaveholding. Writers defending slavery drew on several recurring themes: fear, racism, economics, civil law, and religion. After the slave insurrections of the 1820s, some writers concluded that slavery was an unavoidable social burden that whites had to shoulder to stave off amorality, anarchy, and insurrection. Some claimed that slavery was the appropriate status for an inferior race incapable of governing itself, while others argued that slavery was an economic necessity for the future prosperity of the white middle and upper classes. Many Christians, even those strongly opposed to slavery, came to believe that it was so deeply rooted in southern society and so protected by civil law that the goal of emancipation was far beyond the reach of ordinary individuals. Historian Monica Najar has found that by 1810, many Baptists in the Upper South argued that slavery was a civil matter rather than a moral or religious issue. Nevertheless, attempts to categorize slavery as a completely civil concern failed to silence the ongoing debate over emancipation. To resolve the moral conflict between slaveholding and the Bible's injunction to "do to others as you would have them do to you," some ministers began to argue that God sanctioned slavery.[22]

DIVISION IN THE Presbyterian Church had been brewing for several years before Susan's essay appeared in print. During the 1820s, the New York revivalist Charles Grandison Finney (1792–1875) had developed preaching methods that became known as the New Measures, and among Presbyterians, his followers were dubbed the New School. In contrast to "Old School" Presbyterians, who supported the Calvinist doctrine that Christ died for a chosen few preordained by God, Finney argued that Christ died to make salvation possible for everyone. According to historian Richard Carwardine, Methodists had for some time widely employed many of the methods Finney introduced, but they shocked traditionalists in the Presbyterian Church. Controversial practices included boisterous revivals and public exhortations from the pulpit directed at individuals sitting in a designated area, the "anxious seat." Finney believed that when publicly confronted by the minister before the congregation, the individual sinner could repent and reform.[23]

Finney began preaching against slavery in 1830. "When I first went to New York, I had made up my mind on the question of slavery, and was exceedingly anxious to arouse public attention to the subject," he later recalled. His impassioned preaching won thousands of converts. Most Presbyterians associated with the New School remained committed to a policy of gradual emancipation rather than a policy of immediate abolition, but by putting the issue of slavery before their congregations, Finney and other New School ministers contributed to an increasingly bitter debate among church conservatives, moderates, and abolitionists.[24]

Finney's ministry received substantial support and patronage from several prominent abolitionist leaders, some of whom interpreted the Presbyterian Church's Expression of Views against slavery as a declaration of support for a policy of immediate abolition. This statement, which had been unanimously endorsed by the General Assembly in 1818, enjoined all churches and presbyteries to work toward "a total abolition of slavery." The statement characterized slaveholding as "utterly inconsistent with the law of God which requires us to love our neighbour as ourselves, and as totally irreconcilable with the spirit and principles of the gospel of Christ." Finney's converts and followers included abolitionists Theodore Dwight Weld and Arthur and Lewis Tappan, wealthy New York merchants. In 1832, the Tappan brothers financed the construction of the Broadway Tabernacle to house Finney's ministry. The following year, Arthur Tappan and William Lloyd Garrison founded the American Anti-Slavery Society.[25]

By 1833, petitions on the issue of slaveholding had become a common feature of meetings of the synods and of the General Assembly of the Presbyterian Church. In particular, the Expression of Views against slavery was a bone of contention. Some northern Presbyterian synods grew increasingly uncomfortable with the discrepancy between the church's 1818 antislavery proclamation and southern Presbyterians' growing countenance of slavery. The Expression of Views had directed congregations to discipline church members guilty of separating slave families or of selling professed Presbyterians. But although both those in favor of gradual emancipation and abolitionists had approved the resolution, it was widely ignored in the slaveholding states.[26]

In 1834, the Presbyterian Synod of Kentucky appointed a committee to report on the condition of slavery in the state: the committee found that the church rarely if ever disciplined members for separating slave families through sale. The authors concluded, "Our churches cannot be entirely pure, even from the grossest pollutions of slavery, *until we are willing to pledge ourselves to the destruction of the whole system.*" Other antislavery synods agreed. Throughout the early 1830s, the General Assembly of the Presbyterian Church received a stream of petitions and memorials from synods and individuals asking the church to take action to end slavery. The General Assembly usually referred such petitions to a committee, dragging out the process without any decision.[27]

Despite the General Assembly's stalling tactics, abolition supporters kept up the pressure. In 1835, speaking in support of earlier memorials and petitions, the Reverend Robert Stewart from the Presbytery of Schuyler, Illinois, addressed the delegates: "I hope this Assembly are prepared to come out fully and declare their sentiments, that slaveholding is a most flagrant, and heinous SIN. Let us not pass it by in this indirect way, while so many thousands and tens of thousands of our fellow-creatures are writhing under the lash, often inflicted, too, by ministers and elders of the Presbyterian Church."[28]

Stewart went on to highlight a sensitive issue among Presbyterians: clergy involvement in slaveholding. "In this church, a man may take a free-born child, force it away from its parents, to whom God gave it in charge, saying, 'Bring it up for me,' and sell it as a beast or hold it in perpetual bondage, and not only escape corporeal punishment, but really be esteemed an excellent Christian. Nay, even ministers of the gospel, and Doctors of Divinity, may engage in this unholy traffic, and yet sustain their high and holy calling." In response, the General Assembly simply appointed yet another committee to report on slavery.[29]

Few southern ministers at the 1835 General Assembly wanted to endorse Stewart's call to declare slaveholding a sin. Church congregations had held slaves since the colonial period. The Presbyterian congregation of Edisto Island, South Carolina, received a gift of several slaves in 1732 to be hired out, with their descendants, "for the perpetual maintenance of their yearly labor of a Presbyterian minister." In 1742, elders of Bethel Presbyterian Church started a subscription fund to increase the congregation's pool of slaves. The profits obtained from hiring out these slaves paid the pastor's salary for the next decade, and a decade later, the money earned by slave labor also covered the rent of the pews. As historian Jennifer Oast has pointed out, the practice of "jobbing out" slaves widened the circle of slavery to include whites of a wide range of economic backgrounds. Through congregational slave owning, all members of the church benefited, whether or not they personally owned slaves or even approved of the institution.[30]

The problem of slaveholding was not only theological but also economic. Slaves accounted for a large proportion of some churches' assets, and the market prices for slaves reflected their increasing economic value. Slave prices rose with the cyclical increases in the demand for cotton and fell when the market was in recession, but the overall trend was upward. Prime field hands sold for around $160 in the American colonies in 1750, averaged around $500 in the United States in 1800, and rose to between $1,300 and $1,500 by 1850. Over the long term, investments in slaves appreciated significantly, and through "jobbing out," those assets yielded a steady stream of income to cushion periods of recession. Churches saw the value of their investments in slaves rise over time, as a consequence of both increasing prices and growing slave populations.[31]

In addition, individual ministers frequently owned slaves, giving them strong financial incentives to oppose abolition. The money gained from hiring out slaves could provide a minister with a stable income in retirement, a source of support for his widow, and an inheritance for his heirs. In the absence of any dependents, the minister could direct the executor of his will to sell his slaves and use the proceeds to support missionary work.[32]

If slavery was a sin, as claimed in the church's 1818 statement, then surely, as Stewart argued, all Christians must work to eradicate it, through either gradual emancipation or abolition. But what if slavery were not a sin? Some participants in the 1835 General Assembly rejected Stewart's admonition because they had already come to believe that the Bible sanctioned slavery. The previous year, a meeting of the Presbyterian clergy of South Carolina and Georgia unanimously resolved "that in the opinion of this Synod, Abolition Societies and the principles on which they are formed in the United States, are inconsistent with the best interests of the slaves, the rights of the holders, and the great principles of our political institutions." In October 1835, the Synod of Virginia unanimously adopted a similar resolution: "That we consider the dogma fiercely promulgated by said associations—that slavery as it exists in our slave-holding States is necessarily sinful, and ought to be immediately abolished . . . as directly and palpably contrary to the plainest principles of common sense and common humanity, and to the clearest authority of the word of God." In the judgment of the Virginia synod, all ministers were duty-bound "to follow the example of our Lord and Savior . . . in abstaining from all interference with the state of slavery."[33]

Anticipating more discussion of slavery and a possible call for a vote at the 1836 General Assembly, some individual presbyteries in the slaveholding states issued proslavery resolutions. The Charleston Union Presbytery resolved "that in the opinion of this Presbytery, the holding of slaves, so far from being a SIN in the sight of God, is no where condemned in his Holy Word. . . . They who assume the contrary position, and lay it down as a fundamental principle in morals and religion, that all slaveholding is wrong, proceed upon false principles." The presbytery of Hopewell, South Carolina, instructed its delegates "to use all Christian means to prevent the discussion of domestic slavery in the Assembly—to protest in our name against all acts that involve or approve abolition—and to withdraw from the Assembly and return home, if in spite of their efforts, acts of this character shall be passed." Hopewell Presbytery urged its delegates to adhere to facts that had been "most incontrovertibly established": (1) Slavery was not condemned in the Bible; (2) Emancipation was not mentioned in the Bible; (3) Throughout history, no Christian had ever been excommunicated for owning slaves; (4) Slavery predated the presbytery and had "always existed in our Church without reproof or condemnation"; and (5) "Slavery is a political institution, with which the Church [had] nothing to do."[34]

Arguments erupted between abolitionist and proslavery presbyteries. In 1836, the abolitionist presbytery of Chillicothe, Ohio, addressed a letter to the state clerk of the presbytery of Mississippi, charging that slaveholding was a sin and asking the presbytery to endorse a number of resolutions in favor of abolition. Mississippi minister James Smylie (1780–1853), a slaveholder like many of his brethren, was infuriated. He responded with a proslavery argument based on religious tradition and quotations from Scripture and later expanded his piece into a long pamphlet, *A Review of a Letter from the Presbytery of Chillicothe, to the Presbytery of Mississippi on the Subject of Slavery*. His pamphlet—the most extended defense of slavery prepared by a clergyman to date—was widely distributed throughout churches and theological seminaries. Smylie claimed that the Bible sanctioned slavery and that it could not possibly be evil because so many converted Christians were involved with the institution. "If the buying, selling, and holding of a slave for the sake of gain is a heinous sin and scandal," retorted Smylie, "then verily three-fourths of all the Episcopalians, Methodists, Baptists, and Presbyterians, in eleven States of the Union, are of the devil. They hold, if they do not buy and sell, slaves."[35]

Both the abolitionist and proslavery positions hardened. Abolitionists, many of whom identified with the New School, were very willing to believe that their slaveholding colleagues were "of the devil." The proslavery camp regarded them with fear and loathing. Everyone else in the middle—gradual emancipationists, colonizers interested primarily in evangelism and missionary work, and individuals who remained on the fence—simply wished the agitation would subside. Presbyteries from all regions of the country submitted memorials and petitions to the General

Assembly for consideration at its 1836 meeting and waited anxiously to hear the report of the Committee on Slavery.

In May, the divided committee presented a "majority report" stating that the church had no business interfering with slavery and denying the legitimacy of the 1818 Expression of Views as well as a "minority report" warning that a policy of patient forbearance toward slaveholders threatened to destroy the church. In reference to slavery, the minority report stated, "The church has found herself more deeply involved in its toils, and, in some parts, in danger of being crushed in its folds." Slavery not only continued but was "becoming more and more deeply rooted in the land, and intimately incorporated with the very frame of civil society; and even with the pale of the church, it begins to claim a lodgment, not by indulgence merely, but as of right."[36]

The committee's minority report reflected the Enlightenment views associated with the American Revolution, proposing that "the General Assembly of the Presbyterian church in the United States of America, continue to declare their unwavering and undiminished attachment to those principles of liberty, which are so clearly expressed in the Declaration of Independence, and in the federal and state constitutions of these United States. They do unhesitatingly believe that *all men* are by nature free and equal, and are endowed by their Creator with certain unalienable rights, among which are life, liberty, and the pursuit of happiness."[37]

Fearful of polarization, the majority of delegates to the 1836 General Assembly wished to take no formal position on the matter of slavery and preferred to avoid any discussion at all of the topic. After some heated debate over memorials and petitions on slavery submitted by two presbyteries and scores of individuals, the assembly agreed to divide the Committee on Slavery's majority resolution and vote on the latter part: "Resolved, That this whole subject be indefinitely postponed." It passed by a 154–87 vote.[38]

But of course the arguments raged on. Southern ministers had begun to refer to the 1818 Expression of Views as "the obnoxious resolutions" and declared them invalid. As 1836 went on, Old School leaders interested in excising the New School synods began to agitate for a formal division of the national church.[39]

Women living in the South followed these debates by listening to the discussion in their churches or by reading Virginia's *Richmond Observer*, South Carolina's *Charleston Observer*, or other Presbyterian newspapers. Such publications carried the proceedings and minutes of the General Assembly and local synod meetings. As Peter J. Wallace has shown, although some lay persons contributed articles, most of the writers were ministers or church elders. When Susan read the *Charleston Observer* in 1836, she would have found no female authors. Nevertheless, she had something to say, so she picked up her pen and began to write.[40]

BY JANUARY 1837, Susan had begun to compose an essay urging that the Presbyterian Church remain united. She did not write in her journal between October 22, 1836, and January 1, 1837, so there is no way to know exactly when she began this project, but on January 7, she noted, "I have written all day—oh the moil!" Four days later she confessed, "I have written till a late hour—Sometimes I am tempted to doubt respecting its usefulness." Similar misgivings surfaced the next day: "I write all the time yet I fear it is in vain." Despite her trepidations, she finished the manuscript and on January 17 reported, "I have sent off my address—to the Observer—May it be blessed of the blessed Redeemer."[41]

She grew depressed after three weeks passed with no response and began to question her ambition:

> February 7, 1837—I hear nothing from my letter to the Sisters of our Church—Sometimes I forget that I have written and again I feel humbled that no notice has been taken of it.
> 9—I have been greatly depressed—thoughts of spending so much time and paying so much postage on my letter to the Sisters of the Church has doubtless been one cause—My ambition has been a sin—Oh to be truly humble—Oh to be willing to be anything that God pleases. . . . How have I been disappointed in all my schemes! Nothing has answered my expectation—my literary labours have proved abortive my marriage unhappy—
> 16—. . . ambition too I cannot deny for I am mortified at the rejection.

But her mood changed dramatically when she discovered that the *Charleston Observer* had published her essay in its February 18 issue. Moreover, editor Benjamin Gildersleeve, an Old School Presbyterian minister who opposed dividing the church, placed it on the front page, where no reader could miss it. At nearly five thousand words, it took up two-thirds of the page.[42]

Susan's essay is the only known published writing by a woman arguing against the impending division in the Presbyterian Church. The proposition that a female might publicly weigh in on church politics was controversial at the time. The same year that Susan's essay appeared, Catharine Beecher, arguably the nation's most prominent evangelical woman, proclaimed that women should take no part in public debates on slavery. Also that year, the Presbyterian *Watchman of the South* reprinted Hubbard Winslow's "The Appropriate Sphere of Woman," in which he proclaimed that women should confine themselves to their homes and never sit in judgment on the "affairs of church and state."[43]

To alleviate the concerns of male readers who disapproved of women obliquely expressing an opinion on Presbyterian politics, Gildersleeve pointed out that Susan's essay was aimed at a female audience: "The address of our female correspondent, on the first page of this paper, will be read with interest, and we hope with profit, by many of the sisters in the church to whom it is particularly directed—The strain of piety which pervades it, will be apt to divert attention from some of its minor defects and fix the thoughts upon those important considerations which are embodied in this interesting and timely appeal." Gildersleeve may have hoped to dampen any backlash from male ministers and church elders by highlighting the subordinate and inferior status of a female writer in his newspaper. Susan, of course, immediately zeroed in on the phrase "minor defects": "My address came with an editorial calling the attention of the Sisters to its object but adverting to its minor defects—I am mortified but not sorry that I wrote." She apparently wrote to Gildersleeve to point out that the "minor defects" were typographical errors, because in March, she recorded in her journal that she had received a letter from Gildersleeve "apologizing for my misprinted letter." He never published a correction, however.[44]

Because of Susan's careful couching of her perspective, few male readers likely cared to oppose her in print. She constructed a work of fervent religiosity in which she appealed to Presbyterian women to pray that the church remain united. She drew dozens of examples from the Old Testament to support her contentions that God would listen to women's prayers, that women could make meaningful contributions in the world, and that women's influence could heal the rupture in the church.

Susan argued that the rupture put God to shame, asking, "Is not our own beloved icon bowed down with grief because of the errors and consequent divisions among our brethren? Are we not bound to another by the blood of Jesus? And can there be a stronger bond of union? But does not the afflicted state of our church tear open his bleeding wounds afresh, and thus put him again to open shame?" Men—"our brethren"—had created a rift in the church, and women needed to take up the task of restoring unity. Of course, readers could not have overlooked the fact that her essay was not only a message to women but also an argument to both sexes that the decision of some Presbyterian leaders to effect a formal division in the church was wrong.[45]

She believed that women had an instrumental role in healing the church and that this work could be accomplished through prayer. "Will you not then, my sisters, bare [*sic*] with me, while leaning on the Divine assistance, I humbly attempt to suggest a way in these troublous times, in which we, even *we*, may hope to be instrumental in repairing the breach in the walls of our precious Zion." She skirted controversial ground by overtly referring to women's subordinate social status and studiously avoiding any discussion of the causes of division, and she carefully acknowledged that it was not women's place to teach men: "By what cause, this melancholy breach has been effected, or by whom, it belongs not to us to inquire—full well we know that it pertaineth not to us to teach our respected brethren, much less our venerated fathers in the Gospel—yet if to woman were given the privilege of lingering latest near the cross, and of visiting earliest the sepulcher, surely she will not, cannot, be refused a place before the altar of prayer. . . . That a breach in our spiritual wall exists, and is rapidly desolating all that with us is most fair and beautiful, is a fact of which none of us can be ignorant."[46]

She provided biblical evidence directly counter to contemporary writings that limited a woman's activity to the domestic sphere of her own home. She cited examples of women's heroism, faith, and wisdom, drawing from Old and New Testament stories of Jochebed, Shiprah and Puah, Jael, Deborah, Hannah, Esther, Mary, and Martha. She reminded readers that Deborah had sat in judgment over a house of Israel, that Jael had slain one of Israel's enemies with her own hands, and that women had joined men to repair the walls in Jerusalem.

"Some there be, among us, who with difficulty can be persuaded that there is any utility in the religious efforts of our sex," she wrote. To demonstrate that this opinion lacked foundation, she cited numerous biblical passages in which God listens and acts in response to the prayers of women and chooses women to act as his agents. To those who doubted that the "special mercy" shown to Jochebed, mother of Moses, "might not be expected by those who never move behind the quiet scenes of domestic life," she pointed to passages that highlighted women's work outside the home: "Let such remember the wise hearted women of Israel whose labors were accepted in the erection of the sacred tabernacle. True, we know not their names—It is enough that they are written in heaven; but if example ever were affecting and operative, surely theirs ought to be."[47]

Susan's essay can be interpreted as a protofeminist work. Protofeminism is generally defined as an expression of feminist consciousness in earlier periods and different contexts, and she expressed a clear consciousness of women's subordinate position in a patriarchal society, buttressing her arguments with numerous biblical references and providing examples of earlier women's contributions. Historians traditionally locate the rise of American feminism in the women's political rights movement that developed in the North during the late 1830s and 1840s. Although Susan was not seeking to persuade women to undertake political action, she did aim to engage women in concerted spiritual action through prayer, supporting her argument with examples of women's equality before God.[48]

The impact of her essay on readers is unknown. The *Charleston Observer* printed no letters to the editor in response to the essay. She considered publishing it as a pamphlet but apparently never did so. And by the summer of 1837, her point became moot when the church split. Susan learned of the schism on June 15: after attending a church service in Salisbury, North Carolina, she wrote in her journal, "After sermon I was introduced to the deputation to the General Assembly. I desire to be thankfull that the Church is not divided."[49]

The delegates Susan encountered had just returned from the Presbyterians' national meeting, at which a committee established to "inquire into the expediency of a voluntary division of the Presbyterian Church" had concluded "that the peace and prosperity of the Presbyterian Church in the United States, require a separation of the portions called respectively the Old and New School parties." The committee had recommended that the two groups form separate denominations, with the Old School majority retaining the church's name and corporate property. The General Assembly had voted to excise whole synods and presbyteries associated with the New School. Over the years, Susan had worshipped in both northern and southern Presbyterian congregations, and she had friends in both camps. She was distressed to hear the news. Two years later, she remembered the controversy as "a fearful struggle."[50]

The Presbyterian Church officially divided the following year. The South Amenia Presbyterian Church in New York, where Susan worshipped during her summers on the family farm, went with the New School. North

Carolina's synods went with the Old School. A number of factors contributed to the break between the two groups, including differences in doctrine, disputes over conformity to church policy, questions about the value of the church's association with voluntary associations, concerns over the long-term sustainability of revival movements, and diversity of opinion about the institution of slavery. By and large, however, disputes over slavery overshadowed all other areas of contention, opening a chasm that eventually became impossible to bridge.[51]

Some southern Presbyterian churches had emancipationist ministers during this period, but when they spoke against slavery in public, most individuals highlighted their status as slave owners and disavowed any association with the abolition movement. In 1838 John Witherspoon, a Presbyterian minister from South Carolina who had voted for "the so-called obnoxious resolutions" twenty years earlier, wrote to the *Charleston Observer* to explain that the Expression of Views "was penned, and advocated, and voted for, by *Southern men*. There were *Emancipationists* in that Assembly, but . . . no abolitionists, as known and called at the present day." He claimed that "tens of thousands" of southerners in the western regions of the southern states remained in favor of emancipation "whenever and wherever it can be effected without detriment to the master and injury to the slave." He now proclaimed "publicly, that which I did not state on the floor of Synod, that although a slave holder from my youth up to the present moment, I have been from my youth up, and am now, and ever shall be, a friend to Emancipation."[52]

As a minority group, southern emancipationists such as Witherspoon had little influence in the Old School church. In less than a decade, the two branches of the Presbyterian Church adopted very different positions on slavery. In 1839, the New School General Assembly settled on a statement that characterized slavery as evil and enjoined churches to work toward its elimination. In 1846, in response to abolition agitation within its ranks, the New School adopted a stronger statement: "The system of slavery, as it exists in these United States, viewed either in the laws of the several States which sanction it, or in its actual operation and results in society, is intrinsically an unrighteous and oppressive system, and is opposed to the prescriptions of the law of God, to the spirit and precepts of the gospel, and to the best interests of humanity." In contrast, the Old School branch renounced the idea that slaveholding was a sin, stating at its 1845 meeting, "That slavery existed in the days of Christ and his Apostles is an admitted fact. That they did not denounce the relation itself as sinful, as inconsistent with Christianity; that slaveholders were admitted to membership in the churches organized by the Apostles; that whilst they were required to treat their slaves with kindness, and as rational, accountable, immortal beings, and if Christians, as brethren in the Lord, they were not commanded to emancipate them."[53]

The Methodist and Baptist denominations soon experienced similar schisms over the issue of slaveholding. In 1844, the Southern Methodist Church was formed, and the Southern Baptist Convention was created the following year.[54]

A number of historians have argued that the division of the three major Protestant churches marked the close of the Second Great Awakening. Other scholars, noting the urban revivals of the 1850s, have concluded that the era ended with the Civil War. According to Nathan O. Hatch, "There are more generalizations and less solid data on the dynamics of American religion in this period than in any other in our history." Still, if the spirit of the Second Great Awakening is defined not solely by the presence of revivals but also by a deep-seated belief in the ability of awakened Christians to reform and save the world, then it is reasonable to conclude that the divisions in the evangelical churches meant the end of the Second Great Awakening. During the early decades of that era, the collaboration among reformers reflected a cultural unity of purpose. Whether they hailed from the North, South, or West, American evangelicals, including Susan Nye Hutchison, used the same religious and moral language as they worked to promote education, support for orphans and widows, temperance, and gradual emancipation. Regional vocabularies were virtually indistinguishable. However, this sense of common cause began to unravel in the 1830s. According to Barry Hankins, the rise in abolition agitation and public criticism coincided with a period of stagnation in church membership. Here and there, religious revivals still occurred, but from the mid-1840s to the mid-1850s, overall membership in the Protestant churches declined.[55]

THROUGHOUT THIS PERIOD, Susan maintained her evangelical faith, but after the division of the Presbyterian Church, she appears to have lost her optimism that slaveholding Christians would inevitably take steps to alleviate the lot of enslaved men and women and work toward emancipation. First she decided that she would secretly teach slaves to read. Then she pondered what to do when a slave asked if she would purchase him.

Theologically, Susan aligned squarely with the New School branch of the Presbyterian Church. She rejected the notion, expressed in one sermon she heard, that "God had from the beginning chosen some to eternal life." Instead, she believed that "the divine Master extended the invitation to all"—a position expressed often by Charles G. Finney and other New School ministers. She believed that humans were capable of choosing to obey God's moral laws and live righteously in the world. In fact, her journals are peppered with expressions of dismay about her personal shortcomings in this regard.[56]

Although the Old School Presbyterian Church frowned on religious revivals as unnecessary and undignified spectacles, Susan believed in their power. When she had worked as a common school teacher in Amenia in the winter of 1833, she had invited the minister of the South Amenia Presbyterian Church to preach "a revival sermon" at the schoolhouse, and she continued to promote revivals after returning to North Carolina. In Salisbury, she held prayer meetings at her school and recorded the number of students who had "awakened" and publicly professed their conversion to Christianity. Evangelism pervaded her work with young people, as is evident in an 1838 message she wrote in Mary Steele Ferrand's autograph book urging the young woman toward a personal revival of religious faith: "But there is a glory that endureth, and joys that can not fade, and crowns & harps of everlasting praise, and triumph, now, prepar'd, and ready for the faithful ones. And shall that Crown, oh Mary dear, thy brow adorn? And shall that song of praise be thine?" Susan was delighted to see religious revivals spread through her school in the fall of 1837 and winter of 1838.[57]

After moving to Salisbury, Susan retained many aspects of her earlier ministry in the community. She prayed with the sick and dying, and she sought to convert condemned criminals before they faced the gallows. On December 23, 1837, she visited a Mrs. Moore: "The poor guilty creature burst into a loud cry as I entered confessing her guilt and promising not to sin again—I went to see if she was suffering . . . may Jesus wash her clean from all sin." She comforted widows and on occasion attended births. "Mrs. Pendleton whom I promised to attend during her confinement was tonight ill," wrote Susan on June 2, 1838. "After two she gave birth to a son—I returned about four and lay down pretty nearly exhausted." She visited several prisoners in the Salisbury jail, including one convicted of murdering his wife. Concerned that the condemned man was "insensible as to the great concerns of eternity," she spent the two months before his execution trying to convert him. She noted on April 3, 1837, that he had confessed to his crime, and sixteen days later she wrote, "The prisoner seems to be happy in Jesus." In March of the following year, she resumed visits to the jail to minister to another prisoner.[58]

Criticism of her actions constrained her public behavior, however. Not everyone was pleased with her ministry to prisoners. In 1829 she had visited the jail in Augusta, Georgia, to pray with Jenny, the slave girl convicted of arson and condemned to death, without any complaint from the religious community, but she encountered a very different reaction in Salisbury. Salisbury's community may always have been more conservative about the socially appropriate extent of women's public lay ministry, or social mores might have changed over the preceding decade. In May 1838 she recorded that an Episcopal minister "told me today I had no business at the jail." Susan, however, believed that God alone could judge her actions, writing, "Oh Lord thou knowest if I have erred in going."[59]

In regard to interactions with slaves in public places, social mores had unquestionably altered. When Susan first arrived in Raleigh in 1815, she had often talked and prayed on the streets with free blacks and slaves. But by the late 1830s, a white New York woman following the admonition of her state's Presbyterian synod to bring slaves "into society with those habits of industry that may render them useful citizens" could no longer read the Bible with slaves in the streets without risking censure. By the time Susan had her Salisbury academy up and running, politicians had officially declared citizenship off-limits to free blacks and imposed stiff penalties for anyone teaching slaves to read. Susan continued to record in her journal the number of free blacks and slaves who converted and joined the churches where she worshipped, and she occasionally visited and prayed with old and infirm slaves in the privacy of their own dwellings, but she never again wrote about going out in public to minister to slaves.[60]

Nevertheless, she privately resisted the slave codes. In the summer of 1838 she began to teach a small group of slaves to read, even though doing so violated North Carolina law:

> July 1, 1838—Lord make me wise to love thee better and serve thee
> more then will all be well for time and for eternity—I have today
> stayed from the Sabbath school as Miss Baker will teach my
> class—I have seen however an opportunity of teaching for in
> Col. Lemley's family there are four little servants whom I have
> (with Miss H[ermans]'s help) learned to read in two letters—
> often when, in their zeal to learn, they come for instruction I feel
> too tired to teach them and then I look at the hopelessness of

their condition and see if I hold back there is none to help them, and I exert myself to go on with them in the good work—at three oclock I united with the class in Cathechism and missed a question.[61]

By the time of this entry, Susan had taught this group of slaves to "read in two letters." This phrase refers to a nineteenth-century phonetic teaching method by which students learned to sound out and read words. Students at this level typically could read simple sentences and selected short passages from the Bible.[62]

The secrecy associated with her effort is suggested by the fact that she carved out time for teaching by staying away from the Sabbath school, since she apparently could not schedule regular lessons. In addition, her helper was Susan Hermans, a relative and fellow New Yorker. The motivation and agency of the slaves is evidenced by Susan's reference to their having come to her with a "zeal to learn."

Susan clearly saw teaching slaves to read as an essential moral duty, and her use of the phrase "the hopelessness of their condition" implies that she did not believe religious conversion—which could be achieved without literacy—was sufficient. Without learning to read, slaves would never be prepared for freedom. Moreover, her wording suggests that she believed her students suffered as a consequence of enforced servitude and a lack of education rather than from any inherent trait of inferiority. Messages about the intellectual inferiority of Africans had supported the slave trade from its earliest days, and some southerners continued to advance such arguments to justify slavery. However, the South's antiliteracy laws implied the intellectual equality of blacks and whites. As noted in the school edition of Francis Wayland's *Elements of Moral Science*, a highly popular emancipationist text that eventually superseded Paley's book in the North, "Such laws suppose the capacity of negroes for intellectual culture, and are an implicit confession that it is necessary to degrade their minds in order to keep their bodies in slavery."[63]

Susan and her assistant risked significant punishment. In 1830, the North Carolina Legislature had severely curtailed the rights of free blacks and tightened the restrictions on slaves. Governor John Owen had sent the legislature a copy of David Walker's *Appeal to the Colored Citizens of the World*, explaining that the distribution of Walker's pamphlet represented an attempt to provoke insurrection among slaves and directing the General Assembly to take steps to protect the state's citizens. In response, the assembly removed manumission decisions—judicial processes by which a slave could be freed—from the county courts to the state legislature, passed a quarantine law to prevent free blacks on ships docking in North Carolina ports from communicating with the slaves and free blacks on shore, and directed that any "white man or woman" found teaching slaves to read was subject to a fine of "not less than one hundred dollars, nor more than two hundred dollars" or to imprisonment. In short, had she been caught and convicted, Susan would have gone to jail or paid a fine roughly equal to the annual salary of an academy teacher. In either case, she would have been disgraced, and her career as the respectable head of a female academy would have come to an end. In addition, exposure would have destroyed her plans for her sons.[64]

But Susan saw herself as the slaves' only option: "If I hold back there is none to help them." Her views had changed completely over the preceding three years. Her 1836 essay in the *African Repository and Colonial Journal* had assured readers that southerners not only treated their slaves well materially but also tended to their slaves' salvation and spiritual well-being. "Doubtless it is the imperative duty of masters in our day, as it was in the Apostles," she had written, "to remember that they also have a master in heaven, and by gentleness and kindness to their servants, to do them good for time as well as for eternity; and this I am permitted to say is at present the course pursued by the pious and benevolent owners of slaves in the Southern States." However, after the division of the Presbyterian Church, she came to hold a more pessimistic view of southern benevolence.[65]

Susan's last surviving journal entries are relatively brief, focused primarily on the ebb and flow of life in Charlotte. She jotted down notes about day-to-day school business, interactions with friends and colleagues, her two elder sons' visits during breaks from the Caldwell Academy, and the 1840 presidential campaign. During this period, she rarely wrote about slaves—with one exception.

Among her last entries is a brief description of an event that illustrates one of the most controversial and hotly debated aspects of life in America's slaveholding society: the separation of slave families through sale. In the fall of 1840, a married slave, Ned, asked if she would purchase him, and for a moment she considered the question.

A year earlier, Susan had hired Ned to care for her third son, nine-year-old Adam Alexander. She often referred to the boy as "my poor afflicted darling" because he suffered from daily seizures. In addition, he exhibited some mental impairment: "Sweetest Adam requires a constant attendant. . . . Oh none can tell how one feels who has constant reason to fear the loss of a child's intellect." Her son usually suffered seizures while he slept—sometimes as many as five a night—and required constant care and monitoring.[66]

Ned had a wife and spent evenings with his own family, but he looked after Adam Alexander from dawn to dusk during the week while Susan attended to the business of her school, and Ned accompanied the child to church on Sundays while Susan worshipped with her students. Because Ned could not sit with whites in the segregated churches, he always carried Adam Alexander into the upstairs section reserved for blacks. One Sunday in the spring of 1840, Susan wrote, "Adam attended and sat up stairs with the coloured people—Ned took care of him—he slept a good while in his arms." On another occasion, she was listening to a sermon when she was surprised to hear "a child's voice sounding like Adam's" calling out: "Ned had brought him, and from the black people's gallery he called out 'Mother—Mother.'" She fetched him, and they sat quietly together during the singing. Susan was grateful for Ned's care and relationship with her son.[67]

On November 5, 1840, Susan learned that Ned's master was moving to Georgia and taking Ned. According to Susan, she and Adam Alexander "regretted his departure a great deal." The following day, they were surprised when Ned appeared at their door around dusk: "Adam was wild with joy—he ran to him threw his arms around his neck and burst into loud cries of joy—Ned was so much affected that he expressed a wish that he could stay with him—I believe I would gladly have bought him had I been able to do so on account of my poor little afflicted boy."[68]

In expressing his wish to remain with Adam, Ned deliberately attempted to change his fate. Susan's journal does not mention whether Ned's wife would accompany him to Georgia. The southern states did not recognize marriages among slaves. In the civil courts, slaves could not enter into contracts, make wills, plead their cases, or marry. They might be sold, mortgaged, and removed from one place to another at their master's whim. As historian Marie Jenkins Schwartz has shown, the threat of sale and relocation often forced slaves to engage in complex strategies of negotiation and resistance to avoid or postpone separations among family members.[69] Ned's motivations are unknown: Had he grown to care so much for the boy that he genuinely did not want to leave? Was he more concerned because the move to Georgia would have separated him from his wife and his own family? It is also unknown whether Susan considered Ned's family situation as she struggled with the question of whether she could buy Ned to keep him in Charlotte.

The surviving pages of Susan's journal include no discussion of the moral and financial ramifications of North Carolina's slave codes, but they were considerable. On the one hand, Christians were duty-bound to uphold the institution of marriage, and all of the major Protestant churches had enjoined masters from separating married slaves, though such marriages carried no legal recognition. The separation of slave families was a continuing point of contention in the debates over slavery and abolition. In fact, the trigger event in Harriet Beecher Stowe's *Uncle Tom's Cabin*, which quickly became a best seller after it appeared in 1853, was the desperate escape of a slave mother and her child across an icy river to avoid separation by sale. Purchasing a slave to preserve his marriage could be viewed as an act of Christian benevolence. On the other hand, abolitionists claimed that slaveholding itself was a sin. Moreover, Ned might still be separated from his wife by her owner. In that case, Susan could not even have kept the couple together by setting Ned free. By 1835, North Carolina's slave codes provided that a master wanting to free a slave had to give a one-thousand-dollar bond, file a written petition to the State Superior Court, and publish a notice of intent for six weeks before the manumission. And once freed, the former slave had to leave the state within ninety days; returnees could be arrested and sold back into slavery. Moreover, the purchase price for a slave like Ned would probably have been equivalent to two years' salary for a highly qualified academy teacher. This was an enormous sum, though Susan might have been able to afford it by tightening her belt: the preceding July, she had reviewed her account books and noted, "I find by my settlements that it will take about all that I have made to settle off my debts incurred within the last year." Her school enrolled twenty-four young women, four of whom boarded in her home, and at the end of the year, she had modestly furnished her home, bought two new carpets, paid most of her bills, and helped her brother Meletiah settle a debt. Whatever her reasons—whether she thought that she lacked the money to purchase Ned, whether she could not bring herself to commit the sin of owning a slave even if the purchase would have benefited not only her beloved son but also the slave in question, whether she even seriously considered the idea—she opted not to buy Ned, and she and her son never saw him again.[70]

THE WIDENING GULF among Christians over slavery represented both a theological and a moral crisis. Recent work by historians has emphasized the theological dimension of debates over slaveholding. Based on the writings of clergymen in the United States and abroad, Mark A. Noll has argued that theological disputes over biblical interpretations of slavery were central to the way Americans understood the Civil War. This argument highlights the contemporary discourse of male religious leaders but fails to consider the way schoolrooms as well as churches framed moral lessons. Women who had taught in academies and the higher grades of common schools were very familiar with the lessons on slavery in their moral philosophy textbooks. Harriet Beecher Stowe, who had studied William Paley's moral philosophy text at Litchfield Female Academy and later worked as a teacher with her sister, Catharine Beecher, characterized the problem of slavery as both "a moral and religious question." Susan Nye Hutchison would have agreed with this perspective.[71]

To some Americans, the acrimonious disagreements over emancipation and the division in the churches foreshadowed an inevitable divide in the nation as a whole. Susan referred to the deepening divisions among Christians as the breaking of a "strong fraternal bond." More than a decade later, South Carolina's John C. Calhoun used a similar phrase, describing the bonds within and among the Protestant denominations as "cords that bind." In 1850, in his last speech before the U.S. Congress, Calhoun proclaimed, "The ties which held each denomination together formed a strong cord to hold the whole Union together; but, powerful as they were, they have not been able to resist the explosive effect of slavery agitation." The influence of this growing regional divide is reflected in the migration patterns of northern teachers who came south. Antebellum northerners who went south to teach generally remained in the region for a shorter period than their counterparts who went west. Evidence from teachers' diaries and correspondence from the 1840s and 1850s suggests that slavery played a role in this phenomenon.[72]

Despite her long years in the region, Susan Nye Hutchison did not remain in the South. The year 1845 marked a watershed in her life. She started a new job as principal at Concord Academy, and her oldest two sons, Sylvanus and Ebenezer, graduated from Davidson College at the top of their class after entering three years earlier at ages seventeen and fifteen, respectively. She achieved a long-standing goal and reunited all four of her boys in North Carolina when her youngest son, thirteen-year-old John, came down from New York and enrolled at Davidson. Nevertheless, at some point between 1847 and 1848, Susan returned to New York with her son Adam Alexander, settled down close to the Nye farm, and rejoined the New School Presbyterian congregation in Amenia. Perhaps it had simply become too difficult to teach any longer as an emancipationist in the South, impossible to say the words aloud: "But still slavery is a great evil."[73]

Conclusion

After around thirty years in the South, Susan Nye Hutchison came full circle, returning north to a relatively simple and modest rural life in South Amenia. She lived for twenty-six years after her last extant journal entry. Given her proclivity as a writer, it seems reasonable to believe she continued to record brief notes and reflections on the ebb and flow of her daily life. After all, she had once urged her former student Sarah Frew Davidson to "let every day see *something* written." But if she did leave additional writings, the originals have been lost. Susan may have continued to teach school after returning north: her home and the nearby schoolhouse appear on an 1876 map of South Amenia.[1]

Financially, she was very comfortable. Over the years, she had loaned significant sums of money to her siblings, and she came to hold a mortgage against their share of the family farm. Probably as a result, her sons inherited the farm after the death of her brother Meletiah. At some point Susan purchased a home not far from the Nye farmhouse. She left that house to her sons with the stipulation that her "beloved sister Amanda" would have the use of it during her lifetime, and she directed her executor to pay all of Amanda's debts.[2]

Susan's oldest son, Sylvanus, received a law degree from Davidson College and practiced law for several years in Charlotte before he, too, moved back to Amenia, where he farmed and taught in the little schoolhouse. He later became an elder in Amenia's New School Presbyterian Church. His younger brother Ebenezer studied medicine at the University of Pennsylvania in Philadelphia, graduating in 1848, the same year Adam Alexander died. Two years later, Susan's youngest son, John, was living on the Nye farm.[3]

But all of Susan's sons did not stay in the North. Ebenezer was the first to return to North Carolina, marrying and settling down in Charlotte, where he worked as a doctor, served as a trustee of Davidson College, and became very involved in the affairs of the Old School Presbyterian Church. John followed at the end of 1851. Both Hutchisons were living in the South when the Civil War began.[4]

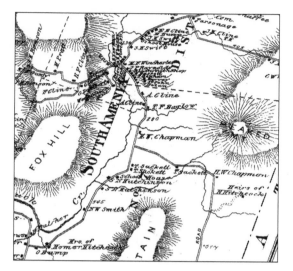

Map excerpt showing the Nye farmhouse and Susan Nye Hutchison's house and school in South Amenia, New York, 1876. Courtesy of Elizabeth Strauss, Amenia Historical Society, Amenia, New York.

There is no evidence to indicate what effect the Civil War had on relationships within the Hutchison family. Scattered evidence provides only brief glimpses of her surviving three sons' later lives. Ebenezer remained in Charlotte until his death sometime after 1880, while Sylvanus remained in the North until he died in 1910. In 1864, John headed west to California, where he found work as a bridge builder. Despite the great distances separating them, all three apparently kept in touch with Susan: "I would acknowledge that one of the sweetest drops in my cup of life has been the thought that my children loved so dearly their old mother," she wrote in her will. "May God's richest blessing rest upon them all."[5]

DURING HER LAST dozen years in North Carolina, Susan Nye Hutchison lifted her family from the brink of poverty and significantly advanced her career. In terms of salary and influence, her position as head of a respected female academy was as close to equity as any woman could achieve in any field or occupation in antebellum society. No woman educator in the South rose higher before midcentury. Earning a living while supporting a family and trying to establish a business—many aspects of Susan's life would seem familiar to twenty-first-century working women. Yet she lived in a very different era. She came of age during the Second Great Awakening, and the significance of her story must be understood in the context of that period.

Some historians have interpreted the Second Great Awakening as a conservative backlash against the radicalism of the American Revolution;

others have emphasized the liberal influence of the British Enlightenment in the work of evangelical social reformers. Scholars have drawn a variety of generalizations about that era, characterizing it as an expression of the American frontier, a response to industrialization, a democratizing movement, or an organizing process. However, it is likely that many "awakenings" occurred, each shaped by the cultural context of a specific time and place. The religious revivals at Connecticut's Yale College and Litchfield Female Academy probably bore little resemblance to populist revivals in southern cane fields. Depending on the minister, congregations might or might not have encountered the liberal ideas of the British Enlightenment in sermons; depending on the school or the teacher, students might or might not have come across such ideas in their lessons.

In its various manifestations, the Second Great Awakening left a number of important legacies in American society. First, the churches of that era created meaningful social and community networks that functioned somewhat like kinship groups, creating bonds among people separated by enormous distances. The bonding and bridging among the churches mobilized people and financial capital for a wide range of reform projects, and that reform impulse—in a more secular guise—continued into the Progressive Era.

This bonding and bridging was particularly important for women, as Susan's experience illustrates. Collaborative relationships among evangelical churches ensured that she always found a warm welcome wherever she traveled. In earlier years, the close bonds within the Presbyterian community in Augusta, Georgia, provided her with an extensive support network and facilitated her separation from an abusive husband. During her later years in North Carolina, the relationships she had developed as a devout Christian educator allowed her to draw prospective students from families that hoped to see their daughters not only learn academic subjects and social skills but also experience religious conversion and spiritual growth. The social capital developed through these networks had both psychic and monetary value. Friendships formed within churches provided emotional support during trying times as well as financial support in the form of school enrollments. Susan's agreement to educate the Morrisons' daughters in exchange for the college education of her sons illustrates the financial benefits that could accrue from this kind of social capital.

The social networks created in the antebellum churches were also important to African Americans, free and slave, and feared by white slaveholders for the potential to facilitate organization and insurrection. The tragic irony of the Second Great Awakening is that leaders in all three major denominations—Methodists, Baptists, and Presbyterians—supported the abolition of slavery just after the American Revolution but abandoned those positions in the face of slaveholders' hostility, in some cases justifying this reversal on the grounds that it represented the only way to evangelize the slaves. Slaves converted by the thousands only to see their marriages disregarded, their families divided, and their independent congregations and preachers forbidden. Susan's journal provides glimpses of these developments, but she may never have witnessed the underground gatherings of worshippers that must have continued after the mid-1830s, sustaining community in hidden places until it could emerge after the Civil War.

Arguably the most important legacy of the Second Great Awakening was the country's educational transformation. Both liberal Protestants and evangelicals emphasized education's importance in teaching young people about God and improving American society. The confluence of these ideas is evident in the evolving, increasingly rigorous course of study in the Female Department of Raleigh Academy and in the courses of study in the female schools Susan later established in Georgia and North Carolina. The close integration of churches and schools helped the spread of education across the country, and the United States came to lead the Western world in educating females.[6]

The education of women has profound implications for the social welfare of a nation's children. Evidence from developing nations reveals that regardless of ethnicity or culture, women tend to invest their resources in ways different from those of men, prioritizing their children's welfare and education. Susan's effort to provide for the education of her sons is an example of this phenomenon.[7]

During the Second Great Awakening, women gained unprecedented access to teaching in the higher grades of common schools and in academies. Females may have been prohibited from the pulpit, but Protestant ministers universally endorsed the idea of women's involvement in benevolent work and teaching. As a result, by the mid-nineteenth century, women had begun to replace men in what had been a male occupation throughout the colonial period.[8]

It is not a coincidence that many of the women who sought to influence Americans' thinking about education and slavery had been teachers. Education provided Emma Willard, Maria Stewart, Angelina Grimké,

Catharine Beecher, Harriet Beecher Stowe, Susan Nye Hutchison, and others with the skills necessary to write and speak effectively in public. Their work as teachers carried them further, allowing them to achieve financial independence, assume positions of relative authority in their communities, voice their opinions in public forums, and write about social and political issues. Such women certainly constituted only a tiny minority; nevertheless, their leadership in benevolent societies and schools and their publications were significant as models for others. The prospect of meaningful work, a comfortable income, and an independent life could motivate others to pursue education and become involved in teaching and social reform. In fact, Susan's journals indicate that she was inspired by the example of other female educators and that she in turn motivated some of the young southern women who were her students or worked as teaching assistants in her schools to become principals of female academies. By the time Susan returned north for the last time, her longtime friend Arabella Bosworth had become the head of New York's Poughkeepsie Female Academy, and Emma Baker, Susan's former teaching assistant from South Carolina, had become the principal of North Carolina's Lenoir Female Academy.[9]

One of the most compelling aspects of Susan's story is her evolution from modest and retiring young teacher to mature and ambitious career woman. Historians have rarely credited antebellum women with career ambitions. Yet based on her journals, she appears to have been far more ambitious and entrepreneurial than her husband or brothers. It took ambition and resolve to leave Raleigh Academy and establish her own school in Georgia, to leave her children in Amenia and return to teaching in the South, to ask for support from wealthy North Carolinians to incorporate a female academy, and to publish her ideas in national journals. She strove to increase her earnings, support her family, educate her children, and rise to a position of social influence. She invested her money in educating her sons and in loans to family members, investments that eventually translated into her sons' success in life. And although Susan often complained in her journals about the difficulties involved in running a school, she derived professional satisfaction from the respect accorded her by parents and community members.

Like all ambitious women of her time, she faced social and cultural constraints. There were limitations to how far a woman could rise in education. Male principals had far greater access to churches' financial resources. When female colleges began to open, only men were hired to lead them. The glass ceiling in higher education established by the mid-1840s endured for more than a century.

In her quest to achieve her goals, Susan sometimes conformed to social conventions and sometimes resisted. Historians have identified the 1820s and 1830s as a period featuring a Cult of Domesticity that idealized women's roles as wives and mothers. In their analysis of the messages in women's magazines and published sermons, scholars have sometimes come close to suggesting that the ideology in published media accurately reflected educated women's lived experience. However, prescriptive messages never mapped particularly well onto individual women's behavior. As when Adam Hutchison faced bankruptcy, economic factors could lead men and women to ignore prescriptive messages about women's work outside the home. How far an individual could transgress the social conventions reflected in contemporary literature depended on the way local communities perceived and acted on those transgressions.

Susan was mindful of the way the local community sometimes monitored her every move, and she both accommodated and resisted social conventions and laws. Whether visiting a prostitute in a brothel or a prisoner in jail, hosting an independent black congregation in her kitchen, managing her children in church, or taking her students to worship on Sundays, her behavior was perpetually subject to scrutiny and possible censure. She knew that transgressing social boundaries could trigger criticism that might damage her career and hurt her family financially, and so she conformed when she felt that doing so was necessary—for example, when she and her husband stopped hosting an independent black congregation that had met in her kitchen, and when she stopped praying with slaves on southern streets. At other times, she resisted, continuing occasionally to visit and pray with slaves in the privacy of their homes and teaching a group of slaves to read.

As an educator, Susan used the ideology of domesticity to strategic effect. She addressed her published essays to other women even as she advanced arguments directed to both sexes. When she claimed to provide "maternal" rather than "paternal" authority over her schools, she used the language of women's separate sphere to justify her leadership of an all-female school. This sort of rhetorical strategy became commonplace in education. Regardless of its power over individual behavior in specific local contexts, the ideology of domesticity did not prevent women from taking up teaching positions in academies and the higher grades of common schools. In later decades, male and female common school reformers leveraged this ideology to justify the movement of women into positions long held by men. By midcentury, state school superintendents in both North and South were interested in staffing their public schools with women, who earned less than men. North Carolina's Calvin Wiley, Connecticut's Henry Barnard, Massachusetts's Horace Mann, and other common school reformers used the language of domesticity to argue that maternal attributes made women especially qualified to teach. Such arguments appear to have helped—by 1900, 55 percent of the public school teachers in the South were women; in New England, that figure was 89 percent. During this time, the gap between men's and women's wages narrowed. Although some historians have claimed that the rhetoric of domesticity led antebellum schools to create differentiated courses of study for females centered on the domestic arts, evidence from published courses of study does not bear out this contention. The large majority of teachers continued to add traditionally male subjects to the female curriculum throughout the antebellum period, with the result that more women were prepared to enter colleges and universities during later decades.[10]

Teachers like Susan Nye Hutchison played an important role in U.S. history, contributing to the expansion of education and the evangelism of the South. In 1815, when she first headed south, less than one-fifth of all southern whites older than sixteen and less than one-tenth of all slaves and free blacks were members of Baptist, Methodist, or Presbyterian churches. Over the next few decades, the number of churches in all regions of the country increased exponentially. The number of schools increased as well, providing instruction in Christian religion along with other subjects. As a result, by the mid-nineteenth century, a majority of southern whites and a growing number of free and enslaved blacks identified as Christians. More than a century after Susan's death in 1867, more than three-quarters of U.S. adults professed a belief in God, making the United States the most religious industrialized nation in the Western world.[11]

The missionary impulse of that era galvanized some American Christians not only to convert and reform their own communities but also to evangelize in other lands. This legacy is evident not only in the pages of Susan's journal but also in the lives of her descendants. Her children and grandchildren became ministers, missionaries, and teachers. Her niece Sarah Louisa Nye, who taught at Susan's Salisbury Academy, eventually established a female school of her own. In 1859, Sylvanus Nye Hutchison fulfilled his mother's long-held wish by enrolling at Princeton Theological

Seminary to train as a Presbyterian minister. After the Civil War, Sylvanus served congregations in Salt Point and Pleasant Plains, New York, before moving to Belvidere, New Jersey. According to his obituary, "Two of his sons are Presbyterian ministers, both now in the Southern Church. The other son and two daughters are influential teachers." One of Susan's grandsons, William E. Hutchison, headed Alabama's Stillman Institute, a Presbyterian school devoted to training African American ministers. Fulfilling one of Susan's long-standing dreams, two of her granddaughters served for a time as missionaries in India.[12]

As Susan's journals illustrate, the zeitgeist of the Second Great Awakening comprised far more than revivals. That era was distinctive in its focus on the way Christians should live in society. The moment of conversion during revival represented the moment of commitment and initiation. The all-important piece that followed was nothing less than an ongoing reaffirmation of a commitment to live justly and righteously in the world. It was often—as Susan sometimes attested—a terrible struggle. She held fast to many of the precepts of the British Enlightenment: a belief in the evils of slavery and in human equality before God, regardless of race; a belief that both men and women were called to reform society and save the world. She strove to balance the dictates of her conscience with her desire to conform to social conventions and her need to support herself and her family. Doing so was never easy, and she did not always color inside the lines society laid out for her.

The struggle over emancipation and abolition undermined one of the long-standing theories in Christian moral philosophy, the belief that the spread of Christianity would usher in a world without slavery. The division of the major Protestant churches portended another sort of metamorphosis: the creation of two Christian nations, one committed to the gradual abolition of slavery and one committed to a slaveholding society. When the Civil War began, the Union and Confederate armies were the most religious in American history because soldiers on both sides were heirs of the Second Great Awakening. On both sides, men read their Bibles and fervently prayed that God would bless their cause before they went forth on the fields of battle and slaughtered one another.[13]

After the Civil War, the social influence of the churches diminished as American culture became more secular. The close relationship that had existed between the preacher's pulpit and the schoolteacher's lectern gradually disappeared. As public school systems spread from coast to coast, squabbling over religious belief and practice erupted in many communities, and schools began to divest themselves of religious influence. While the religious training of children remained the private responsibility of church and family, public school districts gradually eliminated Bible readings and prayer, becoming secular institutions by the second decade of the twentieth century. Americans lost faith that institutional religion could solve deep-seated social problems and unify the country. The churches had utterly failed to solve the problem of slavery, the greatest moral and political issue of that age. To resolve social problems in their communities, men and women increasingly turned to their local, state, and national governments.[14]

In her journals, Susan struggled with the moral dilemmas of her era, often aware of her own shortcomings. As a young single woman, she aspired to make a difference in the world. She felt called to a life of virtue, benevolence, and usefulness. It was an enormously challenging task that became even more daunting after she married and then became a widow with an extended family to support. She often weighed her thoughts, desires, and actions against the precept to live a virtuous life in service to others, and she frequently found herself wanting. As she put it one day in 1839 after spending some time reading the Bible and the memoirs of George Whitfield, "Alas how useless in the Vineyard of the Lord I have been."[15]

Although modern readers might have difficulty identifying with Susan's intense piety and self-criticism, many would empathize with her struggle to advance her career. She was an ambitious woman in an age when women were expected to exhibit modesty and reticence and leave worldly strivings to men. To a surprising degree, we live with the consequences of that era still. As a number of writers have pointed out, many twenty-first-century men and women—much like their nineteenth-century predecessors—do not perceive ambition as a positive character trait in women.[16]

Yet Susan Nye Hutchison's story illustrates the positive outcomes that can accrue when both sexes contribute fully to society. Although full economic and social equality with men was not possible during her lifetime, the ambition that drove her to achieve so much provided benefits in the form of education not only for her own family but also for her students and the slaves she taught in secret. Long after her death in 1867, some southerners remembered her. In 1883, a writer reminisced about his youth in Salisbury and about the town's "female school, managed by a pious and educated lady from New York, Mrs. Susan Nye Hutchison, who taught as fair and lovely a set of girls from Rowan and adjoining counties as ever graced a school room." Reporting her death, the *North Carolina*

Presbyterian stated, "Though many years have elapsed since she left North Carolina, the memory of her many excellences lingers still with those who knew her. Many of the mothers and grandmothers of North Carolina were educated by her, and had something of her own character impressed upon them. Intellectually and morally, she was one of a thousand, and perhaps no one is better remembered, after a long separation, by those who knew her."[17]

Whether through teaching, voluntarism, or acts of benevolence, some nineteenth-century individuals earned the respect of their communities and descendants, a respect marked by an Old Testament phrase that appears on their gravestones. Today it is possible to drive north from New York City along the Hudson River to Poughkeepsie, reversing the route Susan took by water on her first journey south. From Poughkeepsie, the road winds east toward South Amenia through farmland, meadows, woodlands, and small towns. The little graveyard where she lies buried is just up the road from the site of her old schoolhouse. Her simple gravestone is small and sits level with the grass, so overgrown with lichen that it is difficult to make out the inscription below her name. Still, when sunlight falls from the right angle, the phrase becomes clear: *The Righteous Live in Everlasting Remembrance.*[18]

Notes

ABBREVIATIONS

ACGA   *Augusta Chronicle and Georgia Advertiser*

CW   *Carolina Watchman*

GC   *Georgia Courier*

NCSA   Charles L. Coon, ed., *North Carolina Schools and Academies, 1790–1840: A Documentary History* (Raleigh, N.C.: Edwards and Broughton, 1915)

PHS   Presbyterian Historical Society, Philadelphia

RR   *Raleigh Register*

SHC   Southern Historical Collection, Wilson Library, University of North Carolina at Chapel Hill

SM   Session Minutes, First Presbyterian Church of Augusta, Georgia, Records, Presbyterian Historical Society, Philadelphia

SNHJ   Susan Davis Nye Hutchison Journals, Southern Historical Collection, Wilson Library, University of North Carolina at Chapel Hill; North Carolina State Archives, Raleigh

INTRODUCTION

1. SNHJ, September 30, 1833.

2. For factors that led impoverished women to send away their children to family members or to orphanages, see John E. Murray, *Charleston Orphan House*, 1–12.

3. Recent popular books on the importance of women's career ambitions include Sandberg, *Lean In*; Fels, *Necessary Dreams*. For research on negative attitudes toward ambitious women, see the extensive notes to *Lean In*; Rudman and Glick, "Prescriptive Gender Stereotypes"; Phelan and Rudman, "Prejudice toward Female Leaders."

4. "Chemistry Experiments Praised," *RR*, November 10, 1815.

5. Dexter, *Colonial Women of Affairs*. For studies that focus on women's exclusion from antebellum party politics, see Baker, "Domestication of Politics"; Ryan, *Women in Public*, 135–38; McGerr, "Political Style and Women's Power," 866–67. For studies exploring declension in women's access to political equality with men, see Zagarri, *Revolutionary Backlash*. Also see Klinghoffer and Elkis, "'Petticoat

Electors'"; Kerber, *No Constitutional Right*; Zagarri, "Rights of Man and Woman." For studies exploring a backlash against women's public preaching, see Brekus, *Strangers and Pilgrims*; Juster, *Disorderly Women*. For a backlash against women's public speaking in general, see Eastman, *Nation of Speechifiers*, 78.

6. Welter, *Dimity Convictions*; Cott, *Bonds of Womanhood*, 96; Ryan, *Cradle of the Middle Class*, 142; Lebsock, *Free Women of Petersburg*, xv. In *Mere Equals*, McMahon defines "mere equality" as a concept emphasizing women's sexual difference from men while allowing for some degree of social and intellectual equality between the sexes. McMahon concludes that an ideology of domesticity was in full force by 1830.

7. For Virginia women's greater legal autonomy during this period, see Lebsock, *Free Women of Petersburg*. For women's entry into wage work in the Northeast, see Goldin and Sokoloff, "Women, Children, and Industrialization." Also see Kessler-Harris, *Out to Work*, 20–74. For women's increasing civil engagement, see Ryan, *Women in Public*. For the role of education in women's civil engagement, see Kelley, *Learning to Stand and Speak*. Kelley argues that the antebellum rhetoric of domesticity bore little resemblance to the reality of most women's lived experience (22–27). Also see Kelley, "Need of Their Genius"; Gould, "Civil Society." For women's increasing benevolent work, see Ginzberg, *Women and the Work of Benevolence*. For the emergence of women's social activism and politics, see Boylan, *Origins of Women's Activism*. For the rise of women's political engagement and interest in partisan politics, see Lasser and Robertson, *Antebellum Women*; Zboray and Zboray, *Voices without Votes*. For southern women's involvement in partisan politics, see Varon, "Tippecanoe and the Ladies, Too." For women's increasing access to traditionally male school subjects, see Margaret A. Nash, *Women's Education*; Farnham, *Education of the Southern Belle*. For the rise of women among common school and academy teachers, see Perlmann and Margo, *Women's Work?* Also see Kaestle, *Pillars of the Republic*, 123–27. For comparative analysis of the wage structure in common schools and academies and the emerging career ladder for women in education, see Tolley and Beadie, "Socioeconomic Incentives."

8. For example, Kelley briefly refers to the journals to note Susan's activities as a reader and essay writer (*Learning to Stand and Speak*, 264–65). The editors of Sarah Frew Davidson's 1837 journal included a page-long biographical sketch of Susan's life, describing her journals as devoted primarily to education and religious matters along with "daily trivia . . . personal and family struggles, a difficult marriage, and exhausting and often dangerous travel" (*Life in Antebellum Charlotte*, 128–29). Farnham, *Education of the Southern Belle*, devotes ten pages to discussion of Susan's culture shock upon moving to the South, her evangelical piety, her financial difficulties, and the conflicts in her marriage (74–76, 79, 99–103, 168, 169–70). To date, the most extensive treatment of Susan's life is Tolley and Nash, "Leaving Home to Teach."

9. Farnham, *Education of the Southern Belle*, 97–119. Farnham devotes several chapters to antebellum female teachers working in southern schools. Her work is the most extensive to date, and although most of her sources are from the 1840s and 1850s, she provides thumbnail descriptions of a number of earlier women teachers, including Susan Nye Hutchison. Suzanne Lebsock devotes four pages to the twenty free women who conducted their own schools in Petersburg, Virginia, from 1784 to 1820, concluding that school teaching was a serious business for women

during that time (*Free Women of Petersburg*, 172–76). For an introductory overview of academy teaching using some of Hutchison's diary entries as a case study, see Tolley and Nash, "Leaving Home to Teach." A number of important studies have explored women who taught in the West, although most of the primary sources are from after 1835. See Kaufman, *Women Teachers*; Myers, *Westering Women*; Weiler, *Country Schoolwomen*. For the way contemporary gender ideology often justified nineteenth-century women's work in teaching, particularly in the New England common schools, see Clifford, "Man/Woman/Teacher." Also see Nancy Hoffman, *Woman's "True" Profession*.

10. Fox-Genovese, *Within the Plantation Household*, 46. Fox-Genovese cites only one primary source for this claim, the Meta Morris Grimball Journal. Unfortunately, this idea has persisted in the secondary literature. For example, Farnham makes the same claim in *Education of the Southern Belle*, 166, without citing any primary sources. Bryant's entry in volume 20 of the 2012 *New Encyclopedia of Southern Culture* reiterates the conclusion that teaching was "marginally respectable" ("Women, White, Working Class"). For statistics on the numbers of southern slaveholders, see Hahn, *Southern Populism*, 42. For analysis of the relatively high wages afforded female common school and academy teachers, see Tolley and Beadie, "Socioeconomic Incentives." For studies that present evidence of southern women's positive views of teaching, see Jabour, *Scarlett's Sisters*, 61–64, 104–8; Lebsock, *Free Women of Petersburg*, 172–77.

11. See Elizabeth Alden Green, *Mary Lyon*; Lutz, *Emma Willard*; Sklar, *Catharine Beecher*. Beecher and to some extent Willard and Phelps advocated a curriculum for females centered on the domestic tasks of the household. However, before the Civil War, the large majority of private female schools and common schools did not follow this recommendation. For discussion of scholarly debates in curriculum history and analysis of the curriculum in antebellum female schools, see Kim Tolley, *Science Education*, 55–74.

12. Beadie, *Education and the Creation of Capital*, 12–13. Beadie has characterized the Second Great Awakening as an educational movement and an organizing process. Mathews, "Second Great Awakening," argues that the primary difference between the revivals of the First Great Awakening of the colonial period and the Second Great Awakening was their social function. According to Mathews, the Second Great Awakening was both highly local and broadly national in purpose and scope, integrating smaller diverse religious communities into American society at large.

13. Hatch, *Democratization*, interprets the movement as an inevitable outgrowth of the radicalism and social egalitarianism arising from the revolution. Boles, *Religion in Antebellum Kentucky*, explains the widespread appeal of evangelical religion by pointing to its emphasis on the equality of all humans before God. Also see Mathews, *Religion in the Old South*. For an interpretation connecting evangelicalism and the British Enlightenment, see Forbes, "Slavery and the Evangelical Enlightenment." For the evangelism of the early antebellum South, see Najar, *Evangelizing the South*. Butler, *Awash in a Sea of Faith*, argues that as the state's authority in religion declined after the American Revolution, denominational authority expanded, but not as a result of grassroots initiative; instead, denominational leaders strategically

grew their membership to compete with other denominations. Porterfield, *Conceived in Doubt*, further develops this argument, characterizing denominational expansion as authoritarian and reactionary. Also see Heyrman, *Southern Cross*; Noll, *Civil War as a Theological Crisis* (analyzing the theological debates that divided northern and southern clergymen on the eve of the Civil War).

14. This idea builds on the argument in Beadie, *Education and the Creation of Capital*, 72–88. Historians interested in the development of social capital have used the terms "bonding relationships" and "bridging relationships," which may have been coined by Gittell and Vidal in *Community Organizing*. See Putnam and Feldstein, *Better Together*, 34–55; Odom-Reed, *Bonding and Bridging*; Lancee, *Immigrant Performance*.

15. See Bunkers and Huff, *Inscribing the Daily*; Olney, *Autobiography*.

16. Ulrich, *Midwife's Tale*; Van Dyke, *To Read My Heart*. For the role of schools in assigning journal writing to female students, see Blauvelt, "'This Altogather Precious tho Wholy Worthless Book,'" 128; Kerber, *Women of the Republic*, 214; Kelley, "Crafting Subjectivities," 63–64.

17. SNHJ, December 9, 13, 1840.

18. Ibid., August 13, 1815, June 2, 1839.

19. Ibid., April 3, 1829.

20. Reproduced from the transcription prepared by Robert S. Hutchison in 1938. Susan often ended entries with a dash, likely because she planned to return to her journal and write a bit more.

21. SNHJ, March 28, 1833.

22. After preparing his transcription, Robert S. Hutchison returned the original journals to the family member who had loaned them to him, and they were subsequently lost. Dr. Richard H. Marks, Susan Nye Hutchison's great-great-grandson, has family letters written between April 3, 1961, and September 24, 1962, mostly by or to Margaret Hutchison Rennie and Robert S. Hutchison, documenting the unsuccessful search for the missing journals. Marks also possesses photocopies of entries Susan recorded in her *Annual Pocket Remembrancer: For the Year 1818*, along with a sample of entries from 1821 and a typewritten transcript, prepared by Robert S. Hutchison, of a handful of extracts from Susan's last journal, which apparently ran from 1846 until just after 1864. In a document sent to family members in 1968, Robert S. Hutchison explained that he had never possessed the original last journal; he transcribed the brief document from a photocopy. Apparently, most of the entries were illegible. The photocopy of the original last journal also has been lost.

23. Joyner, *Shared Traditions*, 1. For a critical discussion of microhistory, see Magnússon and Szijártó, *What Is Microhistory?* Andrew Abbott's presidential address is in Abbott, "Historicality of Individuals."

24. Perlmann and Margo, *Women's Work?*, 46–49.

CHAPTER 1

1. SNHJ, April 22, 1815.

2. Henry Adams, *History*, 14.

3. SNHJ, April 22, 1815.

4. Stewart, "Barlow Records," 105–6; Reed, *Early History*; "Barlow, Bristol, Fiser/ Fizer, Fish, Mickle, Morse," http://awt.ancestry.com (accessed March 17, 2002).

5. Quinn, "Amenia"; Dwight, *Travels*, 505; Spafford, *Gazetteer*, 123–24.

6. Mann, *Few Thoughts*, 57. For the increase of females in town schools, see Sklar, "Schooling of Girls." Also see Vinovskis and Bernard, *Women in Education*. For the increase in coeducation, see Tyack and Hansot, *Learning Together*.

7. See Beadie, "Tuition Funding." Also see Kaestle, *Pillars of the Republic*; Kaestle, "Common Schools"; Kaestle and Vinovskis, *Education and Social Change*. For the economics of common schooling in the Northeast, see Go and Lindert, "Uneven Rise." For academies, see Sizer, *Age of the Academies*; Beadie and Tolley, *Chartered Schools*, 3–43; Beadie, "Internal Improvement"; Beadie, "Emma Willard's Idea"; Opal, "Exciting Emulation"; George Frederick Miller, *Academy System*.

8. "Record of the Last Will and Testament of Silvanus Nye," recorded December 12, 1844, Dutchess County, New York County Surrogate Court.

9. For parents' motivations for educating their children, see Appleby, "Social Consequences." Also see Kerns, "Antebellum Higher Education," 155–92. Kerns found that from 52.9 to 76.3 percent of students in her sample of New York academies came from farm families. For education in female academies, see Solomon, *In the Company of Educated Women*, 1–61; Margaret A. Nash, *Women's Education*; Beadie, "Internal Improvement"; Kelley, *Learning to Stand and Speak*; Towle, *Vicissitudes*, 18–19.

10. Susan never wrote about her own education, but she made two references to Litchfield. In 1818, during a visit back home, she noted the stage fare (three dollars) from Amenia to Litchfield, and two weeks later, after a visit to the town, she wrote, "At Litchfield rather inclined to fall into the sin of pride" (*Annual Pocket Remembrancer: For the Year 1818*, copy in the possession of Dr. Richard H. Marks of Greenville, North Carolina). Information about alumnae is from Litchfield Female Academy Enrollment Database, Litchfield Female Academy Archives, Litchfield, Connecticut; Vanderpoel, *Chronicles*, 22, 404, 407. For Bosworth, see "Lucy Sheldon—Her Diary," in Vanderpoel, *Chronicles*, 44. Bosworth is also listed in the Litchfield Enrollment Database. She taught in North Carolina for more than six years, in Raleigh Academy, Fayetteville Academy, and Oxford Academy (*NCSA*, 69, 133, 437). By 1833, Bosworth had returned to Poughkeepsie. She and Susan remained friends (SNHJ, November 28, 1829, November 16, 1833, September 10, 12, 1839).

11. "Amenia Presbyterian Church Congregation Minutes, 1749–1816," PHS; SNHJ, January 7, 1833.

12. Vanderpoel, *Chronicles*, 216, 218; Brickley, "Sarah Pierce's Litchfield Female Academy."

13. Lyman Beecher, *Autobiography*, 43; Bacon, *American Church History Series*, 231. For the rise of Enlightenment thought and radicalism during the revolution, see Gordon S. Wood, *Radicalism*; Cotlar, *Tom Paine's America*; Porter, *Creation*, 340–63. For the influence of this ideology on women's social roles, see Kerber, "Republican Mother"; Kerber, *Women of the Republic*; Zagarri, "Morals, Manners, and the Republican Mother"; Berkin, *Revolutionary Mothers*; McMahon, "'Of the Utmost Importance.'" For the resurgence of popular Christianity, see Gordon S. Wood,

Radicalism, 329–36. For the influence of the Second Great Awakening on women's education, see Porterfield, *Mary Lyon*; Sklar, "Founding of Mount Holyoke"; Sklar, *Catharine Beecher*; Boylan, *Sunday School,* 22–59; Kaestle, *Pillars of the Republic,* 30–61. Margaret A. Nash, "Rethinking Republican Motherhood," has documented a range of contemporary rationales, including both secular and religious justifications for female education. In *Women Teachers,* Kaufman has claimed that a mix of economic and missionary motives impelled women sponsored by the Board of National Popular Education, established in 1846, to go west to teach.

14. See Bacon, *American Church History Series*; Noll, *America's God*; Hatch, *Democratization*; Najar, *Evangelizing the South*; Isaac, *Transformation of Virginia.* Scholars have offered many different interpretations of the Second Great Awakening. In "The Significance of the Frontier in American History," Turner characterized the movement as a product of the American frontier. Other scholars have linked it to the Market Revolution and growing middle-class fears and anxieties. See Paul E. Johnson, *Shopkeeper's Millennium.* Ryan, *Cradle of the Middle Class,* places women at the center of religious revivals in Oneida County, New York, arguing that participation in the churches allowed middle-class women to regain some of the social authority they had lost as a result of the transition from a home-based to a market-based economy. Also see Cott, "Young Women."

15. Congregation Minutes, 1749–1816, Amenia Presbyterian Church, PHS. Historians disagree over the extent of lay involvement in the Second Great Awakening. Hatch, *Democratization of American Christianity,* emphasizes grassroots revivalism. For studies that depict the Second Great Awakening as the result of top-down efforts by denominational leaders, see Butler, *Awash in a Sea of Faith*; Porterfield, *Conceived in Doubt* (characterizing denominational expansion as authoritarian and reactionary).

16. Sarah Pierce, "Dialogue between Miss Trusty and Her Pupils," in Vanderpoel, *Chronicles,* 218. For the close connection of evangelicalism and the British Enlightenment during the early decades of the Second Great Awakening, see Forbes, "Slavery and the Evangelical Enlightenment." Also see Bacon, *American Church History Series*; Noll, *America's God*; Hatch, *Democratization*; Isaac, *Transformation of Virginia.*

17. Kelly, *In the New England Fashion,* 75. For the role of academies in developing middle-class social networks, see Beadie, "Internal Improvement"; Beadie, *Education and the Creation of Capital*; Brickley, "Sarah Pierce's Litchfield Female Academy," 323.

18. Vanderpoel, *Chronicles,* 215, 294; Hankins, *Second Great Awakening,* 135–36; Lyman Beecher, *Autobiography,* 183–255. Also see Keller, *Second Great Awakening.* Noll, *America's God,* 269–92, traces the spread of Dwight's legacy through his students.

19. Dwight, *Charitable Blessed,* 6, 23, 28.

20. Weber, *Protestant Ethic*; Beadie, "Internal Improvement"; Walbert, "'Endeavor to Improve Yourself'"; Carter, *Southern Single Blessedness.*

21. Emerson, *Female Education.* Also see Margaret A. Nash, *Women's Education,* 53–76; Kelley, *Learning to Stand and Speak.*

22. Ryan, *Cradle of the Middle Class*, 74–77; Kerber, *Women of the Republic*, 285–87; Freeman, "Religious Revival," 157.

23. Towle, *Vicissitudes*. See Baldwin, "Black Women"; Lindley, *"You Have Stept out of Your Place"*; Brekus, *Strangers and Pilgrims*. Also see Wessinger, *Religious Institutions*; Grammer, *Some Wild Visions*.

24. Freeman, "Religious Revival," 157; Finney, *Lectures on Revivals of Religion*, 239–40; Dee Andrews, *Methodists and Revolutionary America*, 102–3; Juster, *Disorderly Women*; Zagarri, *Revolutionary Backlash*. Zagarri finds that women were increasingly unwelcome in political culture at the turn of the century and that by the 1830s a conservative backlash had developed. Also see Eastman, *Nation of Speechifiers*. Eastman argues that by the 1830s, the notion of separate spheres was fully ascendant. For studies that consider the possibilities for gender equality within radical religious movements, see Porterfield, *Female Piety*; Reis, *Damned Women*.

25. For biographies of these early women preachers, see Towle, *Vicissitudes*; Lee, Elaw, and Foote, *Sisters of the Spirit*; Roberts, *Memoir*.

26. Catharine E. Beecher, *Essay on the Education of Female Teachers*, 266; Tolley and Nash, "Leaving Home to Teach," 165; *Essex Institute Historical Collections* 120 (1984): 234.

27. See Beadie, *Education and the Creation of Capital*, 72–88.

28. Tocqueville, *Democracy in America*, 1:306.

29. SNHJ, February 19, 1834; Demos, *Little Commonwealth*, 62–64.

30. Davis, Easterlin, and Parker, *American Economic Growth*, 24–26; Easterlin, "Factors"; Ryan, *Cradle of the Middle Class*, 55–56; Bishop, *History*, 179.

31. Bishop, *History*, 212, 250; Norton, *Liberty's Daughters*, 17–18; Goldin and Sokoloff, "Women, Children, and Industrialization"; Goldin, "Economic Status"; "Towns of Dutchess County (Population)," www.nyhistory.net (accessed May 9, 2002).

32. "A Female Teacher Wanted," *RR*, November 24, 1814; "Miss Bosworth and Mr. Edmondson Come to Academy," in *NCSA*, 37. Bosworth taught in North Carolina for at least six years (*NCSA*, 69, 133).

33. See Tolley and Beadie, "Socioeconomic Incentives," 44. Also see Perlmann and Margo, *Women's Work?*; Preston, "Domestic Ideology, School Reformers, and Female Teachers." For feminization among music teachers in the South, see Kim Tolley, "Music Teachers." For the number of female schools in North Carolina, see Connor, *North Carolina*, 441.

34. SNHJ, April 22, 1815; Reed, *Early History*, 141; Hallowell, *James and Lucretia Mott*.

35. SNHJ, April 23, 26–27, 1815.

36. Ibid., April 26, 1815.

37. Ibid., April 28, 1815.

38. Ibid., April 29, 30, 1815.

39. Ibid., May 2, 1815; Holland, *History*; Torres, *Historic Resource Study*.

40. SNHJ, May 2, 1815.

41. Ibid., May 2, 3, 1815.

42. Ibid., May 6, 1815.

43. Ibid.

44. Ibid., May 7, 9, 1815; Boles, *Black Southerners*, 157; Historical Census Browser, University of Virginia, Geospatial and Statistical Data Center, http://mapserver.lib.virginia.edu/ (accessed April 12, 2004); McManus, *History*.

45. SNHJ, May 9, 1815.

46. Ibid., May 12, 1815.

47. Ibid.; "Congregation Minutes, 1749–1816, Amenia Presbyterian Church," March 4, 1815, PHS; "Historical Sketch," 14, in "First Presbyterian Church, Raleigh, N.C., Church History, List of Communicants, etc. 1816–1963," PHS. For rules of dismissal, see Lincoln, *Civil Law and the Church*, 487.

48. SNHJ, May 12, 1815.

49. Ibid., May 15, 1815.

50. Ibid., July 9, 1815.

CHAPTER 2

1. See Margaret A. Nash, *Women's Education*. Also see Beadie and Tolley, *Chartered Schools*.

2. Solomon, *In the Company of Educated Women*, 15. For the influence of early republican thinking on northern women's higher education, see Kerber, *Women of the Republic*; Norton, *Liberty's Daughters*; Cott, *Bonds of Womanhood*, 101–25; McMahon, "'Of the Utmost Importance.'" For female academies in the Northeast, see Kelley, *Learning to Stand and Speak*. Also see Scott, "Ever Widening Circle"; Elizabeth Alden Green, *Mary Lyon*. For French schools in Philadelphia, see Kilbride, *American Aristocracy*, 53–77. For southern French schools, see Farnham, *Education of the Southern Belle*, 37–50. Also see Kim Tolley, "Significance of the 'French School.'"

3. Older histories focused primarily on the education of elite families. For depictions of southern academy education as primarily ornamental, see Scott, *Southern Lady*; Fox-Genovese, *Within the Plantation Household*, 256–59; Clinton, *Plantation Mistress*, 130–32; Farnham, *Education of the Southern Belle*.

4. Charles Coon's documentary study, which includes hundreds of full and partial newspaper articles about Raleigh Academy, was useful in this work, and the North Carolina State Archives contains the original newspapers on microfiche, making it possible to check the references and view complete articles in cases where Coon included only excerpts.

5. Battle, *Sketches*; Battle, *Early History*, 21–24.

6. Winifred Gales and Joseph Gales, "Reminiscences," 139, Gales Family Papers, SHC; SNHJ, July 15, 1815.

7. See announcements in *NCSA*, 146, 388–90.

8. See Sizer, *Age of the Academies*; Beadie and Tolley, *Chartered Schools*, 3–43; Kim Tolley, "Chartered School"; Farnham, *Education of the Southern Belle*; Clinton, *Plantation Mistress*, esp. preface. Coeducational academies educated males and females in separate departments. The earliest coeducational academy was North Carolina's New Bern Academy, chartered by the Colonial Assembly in 1766 (Gadski,

History). For the influence of the Enlightenment on American education, see Pangle and Pangle, *Learning of Liberty*.

9. Joseph Gales obituary, *Washington Daily National Intelligencer*, August 28, 1841; Powell, "Diary of Joseph Gales"; Armytage, "Editorial Experience"; Cotlar, "Joseph Gale"; Eaton, "Winifred and Joseph Gales"; Elliott, *Raleigh Register*; Kim Tolley, "Joseph Gales."

10. "Books," *RR*, November 12, 1799; *RR*, June 3, 1800; Winifred Gales and Joseph Gales, "Reminiscences," 140, Gales Family Papers, SHC.

11. SNHJ, June 2–9, 1815; Kelly, "Reading and the Problem of Accomplishment"; Waugh, *North Carolina's Capital*, 34; NCSA, 388–90.

12. For the course of study in Raleigh Academy's male and female departments, see advertisements in *NCSA*, 396–97, 409, 420–21. For comparison of the curriculum in male and female academies, see Kim Tolley, "Mapping the Landscape"; Kim Tolley, *Science Education of American Girls*, 35–94.

13. In 1807, families paid six dollars per quarter to enroll their sons in John Henry Gault's English Seminary ten miles outside of town. In contrast, in 1808, Raleigh Academy charged three dollars per quarter for reading and writing, four dollars for the branches of an English education, and five dollars for those who wanted to study the classics (*NCSA*, 390–91, 514–15; "Lancaster School," *RR*, April 1, 1814; "Raleigh Academy Examinations," *RR*, June 16, 1815). For Lancaster schools in the United States, see Kaestle, *Pillars of the Republic*, 41–42. Kaestle describes the Lancasterian system as the most widespread educational reform in the Western world during the period from 1800 to 1830.

14. SNHJ, June 2, 1815.

15. Ibid., June 9, 1815; Battle, *Early History*, 36.

16. SNHJ, June 9, 1815. For a history of public speaking practice in antebellum female academies, and the significance of this development in terms of women's political engagement, see Kelley, *Learning to Stand and Speak*; Kelley, "'Need of Their Genius.'" Also see Eastman, "Female Cicero." For the practice in Litchfield of men reading female students' graduation speeches, see Brickley, "Sarah Pierce's Litchfield Female Academy," 211.

17. SNHJ, June 9, 1815. I substituted the word "moving" for "pathetic" in the quotation. Nineteenth-century writers used the term "pathetic," derived from "pathos," to denote deep feeling, but this definition has fallen out of use.

18. SNHJ, May 15, 1815.

19. For the curriculum in Litchfield Female Academy, see Brickley, "Sarah Pierce's Litchfield Female Academy," 263–309. For the sciences in antebellum female and coeducational schools, see Warner, "Science Education"; Kim Tolley, *Science Education*, 1–75.

20. Catlow, *Observations*, 59–60; *NCSA*, 2, 18, 61; "From the National Intelligencer," *RR*, November 11, 1805.

21. "Public Examinations in Raleigh Academy," *RR*, June 30, 1806; "Examinations in Raleigh Academy," *RR*, June 4, 1807; "Examinations in Raleigh Academy," *RR*, November 26, 1807; *RR*, January 25, 1811, June 5, November 15, 1815.

22. "School Closing—Patronage, Lancaster Methods, Classes," in *NCSA*, 446–47.

23. "Raleigh Academy Examination and School Closing, June 1822," in ibid., 463–67.

24. Winifred Gales and Joseph Gales, "Reminiscences," 146, Gales Family Papers, SHC; *Laws of the Raleigh Academy*; "Classes and Subjects Taught," in *NCSA*, 464–67; William Gaston is listed as a trustee on 493.

25. Lindley Murray, *English Grammar*, 329; Lindley Murray, *Sequel*, 4, 49, 123.

26. Hedge, *Elements of Logick*, 129.

27. Barber, *Heyday of Natural History*, 21–26; *NCSA*, 421–22.

28. Morse, *Elements*, preface, v; Lindley Murray, *Sequel*, 39–40; SNHJ, August 5, 1834.

29. James Ferguson, *Easy Introduction*; Blair, *Grammar*, vol. 2.

30. Miles and Abrahams, "America's First Chemistry Syllabus-and-Course."

31. "Raleigh: The Semi-Annual Examination," *RR*, November 10, 1815; Kim Tolley, *Science Education*, 35–54.

32. For antebellum women's growing access to literacy, see Hackel and Kelly, *Reading Women*; Kerrison, *Claiming the Pen*; McMahon, *Mere Equals*. For the colonial period, see Monaghan, *Learning to Read and Write*; Lockridge, *Literacy in Colonial New England*. For women's published narratives during the First Great Awakening, see Brekus, *Sarah Osborn's World*, 177–88.

33. Marcet, *Conversations*, 199–200; Kim Tolley, *Science Education*, 62–64; Blair, *Grammar*, v.

34. "School Closing—Change of Teachers," in *NCSA*, 426; "Raleigh Academy," in *NCSA*, 456; "Course of Study in Senior Class," in *NCSA*, 458; Wesleyan Academy, *Catalogue*; Sheldon English and Classical School, *Annual Catalogue*; Mount Holyoke Female Seminary, *Tenth Annual Catalogue*, 12.

35. Norton, "Eighteenth-Century American Women"; Benjamin Franklin, *Autobiography*, 109; essays by Benjamin Rush and Noah Webster in *Essays on Education*, ed. Rudolph. For a history of numeracy, see Cohen, *Calculating People*. For discussion of mental discipline and mathematics, see Margaret A. Nash, *Women's Education*, 84–87. For analysis of antebellum mathematics education in female schools, see Kim Tolley, *Science Education*, 75–94.

36. Published results of examinations in Raleigh Academy's Female Department reveal that students studied bookkeeping in 1822 (*NCSA*, 466). For a survey of the fifty-three cipher books held in the Southern Historical Collection, see Doar, "Cipher Books."

37. Phelps, *Lectures*, 242–43; "Course of Study in Senior Class," in *NCSA*, 458.

38. Phelps, *Lectures*, 238; More, *Strictures*; Bennett, *Strictures*, 21; Furbish, *Some Remarks*, 20.

39. Cohen, *Calculating People*, 143; Fowler, "Educational Services," 133, 147, 147n; Catharine E. Beecher, "Hartford Female Seminary," 69–70; "Misses C. & M. Beecher," *American Mercury*, April 20, 1824.

40. "Miss Nye," *ACGA*, September 20, 1823. Geometry is included in the 1823 course of study of Susan Nye's school in Augusta.

41. "Raleigh Academy: Report of the Examination," *RR*, November 17, 1815; "Teachers for 1821," in *NCSA*, 458.

42. SNHJ, July 5, 1815; Ryan, *Cradle of the Middle Class*, 74–77. For the role of education in developing women's civil engagement, see Kelley, *Learning to Stand and Speak*. Also see Gould, "Civil Society."

43. SNHJ, June 29, 1815.

44. Ibid., May 26, July 1, 2, 18, 1815. In *Education of the Southern Belle*, Farnham described Susan's aversion to dining out on the Sabbath as a cultural difference between northerners and southerners. But in the Presbyterian churches, dining out on Sundays was viewed as a violation of the Sabbath in both regions of the country, and southern congregations disciplined erring members for these sorts of violations, as discussed in chapter 5. Also see Presbyterian Church in the U.S.A., *Constitution* (1806), 436–37.

45. SNHJ, July 3, 1815.

46. Ibid., June 14, July 6, 1815.

47. Ibid., June 1, 1815; Newell, *Memoirs*; Brumberg, *Mission for Life*, 82. Many such narratives appeared in print during this period. For female missionaries, see Ann White, "Counting the Cost"; Robert, *American Women*.

48. More, *Strictures*, 288; Presbyterian Church in the U.S.A., *Constitution* (1806), 437. For discussion of prescriptive literature for women during this period, see Romero, *Home Fronts*. For an overview of the historiography of "separate spheres," see Kerber, "Separate Spheres."

49. SNHJ, June 10, July 16, 1815.

50. Ibid., July 6, 19, 1815.

51. Ibid., July 22, 1815.

52. Ibid.

53. Beadie, *Education and the Creation of Capital*, 55–71. According to entries in Susan's *Annual Pocket Remembrancer: For the Year 1821* (photocopy in possession of Dr. Richard H. Marks, Greenville, North Carolina), she was elected a manager of the Benevolent Society on July 30, and in August of that year she wrote the annual report for the Raleigh Female Tract Society.

54. SNHJ, July 16, 1815; Walters, *American Reformers*, 21–38; Trollope, *Domestic Manners*, 57. For collaboration among evangelicals, see James W. Fraser, *Pedagogue*; Foster, *Errand of Mercy*; Timothy Lawrence Smith, *Revivalism and Social Reform*.

55. Asbury, *Journal*, 2:444; Battle, *Early History*, 64–65. For early Methodist revivals, see Wigger, *Taking Heaven*.

56. SNHJ, July 4, 16, 23, 28, August 5, 1815; "Historical Sketch," 14, First Presbyterian Church, Raleigh, North Carolina, Records, PHS.

57. *NCSA*, 454, 458, 460–61; "New Plan of Studies and Methods," *RR*, December 26, 1823; SNHJ, September 7, 1831, June 14, 1840.

58. Susan's journal never mentions her trip to Augusta; it is reconstructed here from later accounts of her travels and from Stuart, *Three Years*, 152–56. Also see Edward J. Cashin, *Story of Augusta*; Kilbride, *American Aristocracy*, 53–77; Farnham, *Education of the Southern Belle*, 38–43.

59. "Miss Nye," *ACGA*, September 20, 1823. Amanda's name never appeared in these advertisements, probably because she served as Susan's teaching assistant.

60. Edward J. Cashin, *Story of Augusta*, 30, 40, 50, 58; "Classical & English Seminary of Augusta," *ACGA*, June 16, 1824; Charles Grenville, "The Subscriber Respectfully Informs the Public That His School Will Open Again," *ACGA*, October 4, 1823; "A Teacher Wanted for the Lancasterian School," *ACGA*, June 16, 1824; B. B. Hopkins, "Select School for Young Ladies," *ACGA*, October 1, 1823; Julia Hayden, "Tuition," *ACGA*, October 9, 1824.

61. For a brief discussion of Susan's former students who became teachers, see chapter 6.

62. Newell, *Memoirs*, 220, uses nearly the same phrase, "being commended by the prayers of the multitudes," to describe the support and blessing missionaries received before they departed for foreign lands.

63. Finney, *Lectures on Revivals of Religion*, 75; SNHJ, July 16, 1815.

CHAPTER 3

1. Farnham, *Education of the Southern Belle*, 113–18. Farnham analyzed a sample of 134 Mount Holyoke alumnae who taught in the South and compared the results to those from a sample of alumnae who taught in the West.

2. "Death of Mrs. Hutchison," *North Carolina Presbyterian*, April 24, 1867. For a sample of recent studies analyzing contemporary perspectives on slavery and emancipation during the years Susan Nye lived in the South, see Ford, *Deliver Us from Evil*; David Brion Davis, *Problem of Slavery in the Age of Emancipation*; Freehling, *Road to Disunion*. For religious justifications of slavery, see Fox-Genovese and Genovese, "Divine Sanction." For the ideology of benevolent slaveholding, see Gallay, "Origins of Slaveholders' Paternalism"; Gallay, *Formation of a Planter Elite*; Young, *Domesticating Slavery*; Mark M. Smith, *Debating Slavery*, 16–30.

3. SNHJ, July 4, 1815.

4. Ibid.; "Law Intelligence: The State vs. John R. Cook, John Davis, Samuel Bailey, and Wm Heflin (Not Apprehended) on a Charge of Murdering a Negro Man Called Stephen, on the Property of Said Bailey," *Raleigh Star*, October 13, 1815. Also see Kirby, "Horrid Cruelty," 401; Lancaster, *Raleigh*, 140.

5. "Law Intelligence," *Raleigh Star*, October 13, 1815.

6. SNHJ, July 6, 1815.

7. Spafford, "Cruelty and Executive Clemency"; "Raleigh," *Raleigh Star*, October 27, 1815.

8. "Raleigh," *Raleigh Star*, October 27, 1815; Constant Reader, "Miscellany: For the Star," *Raleigh Star*, November 10, 1815.

9. Presbyterian Church in the U.S.A., General Assembly, *Extracts*, 17–18.

10. Ibid., 30. Also see Earl Thompson Jr., "Slavery and Presbyterianism." For similar debates among Methodists, see David Brion Davis, *Problem of Slavery in the Age of Revolution*, 42–47, 196–212. For debates among Baptists, see Najar, "'Meddling with Emancipation.'"

11. Presbyterian Church in the U.S.A., General Assembly, *Digest*, 341–42. See McKivigan, *War against Proslavery Religion*, 44–45. McKivigan notes that the Church's antislavery resolutions remained on the books but were never really enforced.

12. Budros, "Antislavery Movement."

13. Ibid.; Heyrman, *Southern Cross*, 92–93, 138–39.

14. Asbury, *Journal*, 1:495, 3:298. For manumission in the early republican period, see Berlin, *Slaves without Masters*; Bogger, *Free Blacks*; Dunn, "Black Society."

15. Polgar, "'To Raise Them'"; Winch, *Philadelphia's Black Elite*. Also see Newman, *Transformation*; Gary B. Nash and Soderlund, *Freedom by Degrees*; Shane White, *Somewhat More Independent*; Swan, "John Teasman."

16. See Mathews, *Religion in the Old South*, 152. For the colonization movement, see David Brion Davis, *Problem of Slavery in the Age of Emancipation*, 83–185. For black opposition to colonization schemes, see Gary B. Nash, *Forging Freedom*, 101–2, 227–46; Quarles, *Black Abolitionists*, 4–12; Winch, *Philadelphia's Black Elite*.

17. "Colonization Society," *RR*, May 27, 1825; *RR*, January 15, 1818; Joseph and Winifred Gales, "Recollections," North Carolina State Archives, Raleigh. During his years in North Carolina, Gales came to own slaves and view slavery as a necessary evil. For Gales's retreat from radicalism, see Cotlar, "Joseph Gales."

18. See Standenraus, *African Colonization Movement*. For black opposition to colonization schemes, see Gary B. Nash, *Forging Freedom*, 101–2, 227–46; Quarles, *Black Abolitionists*, 3–22. Also see Rhodes and Cary, *Black Press and Protest*, 9–14. The colonization movement, as represented by the ACS, encompassed a complex range of perspectives, as discussed in Burin, *Slavery and the Peculiar Solution*; David Brion Davis, *Problem of Slavery in the Age of Emancipation*, 167–85.

19. Wilson Smith, "William Paley's Theological Utilitarianism"; Susan Nye Hutchison, "Mrs. Hutchison's View," 11; "Female Academy," *Western Carolinian*, February 20, 1836.

20. Paley, *Principles* (1788), 160.

21. Ibid. (1824), 147–48.

22. Ibid., 147.

23. Thomas Jefferson to David Barrow, May 1815, in *Jeffersonian Cyclopedia*, 817; Bernstein, *Thomas Jefferson*, 39–41; Wilson Smith, "William Paley's Theological Utilitarianism." For adaptations of Paley's text designed specifically for use in New England common schools, see Paley, *Boston School Edition*; Paley, *Paley's Moral and Political Philosophy*. For an early northern pro-abolition text containing more than fifty references to Paley, see Parkhurst, *Elements of Moral Philosophy*.

24. Fowler, "Educational Services," 135; Mary Ann Cole to Daniel Cole, June 24, 1821, Chloe Cole to Daniel Hyde Cole, February 22, 1833, both available at http://www.clements.umich.edu/exhibits/online/womened/ColeTroyRead.html (accessed April 12, 2014); Sarah Pierce, "Address at the Close of School, October 29, 1818," in Vanderpoel, *Chronicles*, 178; Hedrick, *Harriet Beecher Stowe*, 26; Fields, *Life and Letters*, 29.

25. "Course of Study for Girls," in *NCSA*, 421; "Valuable English Books," *RR*, June 3, 1800; *Laws of the Raleigh Academy*, 14–15; *NCSA*, xxx, 582, 58, 247. See "Salisbury Female Academy," *CW*, April 16, 1836.

26. The first American edition came out in 1788. Based on my analysis of a sample of twenty-five American editions, I concluded that the chapter on slavery was

unchanged before 1828. See Kim Tolley, "Schoolroom Slavery"; Paley, *Moral Philosophy*, 3:72. For another text that included examination questions, see Paley, *Boston School Edition*.

27. Paley, *Moral Philosophy*, 165–66, 71–73. There is no way to know whether Susan Nye Hutchison ever used Judd's version of Paley's text.

28. See Wilson Smith, "William Paley's Theological Utilitarianism," 417; Paley, *Boston School Edition*, 149–53; Wayland, *Elements of Moral Science* (1835); Vaughn, "Teaching Moral Philosophy"; Jasper Adams, *Elements*, ix, 174, 175. I found no references to Paley's text in newspaper advertisements for North Carolina schools after 1838.

29. Vaughn, "Teaching Moral Philosophy"; Fox-Genovese and Genovese, *Mind of the Master Class*, 569–70; Rivers, *Elements*, xviii.

30. *Annual Pocket Remembrancer: For the Year 1818* and *Annual Pocket Remembrancer: For the Year 1821* (in which Susan notes several visits to "Mrs. Haywood's"), both in possession of Dr. Richard H. Marks, Greenville, North Carolina; Raleigh Female Tract Society, *Fourth Annual Report*; Raleigh Female Benevolent Society, *Revised Constitution*; Lane, *Narrative*.

31. SNHJ, June 7, July 7, 1815; Parish, *Slavery*, 84; Battle, *Early History*, 65. For evangelism among slaves, see Raboteau, *Slave Religion*.

32. Hawkins, *Lunsford Lane*, 289. For brief mentions of worship at the Methodist meetinghouse, see SNHJ, July 4, 6, 16, 1815.

33. Lane, *Narrative*, 6–7. Also see Cornelius, *When I Can Read*. For the efforts of slaves to teach each other, see Heather Andrea Williams, *Self-Taught*. For literacy rates of runaways, see John Hope Franklin and Schweninger, *Runaway Slaves*, 215.

34. North Carolina, *Acts Passed*; Meanders, *Advertisements*, 107; Du Bois, *Black Reconstruction*, 638; Genovese, *Roll, Jordan, Roll*, 563.

35. Genovese, *Roll, Jordan, Roll*, 561–66; Sarah F. Davidson, *Life in Antebellum Charlotte*, 41–42.

36. Genovese, *Roll, Jordan, Roll*, 561–66; Heather Andrea Williams, *Self-Taught*, 1–29.

37. Lane, *Narrative*, 4.

38. SNHJ, August 3, 1815. Also see Baer and Singer, *African American Religion*; John Hope Franklin, *Free Negro*, 58–120; Guion Griffis Johnson, *Ante-Bellum North Carolina*, 515–16, 550; Bowditch, *Slavery and the Constitution*, 23.

39. Genovese, *Roll, Jordan, Roll*, 159–280; Parish, *Slavery*, 81–85.

40. Lane, *Narrative*, 21. Also see Byron, *"Catechism"*; Cornelius, *Slave Missions and the Black Church*.

41. Hawkins, *Lunsford Lane*, 31–32.

42. Lane, *Narrative*, 8.

43. William L. Andrews, *North Carolina Slave Narratives*.

44. Hawkins, *Lunsford Lane*, 282; NCSA, 457, 464–65; SNHJ, September 3, 1839. In her journal entries, Susan never wrote about treating slaves like children. Some historians have characterized Bryan's wording as southern paternalism. For a succinct overview of the debates regarding the meaning of southern paternalism, see Ford, *Deliver Us from Evil*, 145–47, 582–83 (nn. 20, 21). Also see Genovese, *Roll,*

Jordan, Roll, 3–10. I have avoided using the term in this chapter because its gendered nature does not seem to apply to the women described here. Instead, I have used the broader term "benevolent slaveholding" to refer to the ideas expressed in Paley's moral philosophy and in the Presbyterian Church's 1787 and 1818 antislavery resolutions.

45. Lerner, *Grimké Sisters*, 281.

46. Susan Nye Hutchison, "Mrs. Hutchinson's [*sic*] Letter," 155. "Hutchison" is misspelled in both the title and author line.

47. Lane, *Narrative*, 20.

48. Farnham, *Education of the Southern Belle*, 113–18. Susan identified as a northerner in Susan Nye Hutchison, "Mrs. Hutchinson's [*sic*] Letter," 157. In some of her newspaper advertisements from the 1830s, she also sometimes highlighted her experiences visiting Troy Female Seminary in New York, which probably explains why, when southerners wrote about her after her death, they described her as a northern teacher. For mention of her experiences in the North, see "Raleigh Female Academy Examination, 1835," in *NCSA*, 507. For a description of Susan as a northern teacher, see John F. Foard, "Then and Now," *CW*, February 10, 1883.

49. All of Farnham's sources are from the 1840s and 1850s.

50. SNHJ, July 29, 1815.

51. Ibid., May 20, 21, June 3, July 16, 22, 29, 1815.

52. Oakes, "'Whom Have I Oppressed?'"

53. SNHJ, May 9, 1815.

CHAPTER 4

1. "Miss Nye," *ACGA*, September 20, 1823.

2. SNHJ, November 1, 1827, December 25, 1831, May 20, 1829. Susan Nye was admitted to the First Presbyterian Church of Augusta on certificate "of Wm. McPheeters, Raleigh, 4 June 1823" (Catalogue of Members 1822–23, SM). Adam Hutchison's admission to the church is recorded in Catalogue of Members 1820–21, SM. For the admission of his first wife, Elizabeth, on November 22, 1811, see "Members of the Presbyterian Church, Augusta," SM. Elizabeth Anderson (d. October 8, 1819) and Adam Hutchison married on May 3, 1808, and had seven children. Their first three children were baptized in the church: "Record of Baptisms by the Rev. John R. Thompson," SM. According to Susan's May 23, 1827, journal entry, the births of Adam and Elizabeth's children were "not correctly inserted in the family record," so she copied down the birth and death dates from Elizabeth's journal: Alexander (August 7, 1809–February 2, 1810); Adam (February 2, 1811–March 7, 1813); Hannah (December 14, 1812–October 16, 1829); Robert (July 14, 1814–n.d.); John (October 20, 1815–June 20, 1816); Elizabeth (May 26, 1817–1893); Anderson (September 26, 1819–n.d.).

3. SNHJ, December 30, 1826; Susan Nye and Adam Hutchison marriage certificate, February 10, 1825, copy in the possession of Dr. Richard H. Marks of Greenville, North Carolina.

4. Schools enrolling very young children in women's homes were known as "dame schools." See Wyman, "Dame Schools." For the relative lack of dame schools in the South, see Perlmann and Margo, *Women's Work?*, 9, 39–40.

5. Historians have traced the idea of companionate marriage back to the new marriage laws that arose during the Protestant Reformation, especially those that recognized both men's and women's right to divorce and remarriage under certain conditions. See Ozment, *When Fathers Ruled*; Bruce Tolley, *Pastors and Parishioners*, 87–112. For an emerging ideal of companionate marriage in the United States, see Censer, *North Carolina Planters*; Jabour, *Marriage in the Early Republic*. In contrast, Joan Cashin's study of migrating families in the South, *Family Venture*, portrays marriage as less affectionate and companionate. For liberal and conservative views of marriage, see Norton, *Liberty's Daughters*.

6. James Wilson, *Works*, 482. For the influence of Enlightenment ideas on discourse about marriage, see Lewis, "Republican Wife"; Lewis, *Pursuit of Happiness*. For the law of coverture and changes in women's property rights in the mid-nineteenth century, see Shammas, "Re-Assessing the Married Women's Property Acts"; Chused, "Married Women's Property Law"; Salmon, *Women and the Law of Property*.

7. Joseph Lathrop, *Sermons*; Wesley, *Works*, 85; Witherspoon, *Lectures*, 100–101; Jennings, *Married Lady's Companion*, 62–63.

8. Paley, *Principles* (1815), 313; Cott, *Public Vows*.

9. Tocqueville, *Democracy in America*, 2:688, 689.

10. See Kerber, "Separate Spheres." Also see Kerber et al., "Beyond Roles, Beyond Spheres"; McCall and Yacovone, *Shared Experience*; Osterud, *Lives of Farm Women*; Dunaway, *Women, Work, and Family*; Locke and Botting, *Feminist Interpretations*.

11. Lebsock makes this point in *Free Women of Petersburg*, 15–53, concluding that marital relations were fundamentally unequal.

12. SNHJ, June 22, 1827.

13. Ibid., October 1, 8, 9, 17, 1826, May 23, 1827.

14. Ibid., January 1–9, 1827. The Hutchisons hired two slaves, a housekeeper and a wet nurse, to work in the home. Susan nursed Sylvanus until they learned he was not thriving on Susan's milk (ibid., November 13, 1826).

15. Wells, *Origins*, 111–32; Wells, *Women Writers and Journalists*. For discussion of New York family life during this period, see Ryan, *Cradle of the Middle Class*, 233–34. Based on evidence from Oneida County, Ryan argues that before 1830, the family circle was not especially "private" space because men and women were so connected to church, town, and neighborhood communities.

16. Catalogue of Members 1822–23, SM; Augusta (Georgia) First Presbyterian Church, *Memorial*, 27. For demographics in the churches, see Bode, "Transformation."

17. SNHJ, March 12, 22, 24, 1827, October 15, 1829; Waddel, *Memoirs*, 85; Grace Gillam Davidson, *Historical Collections of the Georgia Chapters Daughters of the American Revolution*, 45.

18. SNHJ, December 1, 2, 1827; Augusta (Georgia) First Presbyterian Church, *Memorial*, 36. Some churches permitted women to vote. According to Boles, antebellum Kentucky churches often allowed both black and white men and women to

vote on church matters (*Religion in Antebellum Kentucky*, 125). Similarly, Cornelius has found that in southern all-black churches and slave missions, both free black and slave women voted along with men. However, this practice was far from uniform in the Presbyterian churches (*Slave Missions and the Black Church*, 38; Elizabeth Wilson, *Scriptural View*, 146–47). For a brief contemporary discussion of women's lack of vote in the Presbyterian Church, see Cogswell, *Theological Class Book*, 163. For evidence of women voting, see Nathan Eusebius Wood, *History*, 333–34. For women's limited power in antebellum churches, see Schantz, *Piety in Providence*.

19. SNHJ, February 16, 1827, February 5, November 15, 22, 1828; Graham, *Power of Faith*. For antebellum women's benevolent activity, see Lyerly, *Methodism*, 115–18; Quist, *Restless Visionaries*, 19–102; Lebsock, *Free Women of Petersburg*, 195–216; Carter, *Southern Single Blessedness*; Ginzberg, *Women and the Work of Benevolence*.

20. SNHJ, November 10, December 1, 2, 7, 1826, January 26, 29, February 11, 1827.

21. Ibid., January 27, February 4, June 28, 1827; Catalogue of Members 1822–23, SM. Also see Heyrman, *Southern Cross*, 47–48, 66–69.

22. SNHJ, November 12, 1826, July 1, 1827.

23. Ibid., June 10, 24, 1827. For whites' concerns about independent black churches, see Heyrman, *Southern Cross*, 68–69.

24. "Augusta," *GC*, June 28, 1827; SNHJ, October 7, 11, November 11, 20, 1826.

25. SNHJ, December 12, 1826, February 10, 23, March 8, April 14, 1827.

26. Ibid., April 15, 24, 26, 27, 1827.

27. Ibid., April 18, May 8, 17, 23, July 13, 1827.

28. Ibid., May 17, 1827; Blunt, *American Annual Register*, 492; Cadle, *Georgia Land Surveying*.

29. SNHJ, October 19, 21, 23, 1826, July 21, August 1, 1827.

30. U.S. Bureau of Education, *Report*, 328. Some rural and town districts continued to employ teachers after marriage (Board of National Popular Education, *Annual Report*, 5–10).

31. See Kennedy, *Born Southern*.

32. Proverbs 31:16, 18, 24; Woodworth, "Female Character," 147; Hunter, *Sacred Biography*, 12.

33. For an overview of debates over separate spheres and the colonial "golden age" for women, see Kathleen M. Brown, "Beyond the Great Debates."

34. "Mrs. Adam Hutchison's School," *GC*, September 24, 1827.

35. SNHJ, October 4, 15, 1827; "Mrs. H. Blome," "Mrs. Adam Hutchison's School," "Mrs. Wharton," "The Exercises of Mrs. O'Driscoll & Miss Canuet's Seminary for Young Ladies," all in *GC*, September 24, 27, 1827; "Male & Female Academy," *ACGA*, October 27, 1827.

36. SNHJ, November 3, 15, 1827, October 21, 1829. I have been unable to find the published critical comments Susan refers to in the October 1829 entry. They did not appear in the *Augusta Chronicle and Georgia Advertiser*, and the fall 1829 issues of the *Georgia Courier*, another paper in which she placed advertisements for her school, have not survived. For public scrutiny of antebellum teachers, see Tolley and Nash, "Leaving Home to Teach," 172–76.

37. SNHJ, December 7, 1827, August 1, 26, December 24, 1828, February 27, October 4, 1829.

38. Ibid., December 11, 22, 1827.

39. Ibid., January 6, 9, 1828.

40. Ibid., January 17, 19, 22, February 28, March 31, 1828.

41. Ibid., April 14, 16, 23, 24, 26, 28, 1828.

42. Ibid., May 8, 11, 12, 1828.

43. Ibid., October 16, 1828, January 5, 8, February 9, 1829.

44. Ibid., May 4, July 2, December 27, 1827, February 18, 1828, February 22–24, 1829. For the earlier fires, see "Insurance against Fire," GC, June 11, 1827; "Augusta—FIRE!," ACGA, July 4, 1827.

45. "Augusta—Incendiaries," ACGA, February 25, 1829.

46. SNHJ, April 3, 7, 1829; "Augusta—Volunteer City Guard," GC, March 4, 1829; Edward J. Cashin, Old Springfield, 28–30.

47. SNHJ, April 3, 6, 7, 1829; "Terrible and Awful Conflagration," ACGA, April 4, 1829; "The Fire," ACGA, April 8, 1829.

48. SNHJ, April 11, 1829.

49. Ibid., May 28, 30, June 9, 11, 12, 29, 1829. On the idea of "housekeeping," see Hodes, Sea Captain's Wife, 60.

50. SNHJ, July 30, August 12, 1829. For family boarding, see Brickley, "Sarah Pierce's Litchfield Female Academy," 353–90.

51. SNHJ, August 8, 10, September 19, 1829.

52. Ibid., October 6–7, 1829.

53. Ibid., October 6–16, 1829; "From the New-Haven Journal, 'Directions to Prevent Sickness,'" GC, September 20, 1827. For nineteenth-century medicine, see Rothstein, American Physicians; Steven M. Stowe, Doctoring the South; McMillen, Motherhood.

54. SNHJ, October 16, December 7, 1829.

55. Ibid., November 15, December 22, 1829, January 9, 1830.

56. Ibid., November 6, 10, 1829.

57. Ibid., November 12, 1829; "Augusta," Georgia Constitutionalist, November 24, 1829.

58. ACGA, November 21, 25, 1829.

59. SNHJ, November 28, 1829. The visit to the jail is briefly noted in Edward J. Cashin, Story of Augusta, 58.

60. SNHJ, December 4, 1829. A contemporary portrayal of a dying convert who "desires death" is found in the memoirs of Elizabeth Jones's niece (Waddel, Memoirs, 82).

61. Georgia, Acts Passed, 172; Edward J. Cashin, Old Springfield, 28.

62. Georgia, Acts Passed, 119; Stuart, Three Years, 123; "Augusta," ACGA, June 9, 1830. See also Segal, Black Diaspora, 141.

63. "Fire!," ACGA, November 27, 1829; SNHJ, February 8, 9, 1830.

64. SNHJ, October 16, 1831. I believe Susan uses the term "Marshalls" here to refer to a valance draped over the doorway. For restrictions against black ministers and congregations, see Ford, Deliver Us from Evil, 167–85; Genovese, Roll, Jordan, Roll, 255–79.

65. SNHJ, January 27, 1830.

66. Ibid.

67. Although Susan did not keep a journal between March 26, 1830, and July 24, 1831, subsequent anniversary entries enable the reconstruction of some events during this period. See SNHJ, May 20, June 3, September 1, 1832, September 18, 1833.

68. See Marten, *Children in Colonial America*; John E. Murray, *Charleston Orphan House*; John E. Murray and Herndon, "Markets for Children"; Herndon and Murray, *Children Bound to Labor*. Also see Middleton and Smith, *Class Matters*, 198–212.

69. See Meckel, "Educating a Ministry"; Kennedy, *Born Southern*.

70. Hrdy, *Mothers and Others*.

71. Presbyterian Church in the U.S.A. (Old School), *Book of Public Prayer*, 194; SNHJ, September 1, 1832, September 18, 1833.

CHAPTER 5

1. Robert Stuart Hutchison, "Extracts from the Journal of Susan Nye Hutchison," November 21, 1938, in SNHJ, front matter. Susan never provided details about Adam's abuse; instead, she used phrases such as "Another severe trial of temper" (July 27, 1831).

2. See Mintz and Kellogg, *Domestic Revolutions*, 1–24; Ryan, *Cradle of the Middle Class*, 38–40.

3. There were always exceptions to the legal concept of marital privacy. See Stephanie B. Hoffman, "Behind Closed Doors."

4. See Wyatt-Brown, *Southern Honor*, 272–91; Bardaglio, *Reconstructing the Household*; Hartog, *Man and Wife*.

5. Najar, *Evangelizing the South*, 74.

6. See Lyerly, *Methodism*, 98–99; Wills, *Democratic Religion*; Weaver, "Second Baptist Church, Atlanta"; Ownby, "Church Discipline." Also see Friedman, *Enclosed Garden*.

7. Samuel Miller Jr., *Report*, 134. A number of congregations composed a presbytery, and a number of presbyteries composed a synod, often bounded by state lines. See Presbyterian Church in the U.S.A., *Constitution* (1827), 130; Friedman, *Enclosed Garden*, 5–12; SM, November 22, 1811.

8. SM, January 31, 1828.

9. SM, April 2, 1830.

10. SM, June 15, 1820.

11. SM, February 17, 1808, to October 16, 1837. Friedman, *Enclosed Garden*, 14–15, 77–78, has found a double standard in the sources she examined. Juster, *Disorderly Women*, has drawn a similar conclusion. However, regional differences complicate this picture. Sparks, *On Jordan's Stormy Banks*, 127, has found that church courts in Mississippi sided with women as often as with men in domestic disputes.

12. SM, 1804–37. For men's higher rate of discipline in the churches, see McCurry, *Masters of Small Worlds*, 182–94; Lyerly, *Methodism*, 98–101; Bode, "Transformation." Bode has argued that in Twiggs County, Georgia, men were disciplined more frequently because men's most common sins, such as drunkenness, took place in public. However, McCurry and Lyerly have cited numerous examples in which the

churches also disciplined men for violence against women, acts that often occurred within the privacy of the home.

13. The Session Minutes of the First Presbyterian Church in Augusta do not mention the particulars of Adam Hutchison's suspension, nor do they discuss the couple's separation. This is not unusual, because the minutes do not always consistently record cases of church discipline. According to SM, December 20, 1822, it was common to record cases of church discipline among "the Papers of Session filed away." These records no longer survive. Susan's case is reconstructed from her journal and ultimately substantiated by the fact that the Session officially dismissed her as a member in good standing when she left her husband and took the children back to New York. See Catalogue of Members 1822–23, SM.

14. SNHJ, September 2, October 21, November 1, 1831.

15. Ibid., January 13, June 6, September 7, 18, 1832.

16. Ibid., October 22, 24, 1832. Women discussed the issue in their church groups and benevolent societies, and some northern women had also recently begun to petition the federal government. Within two years, nearly fifteen hundred women from seven northern states submitted petitions to Congress protesting the forced removal of Native Americans. According to Portnoy, *Their Right to Speak*, this was the first national women's petition campaign in U.S. history. Also see Zaeske, *Signatures of Citizenship*. For Cherokee removal, see Daniel Blake Smith, *American Betrayal*.

17. SNHJ, October 27, December 1, 2, 1832, January 11, 1833. See also David Williams, *Georgia Gold Rush*.

18. SNHJ, November 11, December 22, 24, 26, 1832.

19. Ibid., December 4, 1832, March 3, May 3, 1828, January 11, March 20, 1833.

20. Ibid., January 31, February 20–21, April 9, 1833. For tuberculosis in the nineteenth century, see Sheila Rothman, *Living in the Shadow*.

21. SNHJ, March 13, 1833.

22. Schouler, *Treatise*, 69–70; SNHJ, March 18, 1833.

23. SNHJ, April 20, 25, 28, 1833; David Williams, *Georgia Gold Rush*.

24. This speculation is based on the rates of tuition Susan advertised when she taught school in Augusta in 1823 and considers the rates charged by some of her competitors at the time. See "Miss Nye," *ACGA*, September 20, 1823; B. B. Hopkins, "Select School for Young Ladies," *ACGA*, October 1, 1823; Julia Hayden, "Tuition," *ACGA*, October 9, 1824; SNHJ, October 1, 1832, January 10, April 6, 1833.

25. SNHJ, May 2, 3, 1833.

26. Ibid., May 6, 7, 9, 11, 14, 15, 1833.

27. Ibid., May 21, 26, June 1, 1833.

28. Ibid., June 10, 1833.

29. Ibid, June 29, July 3, August 8, 1833.

30. Ibid., August 18, 1833.

31. Hartog, *Man and Wife*, 36; Sievens, *Stray Wives*.

32. SM, November 15, 1830, March 1, 1832, October 31, 1833. The outcome of this case is unknown.

33. Ibid., September 20, October 16, 1837.

34. Daniel D. Smith, *Lectures*, 66; SNHJ, August 18, 29, 1833. For evangelical rhetoric regarding women's moral agency during the Second Great Awakening, see Basch, *Framing American Divorce*, 68–94.

35. SNHJ, October 4, 1833.

36. Cott, *Public Vows*, 49; Daniel D. Smith, *Lectures*, 58.

37. SNHJ, October 4, 7, 1833.

38. Ibid., September 1, 14, 1833.

39. Ibid., September 15, 1833.

40. Ibid., September 27, 30, October 3, 22, 1833.

41. Catalogue of Members 1822–23, SM; Presbyterian Church in the U.S.A., *Constitution* (1827), 420.

42. SNHJ, October 23, 26, 1833.

43. Ibid., October 22–November 16, 1833. The quote is from November 16, 1833.

44. Hartog, *Man and Wife*.

45. SNHJ, November 18, 1833. In New York, women usually taught during a five- or six-month summer term in the common schools, whereas men taught during a shorter four- or five-month winter term. See New York (State), Superintendent of Common Schools, *Annual Report*, 13. Also see Tolley and Beadie, "Socioeconomic Incentives"; Perlmann and Margo, *Women's Work?*, 21–33.

46. SNHJ, November 21, 1833, February 19, March 15, 1834.

47. Ibid., November 27, 1833, January 27, August 8, 11, 12, 1834.

48. Ibid., March 28, 1834.

49. Ibid., December 3, 1833, August 15, 1834.

50. Ibid., February 15, 27, March 6, April 11, 16, 29, 30, 1834.

51. Ibid., May 6, 7, 1834.

52. Ibid., May 20, 24, June 2, 3, 1834.

53. Ibid., June 14, July 27, September 30, October 4, 1834.

54. Ibid., October 11, 13, November 22, 1834.

55. Ibid., October 12, 1836.

56. "Catalogue of the Members of the Presbyterian Church of Augusta from Its Organization in the Year A.D. 1804 by the Rev. Washington McKnight of New York," First Presbyterian Church of Augusta, Georgia, Records, PHS. According to a genealogical entry of the Wing Family of America, Inc., accessed January 11, 2015, from http://wc.rootsweb.ancestry.com, Adam Hutchison died on September 16, 1834, but a September 6, 1840, entry in Susan's journal states he died on September 6, 1834.

57. McCurry, *Masters of Small Worlds*, 192.

58. SNHJ, August 8, 1831.

59. Ibid., February 10, 15, 1837.

60. Ibid., March 23, 1839.

CHAPTER 6

1. SNHJ, October 4, 11, 13, 1834; 1820 Census, Amenia, Dutchess County, New York.

2. SNHJ, July 4, 1833; Susan D. Nye Hutchison to Masters Hutchison, Care of Mr. M. Nye, January 13, 1836, copy in SNHJ typescript.

3. SNHJ, September 2, October 28, November 11, 1834.

4. Ibid., September 2, 1834.

5. For sketches of antebellum teachers working in southern schools, see Lebsock, *Free Women of Petersburg*, 172–76; Farnham, *Education of the Southern Belle*, 33–119. A number of important studies have explored women who taught in the West, although most of the primary sources are from after 1835. See Kaufman, *Women Teachers*; Myers, *Westering Women*; Weiler, *Country Schoolwomen*. For prominent academy founders in the North and Northwest, see Elizabeth Alden Green, *Mary Lyon*; Lutz, *Emma Willard*; Sklar, *Catharine Beecher*.

6. Perlmann and Margo, *Women's Work?*; Tolley and Beadie, "Socioconomic Incentives."

7. Connor, *North Carolina*, 441; North Carolina, Superintendent of Common Schools, *First Annual Report*, 31. For teachers' salaries in New York and North Carolina, see Tolley and Beadie, "Socioeconomic Incentives." For the relatively high salaries paid to female teachers in the South, see Perlmann and Margo, *Women's Work?*, 34–70. For gendered differences in teachers' pay from the colonial period through the early twentieth century, see Preston, "'He Lives as a Master.'"

8. Woodbridge, "Motives," 79–80. For the professionalization of teaching, see Elsbree, *American Teacher*.

9. Beadie, "Emma Willard's Idea Put to the Test"; "Mt. Pleasant," *Richmond Enquirer*, November 24, 1835; *Richmond Enquirer*, December 1, 1835; "Scotland Neck," in *NCSA*, 183. For the influence of Troy Female Seminary, see Scott, "Ever Widening Circle." For other advertisements mentioning faculty members trained at Troy, see *NCSA*, 277–79, 314–47, 335–36. Also see Fairbanks, *Emma Willard and Her Pupils*.

10. See Bailyn, *Education*; Kaestle, *Pillars of the Republic*; Labaree, "Curriculum, Credentials, and the Middle Class." For discussion of the comparatively high salary of female academy teachers, especially in the South, see Tolley and Beadie, "Socio-economic Incentives."

11. SNHJ, October 30, November 1, 2, 8, 1834. For the career ladder in antebellum schools, see Tolley and Beadie, "Socioeconomic Incentives."

12. For the argument that southerners did not view teaching as a respectable occupation for a woman, see Fox-Genovese, *Within the Plantation Household*, 46; Farnham, *Education of the Southern Belle*, 166. For studies that present evidence of southern women's positive views of teaching, see Jabour, *Scarlett's Sisters*, 61–64, 104–8. Also see Lebsock, *Free Women of Petersburg*, 172–77. For statistics on the numbers of southern slaveholders, see Hahn, *Southern Populism*, 42.

13. SNHJ, December 3, 1834. Beman was active in the American Tract Society (American Tract Society, *First Annual Report*, 4).

14. SNHJ, December 3–7, 1834.

15. Ibid., December 8, 1834.

16. Ibid., January 13, July 17, 20, December 31, 1837.

17. Ibid., November 24, 1834.

18. "Female Academy," *RR*, January 6, 1835. The misspelling of her name appears in the original ad, dated November 25, 1834.

19. There is gap in the transcription from December 19, 1834, to August 18, 1836. Robert S. Hutchison noted just after the February 22, 1837, entry that "probably the journal was kept during the period. . . . What became of this portion of the journal is not now known. RSH."

20. Winifred Gales and Joseph Gales, "Reminiscences," 148, Gales Family Papers, SHC. This chronology of events was reconstructed from newspaper advertisements in *NCSA*, 411, 482, 491, 494–95, 534–35. For discussion of Raleigh Academy's collapse, see Kim Tolley, "Chartered School."

21. For Chavis's school, see Guion Griffis Johnson, *Ante-Bellum North Carolina*, 515, 519. Also see Connor, *North Carolina*, 98–99; Knight, "Notes on John Chavis"; Lancaster, *Raleigh*, 89.

22. See Waugh, *North Carolina's Capital*, 53–54.

23. Advertisements for Susan Nye Hutchison's female academy in Raleigh are in *NCSA*, 504–7; SNHJ, January 19, 1828, March 17, 18, 31, April 3, 12, 1834; *Prospectus*. Susan's newspaper advertisements described her school as independent, but her course of study and essay on female education appear in *Prospectus* along with documents related to the male school inhabiting the old academy's original buildings.

24. *Prospectus*, 5.

25. Willard, *Address*, 6.

26. *Prospectus*, 6.

27. Grimké, *Letters*; Wells, *Women Writers and Journalists*, 17–54; Jabour, *Scarlett's Sisters*, 51–55; Pierce, "Why Women Should Be Well Educated," 95.

28. *Prospectus*, 8; Perlmann and Margo, *Women's Work?*, 46–49. According to McMahon, *Mere Equals*, educated New England women ascribed to a cult of domesticity by the 1830s. Also see Ryan, *Cradle of the Middle Class*.

29. *Prospectus*, 6–8. Also see Willard, *Address*, 26; Richards, "Editor's Department."

30. *Prospectus*, 9.

31. Ibid., 11.

32. SNHJ, February 23, 1837, April 29, 1838.

33. *Raleigh Star*, November 12, 1835, quoted in Robert Hutchison, "Susan Davis Nye Hutchison: A School Teacher in North Carolina and Georgia, 1815–1840," 5, typescript, in SNHJ; "Raleigh Academy," *RR*, November 10, 1835.

34. *Raleigh Standard*, February 13, 1835, quoted in Robert Hutchison, "Susan Davis Nye Hutchison," 4; Susan Nye Hutchison to Masters Hutchison, January 13, 1836, SNHJ.

35. Tolley and Nash, "Leaving Home to Teach," 166–67; Farnham, *Education of the Southern Belle*, 97–98; advertisements in *NCSA*, 505–7.

36. Nancy R. White to Mrs. Thomas. L. Cowan and Mrs. Michal Brown, December 30, 1835, SNHJ.

37. Susan Nye Hutchison to Masters Hutchison, January 13, 1836, in SNHJ.

38. Susan's course of study in the first class included arithmetic and algebra, history, the sciences, Paley's moral philosophy, rhetoric, and other subjects, and she charged fifteen dollars per session ("Female Academy," *Western Carolinian*, February 20, 1836; "Female Academy at Salisbury," *RR*, October 8, 1838). Frontis, a native of France, began to teach French at Raleigh Academy in 1818, when

Susan was head of the Female Department ("French for Academy Pupils," in *NCSA*, 452).

39. "Female Academy," *Western Carolinian*, February 20, 1836.

40. For discussion of the way the ideology of domesticity and separate spheres provided legitimacy to women's leadership of independent organizations parallel with men's, see Boydston, Kelley, and Margolis, *Limits of Sisterhood*, 4–5.

41. SNHJ, September 19, 1836. For the higher pay in southern schools, see Perlmann and Margo, *Women's Work?*, 34–70; Tolley and Beadie, "Socioeconomic Incentives," 51–65.

42. SNHJ, September 16, 1836.

43. Ibid., September 22, October 4, 1836; *NCSA*, 124–25, 458.

44. Powers makes this assumption in *"Girl Question,"* 14–15. Similarly, Kessler-Harris, citing Beecher's work, claims that homemaking became professionalized in the 1830s (*Out to Work*, 50). Without citing any references, Eastman, *Nation of Speechifiers*, 78, claims that American writers in the 1820s turned away from the notion of female education as intrinsically valuable and began advocating a differentiated course of study centered on domesticity. For antebellum debates over domesticity in the female curriculum and the increasing rigor of female education in the Northeast, see Kim Tolley, *Science Education*, 55–74. Also see Margaret A. Nash, *Women's Education*; Kelley, *Learning to Stand and Speak*. For a similar trend in the South, see Farnham, *Education of the Southern Belle*.

45. SNHJ, January 7, 1837, January 15, 23, 26, 27, February 2, 3, 20, 1838, January 21, February 7, 1839. For young women's study of mathematics during these years, see Kim Tolley, *Science Education*, 75–94. I am grateful to Professor Eugen Radian, director of the Mathematics Department at Notre Dame de Namur University, for explaining the course level at which a student might encounter eighth-degree equations.

46. SNHJ, July 25, 26, 1837.

47. "Female Academy at Salisbury," *RR*, October 8, 1838; SNHJ, January 22, March 8, 10, April 16, November 10, 17, 1837, January 14, 1838. Kaufman notes that in western communities, one of the most frequently mentioned problems in teachers' diaries was the need to resolve conflicts among different religious denominations competing for members (*Women Teachers*, 33).

48. For the rise of denominational schools and colleges during this period, see Malkmus, "Small Towns, Small Sects"; Beadie, "Toward a History." See also Beadie, *Education and the Creation of Capital*; Beaty, *History*; Gross Alexander et al., *History*, 388; SNHJ, December 2, 28, 1837, January 5, 1838.

49. SNHJ, April 25, 1840.

50. For the effect of the Panic of 1837 on schools, see Tolley and Beadie, "Socioeconomic Incentives," 62–63; Beadie, *Education and the Creation of Capital*, 288–303. According to advertisements in the *RR*, October 8, 1838, and *Western Carolinian*, February 20, 1836, the tuition at Salisbury Academy rose from $15.00 per session in 1836 to $15.50 in 1838.

51. SNHJ, June 13, 1837; Beaty, *History*, 60–67; Edith M. Clark, "Frontis, Stephen," in Powell, *Dictionary of North Carolina Biography*, 2:246–47; Farnham, *Education of the Southern Belle*, 65–66.

52. Beaty, *History*.

53. Presbyterian Church in the U.S.A. (Old School), *Minutes* (1857), 336; Foote, *Sketches*, 518–27; Farnham, *Education of the Southern Belle*, 104–10.

54. For women's status in the antebellum Presbyterian Church, see Boyd and Brackenridge, *Presbyterian Women*, 3–22; Wallace, "'Bond of Union,'" 1:332. Wallace's study focuses on the "Old School" Presbyterian Church, which comprised most of the institutions in the South; for concerns about "feminization" and the social status and salaries of ministers, see 116–29; for 1860 statistics on ministers' salaries, see 125; for debates over parochial education, see 318–45. For the Presbyterian Church's split into "Old School" and "New School" camps, see chapter 7.

55. SNHJ, June 12, December 11, 21, 26, 30, 1837; North Carolina, Department of Public Instruction, *Biennial Report*, 693. Christie Anne Farnham has found that when female educators wanted to offer a college-level education, they sometimes used the title "Seminary" or "Institute" to describe their school in order to gain acceptance for their ventures (*Education of the Southern Belle*, 65). The school's new title was announced in the *Raleigh Register* (*NCSA*, 381). There is no evidence to indicate why the school was chartered as an academy rather than as an institute, as Susan had wanted.

56. SNHJ, October 13, 1838.

57. Ibid., October 18–19, 1838.

58. Ibid., February 28, 1837; Zaeske, *Signatures of Citizenship*; Varon, "Evangelical Womanhood." For the political activism of the Grimkés, see Lerner, *Grimké Sisters*.

59. Rev. Hubbard Winslow, "Appropriate Sphere of Woman," *Watchman of the South*, September 21, 1837; Catharine E. Beecher, *Essay on Slavery and Abolitionism*, 99, 104.

60. Lefler and Newsome, *North Carolina*, 361–62.

61. SNHJ, January 7, 21, 1837, October 3, 23, November 12, 1838; Coon, *Beginnings of Public Education*, 891–92. Susan and Winifred Gales corresponded (see SNHJ, January 5, 1837), but none of their letters have survived. For the role of the *Register* in the common school campaign, see Coon, *Beginnings of Public Education*, 891–92. Twenty of the twenty-four editorials on the 1839 education campaign discussed here appeared in the *Raleigh Register*. Also see Kim Tolley, "Joseph Gales."

62. SNHJ, November 17, December 5, 14, 18, 20, 1838.

63. Ibid., December 25, 1838. Coon was unable to locate a copy of the original memorial (*Beginnings of Public Education*, 824). For advertisements placed by Mary Jones, née Edwards, see Coon, *Beginnings of Public Education*, 41–45. Both Jones and Susan had access to reading material that included reports of national and international news. Jones placed advertisements for her school in seven different North Carolina newspapers, so she probably had access to the national news stories carried in the *Raleigh Register*, which frequently included reprints on political and educational issues from the *National Intelligencer* (Washington, D.C.) and several northern newspapers.

64. Catharine E. Beecher, *Essay on the Education of Female Teachers*; "Female Education"; Massachusetts Department of Education, *Annual Report*, 27, 60. For the influence of Beecher and Mann, see Kaestle, *Pillars of the Republic*, 85–93, 104–82; Sklar, *Catharine Beecher*.

65. See Tolley and Beadie, "Socioeconomic Incentives." Also see Perlmann and Margo, *Women's Work?*

66. SNHJ, May 23, June 11, July 16–17, 1837, January 5, 1838; *NCSA*, 401–3; C. H. Dudley to Albert Hall, March 4, 1835, Ernest Haywood Papers, Series 3, File 143, SHC; Smith and Wilson, *North Carolina Women*, 103–22; Sarah F. Davidson, *Life in Antebellum Charlotte.*

67. SNHJ, January 5, 1839; "Senate Journal, 1838–39," 148, quoted in Coon, *Beginnings of Public Education*, 824.

68. Lefler and Newsome, *North Carolina*, 361–62; Guion Griffis Johnson, *Ante-Bellum North Carolina*, 271–73. Also see Jeffrey, *State Parties and National Politics*, 125–26.

69. Perlmann and Margo, *Women's Work?*, 34–70; see North Carolina, Superintendent of Common Schools, *Second Annual Report*, 37–38; Delia W. Jones, "Necessity."

70. SNHJ, February 28, March 1, 14, April 6, 1839.

71. Ibid., May 17, July 4, 29, 30, 1839.

72. Ibid., October 26, December 20, 1837; *NCSA*, 230–40; Withers, *Semi-Centennial Catalogue*, iii–v; Beaty, *History.* Susan had heard Morrison preach in Raleigh on January 18, 1818 (*Annual Pocket Remembrancer: For the Year 1818* [in possession of Dr. Richard H. Marks, Greenville, North Carolina]).

73. SNHJ, March 21, April 7, 30, 1837. For the interest of evangelicals in promoting Christian piety among their children, see Mathews, *Religion in the Old South*, 115, 123. Also see Walbert, "'Endeavor to Improve Yourself.'"

74. SNHJ, October 5, 14, 15, 1839.

75. Ibid., October 16, 26, 1839. When Susan left Charlotte Academy in 1845, she sold all the furniture she had collected, along with the cow ("Auction at the Charlotte Female Academy," *Mecklenburg Jeffersonian*, August 1, 1845).

76. SNHJ, October 3, 27, November 23, 1840; Sarah F. Davidson, *Life in Antebellum Charlotte.* Farnham mistakenly reports that enrollments continued to decline after Susan moved to Charlotte and concludes that parents found her course offerings less rigorous than at competing schools. However, Farnham's evidence for enrollment comes from Susan's years in Salisbury, and she cites no evidence to support the claim about parents' views (*Education of the Southern Belle*, 102).

77. SNHJ, May 23, October 5, 1840; for students from Georgia and South Carolina, see June 11, July 16, 1837, November 2, 1838, May 23, October 3, 1840.

78. Ibid., July 31, September 6, 1840, January 1, 1841. J. B. Alexander erroneously reports, in *History of Mecklenburg County*, that Susan's tenure at the school only ranged from 1836 to 1839 (19). However, advertisements and announcements demonstrate that she served as principal until the end of the spring session in 1845 (*Mecklenburg Jeffersonian*, September 14, 1841, March 7, August 1, 1845).

79. "Concord Female Academy," *CW*, September 6, 1845; "Charlotte Female Academy," *Mecklenburg Jeffersonian*, September 26, 1845; Wallace, "'Bond of Union,'" 1:339–45.

80. "Charlotte Female Academy," *Mecklenburg Jeffersonian*, September 26, 1845.

1. Susan Nye Hutchison, "Mrs. Hutchinson's [sic] Letter," 156; *African Repository and Colonial Journal* 5 (1830): 331; North Carolina, Constitutional Convention, *Proceedings and Debates*, 80. For the rise of proslavery rhetoric, see Phillips, "Course of the South." For the role of slavery in the division of the Presbyterian Church, see Snay, *Gospel of Disunion*.

2. Gary B. Nash and Soderlund, *Freedom by Degrees*; Zilversmit, *First Emancipation*; David Brion Davis, *Problem of Slavery in the Age of Revolution*. For discussion of the range of emancipationist ideologies among supporters of the American Colonization Society, see Tyler-McGraw, *African Republic*; Brana-Shute and Sparks, *Paths to Freedom*. For the rise of the American Anti-Slavery Society, see Muelder, *Theodore Dwight Weld*, 7–35. For the ideological shift from gradual to immediate emancipation, see David Brion Davis, "Emergence of Immediatism," 238–39.

3. Genovese, *Roll, Jordan, Roll*, 3–7, has defined paternalism in relation to American slavery. For the rise of proslavery paternalism in the South, see Ford, *Deliver Us from Evil*, 505–35. For the role of ministers in promoting this ideology, see Snay, *Gospel of Disunion*; Tise, *Proslavery*; Freehling, *Road to Disunion*, vol. 1. For Cheyney and other northern teachers during this period, see Farnham, *Education of the Southern Belle*, 115–19. For the rise of proslavery evangelicalism, see Daly, *When Slavery Was Called Freedom*.

4. Farnham concluded that Susan's literary efforts were "without success" (*Education of the Southern Belle*, 102), but she apparently did not have access to Susan's published essays.

5. American Anti-Slavery Society, *Second Annual Report*, 32, 62; Wyatt-Brown, "Abolitionists' Postal Campaign," 227. For the role of evangelicals in the antislavery movement, see Wyatt-Brown, *Lewis Tappan*.

6. Wyly-Jones, "1835 Anti-Abolition Meetings"; Benjamin Gildersleeve, "Charleston!," *Charleston Observer*, October 24, 1835; Ford, *Deliver Us from Evil*, 481–97. For John W. Jones's quote, see Gales, *Register of Debates in Congress*, 2035; SNHJ, January 17, February 26, March 14, 1837.

7. Susan Nye Hutchison, "Mrs. Hutchinson's [sic] Letter," 154–57. For the Nullification Crisis, see Freehling, *Road to Disunion*, 1:253–307.

8. Cooper, *Word, Like Fire*; Andrews, Foster, and Harris, *Concise Oxford Companion*; Lerner, *Grimké Sisters*; Portnoy, *Their Right to Speak*, 203–44; Robertson, *Hearts Beating*. Also see Lois A. Brown, "William Lloyd Garrison."

9. Susan Nye Hutchison, "Mrs. Hutchinson's [sic] Letter." For eighteenth-century women evangelical writers, see Brekus, *Sarah Osborn's World*, 177–83. According to Robertson, abolitionist women often faced denunciation when they began offering public lectures to audiences that included both sexes (*Hearts Beating*, 2–3).

10. Gifford, "Thompson, George"; Boston Female Anti-Slavery Society, *Report*, 6–18, 25, 30–51.

11. Boston Female Anti-Slavery Society, *Report*, 61, 50.

12. Susan Nye Hutchison, "Mrs. Hutchinson's [sic] Letter," 154.

13. Ibid., 156.

14. Ibid., 154–55.

15. Ibid., 155–57.

16. Ibid., 156.

17. Ibid., 156–57.

18. Ibid.; Catharine E. Beecher, *Essay on Slavery and Abolitionism*, 101.

19. See SNHJ, May 9, July 29, 1815.

20. Fox-Genovese and Genovese, "Divine Sanction of Social Order." For historians who have argued that a humanitarian ideology of slaveholding emerged in the eighteenth century, see Chaplin, "Slavery and the Principle." For the role of the First Great Awakening in this development, see Gallay, "Origins of Slaveholders' Paternalism"; Gallay, *Formation of a Planter Elite*.

21. Susan Nye Hutchison, "Mrs. Hutchinson's [*sic*] Letter," 155.

22. O'Brien, *Conjectures of Order*; Adam Rothman, *Slave Country*; Najar, "'Meddling with Emancipation'"; David Brion Davis, *Problem of Slavery in the Age of Revolution*. Also see Ambrose, "Of Stations and Relations."

23. See Carwardine, "Second Great Awakening."

24. Finney, *Memoirs*, 324; Carwardine, "Second Great Awakening."

25. Finney, *Memoirs*; Carwardine, "Second Great Awakening." For a contemporary discussion of the 1818 Expression of Views, see Presbyterian Church in the U.S.A., General Assembly, *Digest*, 344, 346. The complete 1818 document is reproduced and discussed in Albert Barnes, *Church and Slavery*, quotations on 54–56.

26. Presbyterian Church in the U.S.A., General Assembly, *Digest*, 344, 346.

27. Presbyterian Synod (Ky.), *Address*, 15; Presbyterian Church in the U.S.A., General Assembly, *Minutes, 1831*, 14, 33.

28. Stewart's comments are in Thompson, Breckinridge, and Burleigh, *Discussion*, 70.

29. Ibid.; Presbyterian Church in the U.S.A., General Assembly, *Minutes, 1835*, 33.

30. Ramsay, *History of South-Carolina*, 558; George Howe, *History*, 256, 280; Oast, "'Worst Kind.'"

31. Engerman, *Cambridge Economic History*, 329–66; Fogel and Engerman, *Time on the Cross*, 59–106; Oast, "'Worst Kind.'"

32. Oast, "'Worst Kind.'" Thompson, Breckinridge, and Burleigh, *Discussion*, 70.

33. Thompson, Breckinridge, and Burleigh, *Discussion*, 76; "Abolition," *African Repository and Colonial Journal* 11 (1835): 370.

34. American Anti-Slavery Society, *Third Annual Report*, 70; "Extract from the Minutes of Hopewell Presbytery," *African Repository and Colonial Journal* 12 (1836): 218.

35. Quoted in Sturge, *Visit*, 186. Also see John Russell Hutchison, *Reminiscences*, 226; Ford, *Deliver Us from Evil*, 519–20; Sparks, *On Jordan's Stormy Banks*.

36. Presbyterian Church in the U.S.A., General Assembly, *Minutes, 1836*, 247–50.

37. Ibid., 248.

38. Ibid., 272–73. Four delegates declined to vote.

39. Wallace, "'Bond of Union,'" 1:48–111. Also see Moorhead, "'Restless Spirit.'" Writers used the phrase "obnoxious resolutions" to describe the Expression of Views in letters and articles in the *Charleston Observer*.

40. Wallace, "'Bond of Union,'" 1:11. Apart from Susan Nye Hutchison, I found no works by female writers in the *Charleston Observer* between 1835 and 1838. All the women writers Wallace identified published in 1840 or later (118–20).

41. SNHJ, January 7, 11, 13, 14, 17, 1837.

42. Susan D. Nye Hutchison, "To the Female Members of the Presbyterian Church," *Charleston Observer*, February 18, 1837.

43. Rev. Hubbard Winslow, "The Appropriate Sphere of Woman," *Watchman of the South*, September 21, 1837.

44. Benjamin Gildersleeve, "Charleston!," *Charleston Observer*, February 18, 1837; SNHJ, February 26, March 14, 1837.

45. Susan D. Nye Hutchison, "To the Female Members of the Presbyterian Church," *Charleston Observer*, February 18, 1837.

46. Ibid.

47. Ibid.

48. Lerner, *Creation of Feminist Consciousness*.

49. SNHJ, June 15, 1837.

50. Ibid., November 8, 1839. Also see Staiger, "Abolitionism."

51. D. W. Lathrop, *Case*; "Statistical Table," Presbyterian Church in the U.S.A. (New School), Synod of New York and New Jersey, *Minutes*, 71; "Statistical Table," Presbyterian Church in the U.S.A., General Assembly, *Minutes, 1839*, 202–76.

52. John Witherspoon, "To the Editor of the Charleston Observer," *Charleston Observer*, March 10, 1838.

53. Presbyterian Church in the U.S.A. (New School), General Assembly, *Minutes*, 22; Albert Barnes, *Church and Slavery*, 83; Presbyterian Church in the U.S.A. (Old School), General Assembly, *Minutes* (1845), 16–17.

54. U.S. Department of the Interior, *Report*, 581; Corbett and Corbett, *Politics and Religion*, 96.

55. Staiger, "Abolitionism"; Gilbert H. Barnes, *Antislavery Impulse*; Sweet, *Religion*, 111; Hankins, *Second Great Awakening*, 18–19; Foster, *Errand of Mercy* (identifying 1837 as the endpoint); Hatch, *Democratization*, 220.

56. SNHJ, March 29, 1840.

57. Ibid., December 22, 1833, November 28, 29, December 3–9, 1837, February 8, 9, 1838; Mary Steele Ferrand Autograph Album, 1837–38, 1894, 1, John Steele Papers, Series 3, Fol. 165, SHC.

58. SNHJ, December 23, 1837, June 2, 1838, April 3, 19, 1837, March 4, June 2, 1838.

59. Ibid., May 5, 1838. If Susan continued to minister to prisoners, she did not note her visits in her journal.

60. Presbyterian Church in the U.S.A., General Assembly, *Extracts*, 30; SNHJ, June 4, 1837, June 3, 1838. For discussion of North Carolina's slave codes, see Guion Griffis Johnson, *Ante-Bellum North Carolina*, 515–16, 550. Also see Cornelius, *When I Can Read*.

61. SNHJ, July 1, 1838.

62. Barnard, "Course of Instruction."

63. See Forbes, "Slavery and the Evangelical Enlightenment," 84–85; Wayland, *Elements of Moral Science* (1858), 198.

64. North Carolina, *Acts Passed*, 11. Also see John Hope Franklin, *Free Negro*, 58–120; Guion Griffis Johnson, *Ante-Bellum North Carolina*, 515–16, 550.

65. Susan Nye Hutchison, "Mrs. Hutchinson's [*sic*] Letter," 156.

66. SNHJ, October 29, 1837, July 17, 1838. The quotes are from April 19, 1837, September 12, 1836.

67. Ibid., April 19, May 20, October 11, November 3, 1840. Note: the April 19 entry is mistakenly labeled as March in the transcript.

68. Ibid., November 5, 6, 1840.

69. Schwartz, *Born in Bondage*.

70. John Hope Franklin, *Free Negro*, 58–120; Guion Griffis Johnson, *Ante-Bellum North Carolina*, 515–16, 550; Pinckney, introduction; SNHJ, July 31, August 28, September 24, October 5, 1840.

71. Noll, *Civil War as a Theological Crisis*; Harriet Beecher Stowe, *Key to Uncle Tom's Cabin*, iii. Also see Miller, Stout, and Wilson, *Religion and the American Civil War*.

72. Susan Nye Hutchison, "Mrs. Hutchinson's [*sic*] Letter," 156; Calhoun, *Works*, 556.

73. "President W. L. Lingle Finds Old Document"; Withers, *Semi-Centennial Catalogue*, 32, 92; Susan Nye Hutchison, "Mrs. Hutchinson's [*sic*] Letter," 157; "Last Will and Testament of Susan D. N. Hutchison, 1868," Dutchess County, New York. According to the *Semi-Centennial Catalogue*, 92, John Grey Hutchison matriculated but never graduated from Davidson. The *Catalogue* mistakenly gives Sylvanus's and Ebenezer's graduation date as 1848. The correct 1845 date is reported in "President W. L. Lingle Finds Old Document" and is also shown on a copy of Sylvanus's graduation certificate, in possession of Dr. Richard H. Marks of Greenville, North Carolina. Susan had returned to New York by April 18, 1848, when her son Adam Alexander died; he is buried in the South Amenia cemetery. According to the 1850 census, Susan, her sister Amanda, and her youngest son, John Grey Hutchison, were living on the farm with her brother Meletiah in South Amenia.

CONCLUSION

1. Sarah F. Davidson, *Life in Antebellum Charlotte*, 43. "Last Will and Testament of Meletiah Nye" and "Record of the Last Will and Testament of Susan D. N. Hutchison," Dutchess County, New York.

2. "Last Will and Testament of Meletiah Nye" and "Record of the Last Will and Testament of Susan D. N. Hutchison," Dutchess County, New York. Susan's mother, Sylvania Barlow Nye, died on October 15, 1838, and her father, Sylvanus Nye, died on March 5, 1841 (Nye, *Genealogy*), and left the farm to Susan's brother Meletiah ("Last Will and Testament of Sylvanus Nye, recorded December 12, 1844," Dutchess County, New York). Susan's brother Shubal, who had struggled financially for years, received "a mountain lot in Kent, CT." To his three surviving daughters, Sarah, Susan, and Amanda, Sylvanus left "half of house and northside of house for garden. Things necessary for comfort. Wood at the door, 10 lbs. wool, 10 lbs. flax, a cow and her keep, 6 bu[shels] wheat, 6 [bushels] corn, own pork, yearly household goods

and furniture." When Susan returned to Amenia, she apparently purchased the former residence of Amenia's first known physician, Dr. John Chamberlain (Barlow,
History, 7, 73).

3. Information about Susan's sons is drawn from "President W. L. Lingle Finds Old
Document"; Withers, *Semi-Centennial Catalogue*, 32, 92; University of Pennsylvania,
Department of Medicine, Society of the Alumni, *Catalogue*; 1850 U.S. Census; "South
Amenia Rejoices," *New York Observer*, December 23, 1909; "Obituary, Sylvanus Nye
Hutchison," *New York Observer*, May 5, 1910; transcript of Susan's last journal (in pos-
session of Dr. Richard H. Marks, Greenville, North Carolina).

4. "President W. L. Lingle Finds Old Document"; University of Pennsylvania,
Department of Medicine, Society of the Alumni, *Catalogue*. Withers, *Semi-Centennial
Catalogue*, 92, reports that John Grey Hutchison enlisted in the Confederate Army
and was imprisoned at Fort Warren. According to the transcribed entries in Susan's
last journal, John left for the South on December 26, 1851, but returned to Amenia
sometime in the summer of 1862: on August 12, 1862, she wrote, "Today is a day of
deep sorrow. My dear youngest son (John) left me going away I know not whither to
escape being compelled to take arms against his native South." On October 15, "John
came home again." Then, in an undated 1864 entry, she noted, "John left New York on
a crowded steamboat for California. There were 800 passengers." I found no record of
John Grey Hutchison's Confederate service.

5. Taylor, *Divided Family*, 152–54; "Record of the Last Will and Testament of
Susan D. N. Hutchison."

6. Go and Lindert, "Uneven Rise"; Albisetti, Goodman, and Rogers, *Girls' Secondary
Education*; Perlmann and Margo, *Women's Work?*

7. Schultz, "Returns to Women's Education," 51–57.

8. Perlmann and Margo, *Women's Work?*; Tolley and Beadie, "Socioeconomic
Incentives."

9. "Some Landmarks of Dutchess County," *Architectural Record* 45 (January–
June 1919): 477; "Lenoir Female Academy," *CW*, August 21, 1846.

10. For discussion of the way school reformers used the language of domes-
ticity to promote the hiring of women in common schools, see Nancy Hoffman,
Woman's "True" Profession. For Calvin Wiley's use of this rhetoric in North
Carolina, see North Carolina, Superintendent of Common Schools, *Second
Annual Report*, 37–38. For Catharine Beecher, see Sklar, *Catharine Beecher*. For
statistics on women teachers and teachers' wages, see Perlmann and Margo,
Women's Work?, 90, 142–43. For the rise of higher mathematics in female private
schools and public high schools during the nineteenth century, see Kim Tolley,
Science Education, 75–94.

11. Heyrman, *Southern Cross*, 5–6, 264–66; DeBow, *Statistical View*; Noll, *Civil
War as a Theological Crisis*, 17–29; McPherson, afterword, 409; Hatch, *Democratization*, 210–11.

12. SNHJ, November 20, 1840; "President W. L. Lingle Finds Old Document";
Withers, *Semi-Centennial Catalogue*, 32, 92; "South Amenia Rejoices," *New York
Observer*, December 23, 1909, 837; "Obituary, Sylvanus Nye Hutchison," *New York
Observer*, May 5, 1910, 574; Patterson, *Patterson's American Educational Directory*, 561.

13. McPherson, afterword.

14. See Christian Smith, *Secular Revolution*. For the secularization of public schools, see Tyack, "Kingdom"; Jorgenson, *State and the Non-Public School*. For an overview of historiography, see Perko, "Religious Schooling." For Americans' turn to secular rather than religious petitions and political involvement, see Walters, *American Reformers*, 193–217.

15. SNHJ, May 12, 1839.

16. For example, see Sandberg, *Lean In*; Fels, *Necessary Dreams*.

17. John F. Foard, "Then and Now," *CW*, February 10, 1883; "Death of Mrs. Hutchison," *North Carolina Presbyterian*, April 24, 1867. Also see J. B. Alexander, *History of Mecklenburg County*, 19, 325; Tompkins, *History*, 114.

18. Psalm 112:6.

Bibliography

MANUSCRIPT COLLECTIONS

Chapel Hill, North Carolina
    Wilson Library, University of North Carolina
        Southern Historical Collection
            Gales Family Papers
            Ernest Haywood Papers
            Susan Davis Nye Hutchison Journals
            Raleigh Academy Trustees' Resolutions
            Martha Ryan Cipher Book
            John Steele Papers
Litchfield, Connecticut
    Litchfield Female Academy Archives
Philadelphia, Pennsylvania
    Presbyterian Historical Society
        First Presbyterian Church of Amenia, New York, Records, 1749–1989
        First Presbyterian Church of Augusta, Georgia, Records, 1804–1969
        First Presbyterian Church of Raleigh, North Carolina, Records, 1816–1963
Raleigh, North Carolina
    North Carolina State Archives
        Gales Papers
        Susan Davis Nye Hutchison Journal (vol. 1)
Worcester, Massachusetts
    American Antiquarian Society
        School Catalog Collection

NEWSPAPERS

African Repository and Colonial Journal, Washington, D.C., 1835–40

American Annals of Education, Boston, Massachusetts, 1831–40

American Mercury, Connecticut, 1823

American Sunday School Teachers' Magazine, 1830

Augusta Chronicle, Georgia, 1834–37

Augusta Chronicle and Georgia Advertiser, Georgia, 1830–31

Carolina Watchman, North Carolina, 1836–49

Charleston Observer, South Carolina, 1835–38

Daily National Intelligencer, Washington, D.C., 1840–41

Davidsonian, Charlotte,
North Carolina, 1931
Georgia Constitutionalist, 1825–27,
1832–34
Macon Telegraph, Georgia, 1828, 1832–35
Mecklenburg Jeffersonian, North
Carolina, 1841–46

Raleigh Register, North Carolina,
1800–1840
Raleigh Standard, North Carolina, 1835
Raleigh Star, North Carolina, 1815–30
Richmond Enquirer, Virginia, 1835–37
Western Carolinian, North Carolina,
1835–40

BOOKS, ARTICLES, DISSERTATIONS, AND ONLINE SOURCES

Abbott, Andrew. "The Historicality of Individuals." *Social Science History* 29 (Spring 2005): 1–13.

Adams, Henry. *History of the United States during the First Administration of Jefferson.* Vol. 1. New York: Scribner's, 1921.

Adams, Jasper. *Elements of Moral Philosophy.* Cambridge, Mass.: Folsom, Wells, and Thurston, 1837.

Albisetti, James C., Joyce Goodman, and Rebecca Rogers, eds. *Girls' Secondary Education in the Western World: From the 18th to the 20th Century.* New York: Palgrave Macmillan, 2010.

Alexander, Gross, James B. Scouller, R. V. Foster, and Thomas Cary Johnson. *A History of the Methodist Church, South; the United Presbyterian Church; the Cumberland Presbyterian Church; and the Presbyterian Church, South, in the United States.* New York: Christian Literature, 1894.

Alexander, J. B. *The History of Mecklenburg County, from 1740 to 1900.* Charlotte, N.C.: Observer, 1902.

Ambrose, Douglas. "Of Stations and Relations: Proslavery Christianity in Early National Virginia." In *Religion and the Antebellum Debate over Slavery*, edited by John R. McKivigan and Mitchell Snay, 35–67. Athens: University of Georgia Press, 1998.

American Anti-Slavery Society. *Second Annual Report of the American Anti-Slavery Society; With the Speeches Delivered at the Anniversary Meeting, Held in the City of New-York on the 12th May, 1835.* New York: Door, 1835.

———. *Third Annual Report of the American Anti-Slavery Society.* New York: Dorr, 1836.

American Bible Society. *Annual Report of the American Bible Society.* Vol. 45. New York: American Bible Society, 1860.

American Board of Commissioners for Foreign Missions. *Report of the American Board of Commissioners for Foreign Missions: Presented at the Twenty-Eighth Annual Meeting: Held in the City of Newark, N.J., September 13, 14, and 15, 1837.* Boston: Crocker and Brewster, 1837.

American Colonization Society. "Extract from the Minutes of Hopewell Presbytery." *African Repository and Colonial Journal* 12 (1836): 218.

———. "Review of Mr. Pinkney's Address." *African Repository and Colonial Journal* 5 (1830): 331.

American Sunday School Union. *Union Questions of Select Portions of Scripture from the Old and New Testaments.* Vol. 3. Philadelphia: American Sunday-School Union, 1830.

American Tract Society. *First Annual Report of the American Tract Society, Instituted at New York, 1825.* New York: Fanshaw, 1826.

Andrews, Dee. *The Methodists and Revolutionary America, 1760–1800: The Shaping of an Evangelical Culture.* Princeton: Princeton University Press, 2000.

Andrews, William L., ed. *North Carolina Slave Narratives: The Lives of Moses Roper, Lunsford Lane, Moses Grandy, and Thomas H. Jones.* Chapel Hill: University of North Carolina Press, 2003.

Andrews, William L., Frances Smith Foster, and Trudier Harris, eds. *The Concise Oxford Companion to African American Literature.* New York: Oxford University Press, 2001.

Appleby, Joyce. "The Social Consequences of American Revolutionary Ideals in the Early Republic." In *The Middling Sorts: Explorations in the History of the American Middle Class,* edited by Burton J. Bledstein and Robert D. Johnston, 32–49. New York: Psychology Press, 2001.

Armytage, W. H. G. "The Editorial Experience of Joseph Gales, 1786–1794." *North Carolina Historical Review* 28 (July 1951): 332–61.

Asbury, Francis. *Journal of Rev. Francis Asbury, Bishop of the Methodist Episcopal Church.* New York: Eaton and Mains, 1800.

Augusta (Georgia) First Presbyterian Church. *Memorial of the Centennial Anniversary of the First Presbyterian Church, Augusta, Georgia: The Anniversary Exercises May Fifteenth to Eighteenth, 1904.* Philadelphia: Allen, Lane, and Scott, 1904.

Bacon, Leonard Woolsey. *The American Church History Series: A History of American Christianity.* New York: Scribner's, 1898.

Baer, Hans A., and Merrill Singer. *African American Religion: Varieties of Protest and Accommodation.* Knoxville: University of Tennessee Press, 2002.

Bailyn, Bernard. *Education in the Forming of American Society: Needs and Opportunities for Study.* Chapel Hill: University of North Carolina Press, 1960.

Baker, Paula C. "The Domestication of Politics: Women and American Political Society, 1780–1920." *American Historical Review* 89 (June 1984): 620–47.

Baldwin, Lewis V. "Black Women and African Union Methodism, 1813–1983." *Methodist History* 21 (July 1983): 225–37.

Barber, Lynn. *The Heyday of Natural History, 1820–1870.* New York: Doubleday, 1980.

Bardaglio, Peter W. *Reconstructing the Household: Families, Sex, and the Law in the Nineteenth-Century South.* Chapel Hill: University of North Carolina Press, 1995.

Barlow, Ruth E. *A History of the South Amenia Presbyterian Church of Union Society.* Amenia, N.Y.: Union Society, 1959.

Barnard, Henry, ed. "Course of Instruction in the Common Schools of Prussia and Wirtemberg." *Connecticut Common School Journal and Annals of Education* 1 (April 1, 1839): 134–36.

————. "Report of the Secretary of the Board." *Connecticut Common School Journal* 1 (June 1, 1839): 155–96.

Barnes, Albert. *The Church and Slavery*. Philadelphia: Parry and McMillan, 1857.

Barnes, Gilbert H. *The Antislavery Impulse, 1830–1844*. 1933; reprint, Gloucester, Mass.: Smith, 1957.

Basch, Norma. *Framing American Divorce: From the Revolutionary Generation to the Victorians*. Berkeley: University of California Press, 2001.

Battle, Kemp P. *The Early History of Raleigh, the Capital City of North Carolina: A Centennial Address Delivered by Invitation of the Committee on the Centennial Celebration of the Foundation of the City*. Raleigh, N.C.: Edwards and Broughton, 1893.

————. *Sketches of the Early History of the City of Raleigh: Centennial Address, Fourth of July, 1876*. Raleigh, N.C.: Raleigh News, 1877.

Beadie, Nancy. *Education and the Creation of Capital in the Early American Republic*. New York: Cambridge University Press, 2010.

————. "Emma Willard's Idea Put to the Test: The Consequences of State Support of Female Education in New York, 1819–67." *History of Education Quarterly* 33 (Winter 1993): 543–62.

————. "Internal Improvement: The Structure and Culture of Academy Expansion in New York State in the Antebellum Era, 1820–1860." In *Chartered Schools*, edited by Beadie and Tolley, 89–116.

————. "Toward a History of Education Markets in the United States: An Introduction." *Social Science History* 32 (Spring 2008): 47–74.

————. "Tuition Funding for Common Schools: Education Markets and Market Regulation in Rural New York, 1815–1850." *Social Science History* 32 (Spring 2008): 107–34.

Beadie, Nancy, and Kim Tolley, eds. *Chartered Schools: Two Hundred Years of Independent Academies in the United States, 1727–1925*. New York: Routledge, 2002.

Beaty, Mary D. *A History of Davidson College*. Davidson, N.C.: Briarpatch, 1988.

Beecher, Catharine E. *An Essay on Slavery and Abolitionism in Reference to the Duty of American Females*. Philadelphia: Perkins, 1837.

————. *An Essay on the Education of Female Teachers*. New York: Van Nostrand and Dwight, 1835.

————. "Hartford Female Seminary and Its Founder." *American Journal of Education* 28 (1878): 65–86.

Beecher, Lyman. *Autobiography, Correspondence, Etc., of Lyman Beecher, D.D*. Vol. 1. New York: Harper, 1864.

Bennett, John. *Strictures on Female Education*. 1795; reprint, New York: Source Book Press, 1971.

Berkin, Carol. *Revolutionary Mothers: Women in the Struggle for America's Independence*. New York: Random House, 2006.

Berlin, Ira. *Slaves without Masters: The Free Negro in the Antebellum South*. New York: Oxford University Press, 1974.

Bernstein, Richard B. *Thomas Jefferson*. New York: Oxford University Press, 2005.

Birney, James Gillespie. *Letters of James Gillespie Birney, 1831–1857*. Vol. 1. New York: Appleton-Century, 1938.

Bishop, J. Leander. *A History of American Manufactures from 1608 to 1860*. Philadelphia: Young, 1864.

Blair, David. *A Grammar of the Principles and Practice of Chemistry*. Vol. 2. London: Phillips, 1810.

Blauvelt, Martha Tomhave. "'This Altogather Precious tho Wholy Worthless Book': The Diary of Mary Guion, 1800–1852." In *Anxious Power: Reading, Writing, and Ambivalence in Narrative by Women*, edited by Carol J. Singley and Susan Elizabeth Sweeney, 125–42. Albany: State University of New York Press, 1993.

Blunt, Joseph. *American Annual Register*. Vol. 2. New York: Blunt and Blunt, 1828.

Board of National Popular Education. *Annual Report of the General Agent of the Board of National Popular Education, with the Constitution of the Board*. Cincinnati: Franklin, 1848.

Bode, Frederick A. "The Transformation of Evangelical Communities in Middle Georgia: Twiggs County, 1820–1861." *Journal of Southern History* 60 (November 1994): 711–48.

Bogger, Tommy. *Free Blacks in Norfolk, Virginia, 1790–1860: The Darker Side of Freedom*. Charlottesville: University Press of Virginia, 1997.

Boles, John B. *Black Southerners, 1619–1869*. Lexington: University Press of Kentucky, 1984.

———. *Religion in Antebellum Kentucky*. Lexington: University Press of Kentucky, 1976.

Boston Female Anti-Slavery Society. *Report of the Boston Female Anti-Slavery Society, with a Concise Statement of Events, Previous and Subsequent to the Annual Meeting of 1835*. Boston: Boston Female Anti-Slavery Society, 1836.

Bowditch, William Ingersoll. *Slavery and the Constitution*. Boston: Wallcut, 1849.

Boyd, Lois A., and R. Douglas Brackenridge. *Presbyterian Women in America: Two Centuries of a Quest for Status*. 2nd ed. Westport, Conn.: Greenwood, 1996.

Boydston, Jeanne, Mary Kelley, and Anne Margolis. *The Limits of Sisterhood: The Beecher Sisters on Women's Rights and Woman's Sphere*. Chapel Hill: University of North Carolina Press, 1988.

Boylan, Anne M. *The Origins of Women's Activism: New York and Boston, 1797–1840*. Chapel Hill: University of North Carolina Press, 2002.

———. *Sunday School: The Formation of an American Institution, 1790–1880*. New Haven, Conn.: Yale University Press, 1988.

Brana-Shute, Rosemary, and Randy J. Sparks, eds. *Paths to Freedom: Manumission in the Atlantic World*. Columbia: University of South Carolina Press, 2009.

Brekus, Catherine. *Sarah Osborn's World: The Rise of Evangelical Christianity in Early America*. New Haven, Conn.: Yale University Press, 2013.

———. *Strangers and Pilgrims: Female Preaching in America, 1740–1845*. Chapel Hill: University of North Carolina Press, 1998.

Bremer, Fredrika. *The Homes of the New World: Impressions of America*. Vol. 1. New York: Harper, 1853.

Brickley, Lynne Templeton. "Sarah Pierce's Litchfield Female Academy, 1792–1833." Ed.D. diss., Harvard University, 1985.

Brown, Kathleen M. "Beyond the Great Debates: Gender and Race in Early America." In *The Challenge of American History*, edited by Louis P. Masur, 96–124. Baltimore: Johns Hopkins University Press, 1999.

Brown, Lois A. "William Lloyd Garrison and Emancipatory Feminism in Nineteenth-Century America." In *William Lloyd Garrison at Two Hundred: History, Legacy, and Memory*, edited by James Brewer Steward, 41–76. New Haven, Conn.: Yale University Press, 2008.

Brumberg, Joan Jacobs. *Mission for Life: The Judson Family and American Evangelical Culture*. New York: New York University Press, 1984.

Bryant, Gary E. "Women, White, Working Class." In *New Encyclopedia of Southern Culture*, vol. 20, *Social Class*, edited by Charles Reagan Wilson, 303–6. Chapel Hill: University of North Carolina Press, 2012.

Budros, Art. "The Antislavery Movement in Early America: Religion, Social Environment, and Slave Manumissions." *Social Forces* 84 (December 2005): 937–62.

Bunkers, Suzanne L., and Cynthia Anne Huff, eds. *Inscribing the Daily: Critical Essays on Women's Diaries*. Amherst: University of Massachusetts Press, 1996.

Burin, Eric. *Slavery and the Peculiar Solution: A History of the American Colonization Society*. Gainesville: University Press of Florida, 2008.

Butler, John. *Awash in a Sea of Faith*. Cambridge: Harvard University Press, 1990.

Byron, Tammy K. *"A Catechism for Their Special Use": Slave Catechisms in the Antebellum South*. Fayetteville: University of Arkansas Press, 2008.

Cadle, Farris W. *Georgia Land Surveying History and Law*. Athens: University of Georgia Press, 1991.

Calhoun, John C. *The Works of John C. Calhoun*. Vol. 4. New York: Appleton, 1854.

Carter, Christine Jacobson. *Southern Single Blessedness: Unmarried Women in the Urban South, 1800–1865*. Urbana: University of Illinois Press, 2006.

Carwardine, Richard. "The Second Great Awakening in the Urban Centers: An Examination of Methodism and the 'New Measures.'" *Journal of American History* 59 (September 1972): 327–40.

Cashin, Edward J. *Old Springfield: Race and Religion in Augusta, Georgia*. Augusta, Ga.: Springfield Village Park Foundation, 1995.

———. *The Story of Augusta*. 1980; reprint, Spartanburg, S.C.: Reprint Company, 1991.

Cashin, Joan. *A Family Venture: Men and Women on the Southern Frontier*. New York: Oxford University Press, 1991.

Catlow, Samuel. *Observations on a Course of Instruction, for Young Persons in the Middle Classes of Life*. Sheffield, U.K.: Gales, 1793.

Censer, Jane Turner. *North Carolina Planters and Their Children, 1800–1860*. Baton Rouge: Louisiana State University Press, 1984.

Chambers-Schiller, Lee Virginia. *Liberty a Better Husband: Single Women in America: The Generations of 1780–1840*. New Haven, Conn.: Yale University Press, 1984.

Chaplin, Joyce E. "Slavery and the Principle of Humanity: A Modern Idea in the Early Lower South." *Journal of Social History* 24 (December 1990): 299–315.

Chused, Richard H. "Married Women's Property Law, 1800–1850." *Georgetown Law Journal* 71 (June 1983): 1359–1425.

Clancy, James. *A Treatise of the Rights, Duties, and Liabilities of Husband and Wife, at Law and in Equity*. New York: Treadway and Bogert, 1828.

Clifford, Geraldine J. "Man/Woman/Teacher: Gender, Family, and Career in American Educational History." In *American Teachers: Histories of a Profession at Work*, edited by Donald Warren, 293–343. New York: Macmillan, 1989.

Clinton, Catherine. *The Plantation Mistress: Woman's World in the Old South*. New York: Pantheon, 1982.

Cogswell, William. *The Theological Class Book: Containing a System of Divinity in the Form of Question and Answer, with Scriptural Proofs Designed for Theological Classes and the Higher Classes in Sabbath Schools*. Boston: Crocker and Brewster, 1838.

Cohen, Patricia Cline. *A Calculating People: The Spread of Numeracy in Early America*. Chicago: University of Chicago Press, 1982.

Connor, R. D. W. *North Carolina: Rebuilding an Ancient Commonwealth, 1584–1925*. Vol. 1. Chicago: American Historical Society, 1929.

Coon, Charles L., ed. *The Beginnings of Public Education in North Carolina: A Documentary History, 1790–1840*. Vol. 2. Raleigh, N.C.: Edwards and Broughton, 1908.

———, ed. *North Carolina Schools and Academies, 1790–1840: A Documentary History*. Raleigh, N.C.: Edwards and Broughton, 1915.

Cooper, Valerie C. *Word, Like Fire: Maria Stewart, the Bible, and the Rights of African Americans*. Charlottesville: University of Virginia Press, 2011.

Corbett, Michael, and Julia Mitchell Corbett. *Politics and Religion in the United States*. New York: Garland, 1999.

Cornelius, Janet Duitsman. *Slave Missions and the Black Church in the Antebellum South*. Columbia: University of South Carolina Press, 1999.

———. *When I Can Read My Title Clear: Literacy, Slavery, and Religion in the Antebellum South*. Columbia: University of South Carolina Press, 1991.

Cotlar, Seth. "Joseph Gales and the Making of the Jeffersonian Middle Class." In *The Revolution of 1800: Democracy, Race, and the New Republic*, edited by James Horn, Jan Ellen Lewis, and Peter S. Onuf, 331–59. Charlottesville: University of Virginia Press, 2002.

———. *Tom Paine's America: The Rise and Fall of Transatlantic Radicalism in the Early Republic*. Charlottesville: University of Virginia Press, 2011.

Cott, Nancy F. *The Bonds of Womanhood: "Women's Sphere" in New England, 1780–1835*. New Haven, Conn.: Yale University Press, 1977.

———. *Public Vows: A History of Marriage and the Nation*. Cambridge: Harvard University Press, 2002.

———. "Young Women in the Second Great Awakening in New England." *Feminist Studies* 3 (Autumn 1975): 15–29.

Curtis, Thomas, ed. *The London Encyclopaedia; or, Universal Dictionary of Science, Art, Literature, and Practical Mechanics, Comprising a Popular View of the Present State of Knowledge.* Vol. 14. London: Tegg, 1839.

Daly, John Patrick. *When Slavery Was Called Freedom: Evangelicalism, Proslavery, and the Causes of the Civil War.* Lexington: University Press of Kentucky, 2002.

Davidson, Grace Gillam, comp. *Historical Collections of the Georgia Chapters Daughters of the American Revolution.* Vol. 2, *Records of Richmond County, Georgia, Formerly Saint Paul's Parish.* 1929; reprint, Baltimore: Clearfield, 1995.

Davidson, Sarah F. *A Life in Antebellum Charlotte: The Private Journal of Sarah F. Davidson.* Edited by Karen M. McConnell, Janet S. Dyer, and Ann Williams. Charleston, S.C.: History Press, 2005.

Davis, David Brion. "The Emergence of Immediatism in British and American Antislavery Thought." *Mississippi Valley Historical Review* 49 (September 1962): 209–30.

———. *The Problem of Slavery in the Age of Emancipation.* New York: Knopf, 2014.

———. *The Problem of Slavery in the Age of Revolution, 1770–1823.* Ithaca: Cornell University Press, 1975.

Davis, Lance E., Richard A. Easterlin, and William N. Parker, eds. *American Economic Growth: An Economist's History of the United States.* New York: Harper and Row, 1972.

DeBow, J. D. B. *Statistical View of the United States . . . Being a Compendium of the Seventh Census.* Washington, D.C.: Tucker, 1854.

Demos, John. *A Little Commonwealth: Family Life in Plymouth Colony.* 1970; reprint, New York: Oxford University Press, 2000.

Dexter, Elisabeth Anthony. *Colonial Women of Affairs: Women in Business and the Professions in America before 1776.* New York: Kelley, 1972.

Doar, Ashley K. "Cipher Books in the Southern Historical Collection." Master's thesis, University of North Carolina at Chapel Hill, 2006. Available at http://ils.unc.edu/MSpapers/3160.pdf. Accessed June 2, 2009.

Douglass, Frederick. *Narrative of the Life of Frederick Douglass, an American Slave, Written by Himself.* London: Collins, 1832.

Du Bois, W. E. B. *Black Reconstruction in America, 1860–1880.* 1935; reprint, New York: Free Press, 1992.

Dunaway, Wilma A. *Women, Work, and Family in the Antebellum Mountain South.* New York: Cambridge University Press, 2008.

Dunn, Richard. "Black Society in the Chesapeake, 1776–1810." In *Slavery and Freedom in the Age of the American Revolution,* edited by Ira Berlin and Ronald Hoffman, 49–82. Charlottesville: University Press of Virginia for the U.S. Capitol Historical Society, 1983.

Dwight, Timothy. *The Charitable Blessed: A Sermon, Preached in the First Church in New Haven, August 8, 1810.* New Haven, Conn.: Sidney's, 1810.

———. *Theology: Explained and Defended, in a Series of Sermons.* Edited by Sereno Edwards Dwight. New Haven, Conn.: Dwight, 1839.

———. *Travels in New-England and New York.* New Haven, Conn.: Dwight, 1821.

Easterlin, Richard A. "Factors in the Decline of Farm Family Fertility in the United States: Some Preliminary Research Results." *Journal of American History* 63 (December 1976): 600–614.

Eastman, Carolyn. "The Female Cicero: Young Women's Oratory and Gendered Public Participation in the Early American Republic." *Gender and History* 19 (August 2007): 260–83.

———. *A Nation of Speechifiers: Making an American Public after the Revolution.* Chicago: University of Chicago Press, 2010.

Eaton, Clement. "Winifred and Joseph Gales, Liberals in the Old South." *Journal of Southern History* 10 (November 1944): 461–74.

Elliott, Robert Neal, Jr. *The Raleigh Register, 1799–1863.* Chapel Hill: University of North Carolina Press, 1955.

Elsbree, Willard S. *The American Teacher: Evolution of a Profession in a Democracy.* New York: American Book, 1939.

Emerson, Joseph. *Female Education: A Discourse, Delivered at the Dedication of the Seminary Hall in Saugus, January 14, 1822.* Boston: Armstrong and Crocker & Brewster, 1823.

Engerman, Stanley Lewis. *The Cambridge Economic History of the United States.* Vol. 1. New York: Cambridge University Press, 2000.

Fairbanks, Mary J., ed. *Emma Willard and Her Pupils; or, Fifty Years of the Troy Female Seminary, 1822–1872.* New York: Sage, 1898.

Farnham, Christie Anne. *The Education of the Southern Belle: Higher Education and Student Socialization in the Antebellum South.* New York: New York University Press, 1994.

Fels, Anna. *Necessary Dreams: Ambition in Women's Changing Lives.* New York: Pantheon, 2004.

"The Female Character." *Ladies' Literary Cabinet,* March 18, 1820, 147–48.

"Female Education, No. II." *Western Academician and Journal of Education and Science* (1837–38): 478–80. Edited by John W. Picket.

Ferguson, Adam. *Institutes of Moral Philosophy.* New ed. Mentz and Frankfort, Ger.: Schiller, 1786.

Ferguson, James. *An Easy Introduction to Astronomy for Young Gentlemen and Ladies.* Philadelphia: M'Laughlin, 1805.

Fields, Annie. *Life and Letters of Harriet Beecher Stowe.* Cambridge, Mass.: Riverside, 1897.

Finney, Charles G. *Lectures on Revivals of Religion.* New York: Leavitt, Lord, 1835.

———. *Lectures on Systematic Theology: Embracing Lectures on Moral Government, Together with Atonement, Moral and Physical Depravity, Regeneration, Philosophical Theories, and Evidences of Regeneration.* Oberlin, Ohio: Fitch, 1847.

———. *Memoirs of Rev. Charles G. Finney.* New York: Barnes, 1876.

First Presbyterian Church, Troy, New York. *Brief Account of the Origins and Progress of the Divisions in the First Presbyterian Church; Containing Also Strictures upon the New Doctrines Preached by the Rev C. G. Finney and N. S. S. Beman, with a Summary Relation of the Trial of the Latter before the Troy*

Presbytery, by a Member of the Late Church and Congregation. Troy, N.Y.: Tuttle and Richards, 1827.

Fitzhugh, George. *Sociology for the South; or, The Failure of Free Society*. Richmond, Va.: Morris, 1854.

Fogel, Robert William, and Stanley L. Engerman. *Time on the Cross: The Economics of American Negro Slavery*. Boston: Little, Brown, 1974.

Foote, William Henry. *Sketches of North Carolina*. Carlisle, Mass.: Applewood, 1846.

Forbes, Robert P. "Slavery and the Evangelical Enlightenment." In *Religion and the Antebellum Debate over Slavery*, edited by John R. McKivigan and Mitchell Snay, 68–108. Athens: University of Georgia Press, 1998.

Ford, Lacy K. *Deliver Us from Evil: The Slavery Question in the Old South*. New York: Oxford University Press, 2009.

Foster, Charles I. *An Errand of Mercy: The Evangelical United Front, 1790–1837*. Chapel Hill: University of North Carolina Press, 1960.

Fowler, Henry. "Educational Services of Mrs. Emma Willard." *American Journal of Education* 6 (1859): 125–68.

Fox-Genovese, Elizabeth. *Within the Plantation Household: Black and White Women of the Old South*. Chapel Hill: University of North Carolina Press, 1988.

Fox-Genovese, Elizabeth, and Eugene D. Genovese. "The Divine Sanction of Social Order: Religious Foundations of the Southern Slaveholders' World View." *Journal of the American Academy of Religion* 55 (Summer 1987): 211–33.

———. *The Mind of the Master Class: History and Faith in the Southern Slaveholders' Worldview*. New York: Cambridge University Press, 2005.

Franklin, Benjamin. *The Autobiography of Benjamin Franklin*. Philadelphia: Lippincott, 1868.

Franklin, John Hope. *The Free Negro in North Carolina, 1790–1860*. Chapel Hill: University of North Carolina Press, 1995.

Franklin, John Hope, and Loren Schweninger. *Runaway Slaves: Rebels on the Plantation*. New York: Oxford University Press, 1999.

Fraser, James W. *Pedagogue for God's Kingdom: Lyman Beecher and the Second Great Awakening*. Lanham, Md.: University Press of America, 1985.

Fraser, Walter J. *Savannah in the Old South*. Athens: University of Georgia Press, 2003.

Freehling, William W. *The Road to Disunion*. New York: Oxford University Press, 1990.

Freeman, Jonathan. "The Religious Revival at Bridgeton, N.J. in 1817." *Journal of the Presbyterian Historical Society* 7 (September 1913): 155–57.

Friedman, Jean E. *The Enclosed Garden: Women and Community in the Evangelical South, 1830–1900*. Chapel Hill: University of North Carolina Press, 1990.

Furbish, James. *Some Remarks on Education, Textbooks, Etc.* Portland, Me.: Shirley and Hyde, 1828.

Gadski, Mary Ellen. *The History of the New Bern Academy*. New Bern, N.C.: Tryon Palace Commission, 1986.

Gales, Joseph, ed. *Register of Debates in Congress, Comprising the Leading Debates and Incidents of the First Session of the Twenty-Fourth Congress*. Washington, D.C.

UNT Digital Library. http://digital.library.unt.edu/ark:/67531/metadc30765/. Accessed February 17, 2015.

Gallay, Allan. *The Formation of a Planter Elite: Jonathan Bryan and the Southern Colonial Frontier*. Athens: University of Georgia Press, 1989.

———. "The Origins of Slaveholders' Paternalism: George Whitfield, the Bryan Family, and the Great Awakening in the South." *Journal of Southern History* 53 (August 1987): 369–94.

Genovese, Eugene D. *Roll, Jordan, Roll: The World the Slaves Made*. New York: Vintage, 1976.

Georgia. *Acts of the General Assembly of Georgia, Passed in Milledgeville at an Annual Session in November and December, 1829*. Milledgeville, Ga.: Camak and Ragland, 1830.

Gifford, Ronald M. "Thompson, George." *American National Biography Online October 2007 Update*. http://www.anb.org/articles/15/15-01311.html?from=../15/15-00706.html&from_nm=Truth%2C%20Sojourner. Accessed August 10, 2011.

Ginzberg, Lori D. *Women and the Work of Benevolence: Morality, Politics, and Class in the Nineteenth-Century United States*. New Haven, Conn.: Yale University Press, 1990.

Gittell, Ross, and Avis Vidal. *Community Organizing: Building Social Capital as a Development Strategy*. Thousand Oaks, Calif.: Sage Publications, 1998.

Go, Sun, and Peter Lindert. "The Uneven Rise of American Public Schools to 1850." *Journal of Economic History* 70 (March 2010): 1–26.

Goldin, Claudia. "The Economic Status of Women in the Early Republic: Quantitative Evidence." *Journal of Interdisciplinary History* 16 (Winter 1986): 375–404.

Goldin, Claudia, and Kenneth Sokoloff. "Women, Children, and Industrialization in the Early Republic: Evidence from the Manufacturing Censuses." *Journal of Economic History* 42 (December 1982): 741–74.

Gould, Philip. "Civil Society and the Public Woman." *Journal of the Early Republic* 28 (Spring 2008): 29–46.

Graham, Isabella. *The Power of Faith: Exemplified in the Life and Writings of the Late Mrs. Isabella Graham of New York*. New York: Seymour, 1816.

Grammer, Elizabeth Elken. *Some Wild Visions: Autobiographies by Female Itinerant Evangelists in Nineteenth-Century America*. New York: Oxford University Press, 2002.

Green, Elizabeth Alden. *Mary Lyon and Mount Holyoke: Opening the Gates*. Hanover, N.H.: University Press of New England, 1979.

Green, Fletcher. *The Role of the Yankee in the Old South*. Athens: University of Georgia Press, 1972.

Grimké, Sarah Moore. *Letters on the Equality of the Sexes and the Condition of Woman, Addressed to Mary S. Parker, President of the Boston Female Anti-Slavery Society*. Boston: Knapp, 1838.

Hackel, Heidi Brayman, and Catherine E. Kelly, eds. *Reading Women: Literacy, Authorship, and Culture in the Atlantic World, 1500–1800*. Philadelphia: University of Pennsylvania Press, 2008.

Hahn, Steven. *Southern Populism: Yeoman Farmers and the Transformation of the Georgia Upcountry, 1850–1890*. New York: Oxford University Press, 2006.

Hallowell, Anna Davis, ed. *James and Lucretia Mott: Life and Letters*. New York: Houghton Mifflin, 1884.

Hankins, Barry. *The Second Great Awakening and the Transcendentalists*. Westport, Conn.: Greenwood, 2004.

Hardesty, Nancy. *Women Called to Witness: Evangelical Feminism in the 19th Century*. Nashville, Tenn.: Abingdon, 1984.

Hartog, Hendrik. *Man and Wife in America: A History*. Cambridge: Harvard University Press, 2002.

Harvey, Paul. *Freedom's Coming: Religious Culture and the Shaping of the South from the Civil War through the Civil Rights Era*. Chapel Hill: University of North Carolina Press, 2005.

Hatch, Nathan O. *The Democratization of American Christianity*. New Haven, Conn.: Yale University Press, 1991.

Hawkins, William G. *Lunsford Lane; or, Another Helper from North Carolina*. Boston: Crosby and Nichols, 1863.

Hedge, Levi. *Elements of Logick; or, A Summary of the General Principles and Different Modes of Reasoning*. Boston: Gray, Little, and Wilkins, 1827.

Hedrick, Joan D. *Harriet Beecher Stowe: A Life*. New York: Oxford University Press, 1995.

Herndon, Ruth Wallis, and John E. Murray. *Children Bound to Labor: The Pauper Apprentice System in Early America*. Ithaca: Cornell University Press, 2009.

Hewitt, Nancy A. "The Perimeters of Women's Power in American Religion." In *The Evangelical Tradition in America*, edited by Leonard I. Sweet, 233–56. Macon: Mercer University Press, 1984.

Heyrman, Christine Leigh. *Southern Cross: The Beginnings of the Bible Belt*. Chapel Hill: University of North Carolina Press, 1998.

Hodes, Martha. *The Sea Captain's Wife: A True Story of Love, Race, and War in the Nineteenth Century*. New York: Norton, 2006.

Hodgson, Adam. *Remarks during a Journey through North America in the Years 1819, 1820, and 1821*. New York: Whiting, 1823.

Hoffman, Nancy, ed. *Woman's "True" Profession: Voices from the History of Teaching*. Old Westbury, N.Y.: Feminist Press, 1981.

Hoffman, Stephanie B. "Behind Closed Doors: Impotence Trials and the Trans-Historical Right to Marital Privacy." *Boston University Law Review* 89 (December 2009): 1725–52.

Holland, F. Ross, Jr. *A History of the Cape Hatteras Light Station*. Washington, D.C.: National Park Service, Division of History, Office of Archeology and Historic Preservation, 1968.

Howe, Daniel Walter. *What Hath God Wrought: The Transformation of America, 1815–1848*. New York: Oxford University Press, 2007.

Howe, George. *History of the Presbyterian Church in South Carolina*. Vol. 1. Columbia, S.C.: Duffie and Chapman, 1870.

Hrdy, Sarah Blaffer. *Mothers and Others: The Evolutionary Origins of Mutual Understanding*. Cambridge: Harvard University Press, 2009.

Hunter, Henry. *Sacred Biography; or, The History of the Patriarchs*. Vol. 1. New York: Collins and Hanay, 1828.

Hutcheson, Francis. *A System of Moral Philosophy, in Three Books*. Vol. 1. London, 1755.

Hutchison, John Russell. *Reminiscences, Sketches, and Addresses Selected from My Papers during a Ministry of Forty-Five Years in Mississippi, Louisiana, and Texas*. Houston: Cushing, 1874.

Hutchison, Susan Nye. "Mrs. Hutchinson's [*sic*] Letter." *African Repository and Colonial Journal* 12 (1836): 154–57.

———. "Mrs. Hutchison's View of Female Education." In *Prospectus*, 5–12.

———. "To the Female Members of the Presbyterian Church." *Charleston Observer*, February 18, 1837.

Isaac, Rhys. *The Transformation of Virginia, 1740–1790*. Chapel Hill: University of North Carolina Press, 1999.

Jabour, Anya. *Marriage in the Early Republic: Elizabeth and William Wirt and the Companionate Ideal*. Baltimore: Johns Hopkins University Press, 1998.

———. *Scarlett's Sisters: Young Women in the Old South*. Chapel Hill: University of North Carolina Press, 2007.

Jefferson, Thomas. *The Jeffersonian Cyclopedia: A Comprehensive Collection of the Views of Thomas Jefferson*. Edited by J. P. Foley. New York: Funk and Wagnalls, 1900.

Jeffrey, Thomas E. *State Parties and National Politics: North Carolina, 1815–1861*. Athens: University of Georgia Press, 2012.

Jennings, Samuel K. *The Married Lady's Companion; or, Poor Man's Friend: In Four Parts*. New York: Dow, 1808.

Johnson, Guion Griffis. *Ante-Bellum North Carolina: A Social History*. Chapel Hill: University of North Carolina Press, 1937.

Johnson, Oliver. "Recollections of an Abolitionist, in the N.Y. Tribune." *Unity: Freedom, Fellowship and Character in Religion*, August 1, 1879, 168–69.

Johnson, Paul E. *A Shopkeeper's Millennium: Society and Revivals in Rochester, New York, 1815–1837*. 1978; reprint, New York: Hill and Wang, 2004.

Jones, Delia W. "Necessity of Female Education: An Essay by Mrs. Delia W. Jones, Read before the State Educational Association, at Statesville, July 8th, 1858." *North-Carolina Journal of Education* 1 (September 1858): 263–67.

Jorgenson, Lloyd P. *The State and the Non-Public School, 1825–1925*. Columbia: University of Missouri Press, 1987.

Joyner, Charles W. *Shared Traditions: Southern History and Folk Culture*. Urbana: University of Illinois Press, 1999.

Juster, Susan. *Disorderly Women: Sexual Politics and Evangelicalism in Revolutionary New England*. Ithaca: Cornell University Press, 1996.

Kaestle, Carl F. "Common Schools before the Common School Revival: New York Schooling in the 1790s." *History of Education Quarterly* 12 (Winter 1972): 465–500.

———. *Pillars of the Republic: Common Schools and American Society, 1780–1860.*
New York: Hill and Wang, 1983.

Kaestle, Carl F., and Maris A. Vinovskis. *Education and Social Change in Nineteenth-Century Massachusetts.* New York: Cambridge University Press, 2009.

Kaufman, Polly Welts. *Women Teachers on the Frontier.* New Haven, Conn.: Yale University Press, 1984.

Keller, Charles Roy. *The Second Great Awakening in Connecticut.* New Haven, Conn.: Yale University Press, 1942.

Kelley, Mary. "Crafting Subjectivities: Women, Reading, and Self-Imagining." In *Reading Women,* edited by Hackel and Kelly, 55–78.

———. *Learning to Stand and Speak: Women, Education, and Public Life in America's Republic.* Chapel Hill: University of North Carolina Press, 2008.

———. "'The Need of Their Genius': Women's Reading and Writing Practices in Early America." *Journal of the Early Republic* 28 (Spring 2008): 1–82.

Kelly, Catherine E. *In the New England Fashion: Reshaping Women's Lives in the Nineteenth Century.* Ithaca: Cornell University Press, 2002.

———. "Reading and the Problem of Accomplishment." In *Reading Women,* edited by Hackel and Kelly, 124–50.

Kennedy, V. Lynn. *Born Southern: Childbirth, Motherhood, and Social Networks in the Old South.* Baltimore: Johns Hopkins University Press, 2010.

Kerber, Linda K. *No Constitutional Right to Be Ladies: Women and the Obligations of Citizenship.* New York: Hill and Wang, 1998.

———. "The Republican Mother: Women and the Enlightenment—An American Perspective." *American Quarterly* 28 (Summer 1976): 187–205.

———. "Separate Spheres, Female Worlds, Woman's Place: The Rhetoric of Women's History." In *Toward an Intellectual History of Women: Essays by Linda Kerber,* 159–99. Chapel Hill: University of North Carolina Press, 1997.

———. *Women of the Republic: Intellect and Ideology in Revolutionary America.* Chapel Hill: University of North Carolina Press, 1980.

Kerber, Linda K., Nancy F. Cott, Robert Gross, Lynn Hunt, Carroll Smith-Rosenberg, and Christine M. Stansell. "Beyond Roles, Beyond Spheres: Thinking about Gender in the Early Republic." *William and Mary Quarterly,* 3rd ser., 46 (July 1989): 565–85.

Kerns, Kathryn. "Antebellum Higher Education for Women in Western New York State." Ph.D. diss., University of Pennsylvania, 1993.

Kerrison, Catherine. *Claiming the Pen: Women and Intellectual Life in the Early American South.* Ithaca: Cornell University Press, 2006.

Kessler-Harris, Alice. *Out to Work: A History of Wage-Earning Women in the United States.* New York: Oxford University Press, 1982.

Kilbride, Daniel. *An American Aristocracy: Southern Planters in Antebellum Philadelphia.* Columbia: University of South Carolina Press, 2006.

Kirby, R. S. "Horrid Cruelty, in the Murder of a Slave in America." *Kirby's Wonderful and Eccentric Museum; or, Magazine of Remarkable Characters, Including All the Curiosities of Nature and Art, from the Remotest Period to the Present Time, Drawn from Every Authentic Source* 6 (1820): 400–402.

Klinghoffer, Judith Apter, and Lois Elkis. "'The Petticoat Electors': Women's Suffrage in New Jersey." *Journal of the Early Republic* 12 (Summer 1992): 159–93.

Knight, Edgar W. "Notes on John Chavis." *North Carolina Historical Review* 7 (July 1930): 326–45.

Labaree, David F. "Curriculum, Credentials, and the Middle Class: A Case Study of a Nineteenth Century High School." *Sociology of Education* 59 (January 1986): 42–57.

Lancaster, Marshall. *Raleigh: An Unorthodox History of North Carolina's Capital.* Asheboro, N.C.: Down Home, 1992.

Lancee, Bram. *Immigrant Performance in the Labour Market: Bonding and Bridging Social Capital.* Amsterdam: Amsterdam University Press, 2012.

Lane, Lunsford. *The Narrative of Lunsford Lane, Formerly of Raleigh, N.C.* Boston: Torrey, 1842.

Lasser, Carol, and Stacey Robertson. *Antebellum Women: Private, Public, Partisan.* Lanham, Md.: Rowman and Littlefield, 2010.

Lathrop, D. W. *The Case of the General Assembly of the Presbyterian Church in the United States of America, before the Supreme Court of the Common wealth of Pennsylvania, Impartially Reported by Disinterested Stenographers, Including All the Proceedings, Testimony, and Arguments at Nisi Prius, and before the Court in Bank, with the Charge of Judge Rogers, the Verdict of the Jury, and the Opinion of Chief Justice Gibson.* Philadelphia: McElroy, 1839.

Lathrop, Joseph. *Sermons on Various Subjects, Evangelical, Devotional, and Practical, Adapted to the Promotion of Christian Piety, Family Religion, and Youthful Virtue.* Worcester, Mass.: Thomas, 1810.

Laws of the Raleigh Academy: With the Plan of Education Annexed. Raleigh: Gales and Seaton, 1822.

Lebsock, Suzanne. *The Free Women of Petersburg: Status and Culture in a Southern Town, 1784–1860.* New York: Norton, 1984.

Lee, Jarena, Zilpha Elaw, and Julia A. J. Foote. *Sisters of the Spirit: Three Black Women's Autobiographies of the Nineteenth Century.* Edited and introduction by William L. Andrews. Bloomington: Indiana University Press, 1986.

Lefler, Hugh Talmage, and Albert Ray Newsome. *North Carolina: The History of a Southern State.* Chapel Hill: University of North Carolina Press, 1973.

Lerner, Gerda. *The Creation of Feminist Consciousness: From the Middle Ages to Eighteen-Seventy.* New York: Oxford University Press, 1993.

———. *The Grimké Sisters from South Carolina: Pioneers for Women's Rights and Abolition.* New York: Oxford University Press, 1998.

Lewis, Jan. *The Pursuit of Happiness: Family and Values in Jefferson's Virginia.* New York: Cambridge University Press, 1983.

———. "The Republican Wife: Virtue and Seduction in the Early Republic." *William and Mary Quarterly,* 3rd ser., 44 (October 1987): 689–721.

Lincoln, Charles Zebina. *The Civil Law and the Church.* New York: Abingdon Press, 1916.

Lindley, Susan Hill. *"You Have Stept out of Your Place": A History of Women and Religion in America.* Louisville, Ky.: Westminster John Knox, 1996.

Locke, Jill, and Eileen Hunt Botting, eds. *Feminist Interpretations of Alexis de Tocqueville*. University Park: Pennsylvania State University Press, 2009.

Lockridge, Kenneth A. *Literacy in Colonial New England: An Enquiry into the Social Context of Literacy in the Early Modern West*. New York: Norton, 1974.

Lutz, Alma. *Emma Willard: Daughter of Democracy*. Boston: Houghton Mifflin, 1929.

Lyerly, Cynthia Lynn. *Methodism and the Southern Mind, 1770–1810*. New York: Oxford University Press, 2006.

Lyons, Clare A. *Sex among the Rabble: An Intimate History of Gender and Power in the Age of Revolution, Philadelphia, 1730–1830*. Chapel Hill: University of North Carolina Press, 2006.

Maffly-Kipp, Laurie F. "An Introduction to the Church in the Southern Black Community." May 2001. *Documenting the American South*. http://docsouth.unc .edu/church/intro.html. Accessed December 9, 2014.

Magnússon, Sigurður Gylfi, and István M. Szijártó. *What Is Microhistory? Theory and Practice*. London: Routledge, 2013.

Malkmus, Doris. "Small Towns, Small Sects, and Coeducation in Midwestern Colleges, 1853–1861." *History of Higher Education Annual* 22 (2002): 33–65.

Mann, Horace. *A Few Thoughts on the Powers and Duties of Woman: Two Lectures*. Syracuse, N.Y.: Hall, Mills, 1853.

Marcet, Jane. *Conversations on Chemistry, in Which the Elements of That Science Are Familiarly Explained and Illustrated*. New Haven, Conn.: Sidney's, 1809.

Marten, James Alan. *Children in Colonial America*. New York: New York University Press, 2007.

Mason, Matthew. *Slavery and Politics in the Early American Republic*. Chapel Hill: University of North Carolina Press, 2006.

Massachusetts. Department of Education. *Annual Report of the Board of Education, Together with the First Annual Report of the Secretary of the Board*. Boston: Dutton and Wentworth, 1838.

Mathews, Donald G. *Religion in the Old South*. Chicago: University of Chicago Press, 1979.

———. "The Second Great Awakening as an Organizing Process, 1780–1830: An Hypothesis." *American Quarterly* 21 (Spring 1969): 23–43.

McCall, Laura, and Donald Yacovone, eds. *A Shared Experience: Men, Women, and the History of Gender*. New York: New York University Press, 1998.

McCurry, Stephanie. *Masters of Small Worlds: Yeoman Households, Gender Relations, and the Political Culture of the Antebellum South Carolina Low Country*. New York: Oxford University Press, 1995.

McGerr, Michael E. "Political Style and Women's Power, 1830–1930." *Journal of American History* 77 (December 1990): 864–85.

McKivigan, John R. *The War against Proslavery Religion: Abolitionism and the Northern Churches, 1830–1865*. Ithaca: Cornell University Press, 1984.

McMahon, Lucia. *Mere Equals: The Paradox of Educated Women in the Early American Republic*. Ithaca: Cornell University Press, 2012.

———. "'Of the Utmost Importance to Our Country': Women, Education, and Society, 1780–1820." *Journal of the Early Republic* 29 (Fall 2009): 475–506.

McManus, Edgar J. *A History of Negro Slavery in New York*. Syracuse, N.Y.: Syracuse University Press, 1966.

McMillen, Sally G. *Motherhood in the Old South: Pregnancy, Childbirth, and Infant Rearing*. Baton Rouge: Louisiana State University Press, 1990.

McPherson, James M. Afterword to *Religion and the American Civil War*, edited by Randall M. Miller, Harry S. Stout, and Charles Reagan Wilson, 408–11. New York: Oxford University Press, 1998.

Meanders, Daniel, comp. *Advertisements for Runaway Slaves in Virginia, 1801–1820*. New York: Garland, 1997.

Meckel, Richard A. "Educating a Ministry of Mothers: Evangelical Maternal Associations, 1815–1860." *Journal of the Early Republic* 2 (Winter 1882): 403–23.

Melish, Joanne Pope. *Disowning Slavery: Gradual Emancipation and "Race" in New England, 1780–1860*. Ithaca: Cornell University Press, 1998.

Middleton, Simon, and Billy G. Smith. *Class Matters: Early North America and the Atlantic World*. Philadelphia: University of Pennsylvania Press, 2008.

Miles, Wyndham D., and Harold J. Abrahams. "America's First Chemistry Syllabus-and-Course for Girls." *School Science and Mathematics* 58 (February 1958): 111–18.

Mill, John Stuart. "The Spirit of the Age." In *The Spirit of the Age: Victorian Essays*, edited by Gertrude Himmelfarb, 50–79. New Haven, Conn.: Yale University Press, 2007.

Miller, George Frederick. *The Academy System of the State of New York*. Albany, N.Y.: Lyon, 1922.

Miller, Randall M., Harry S. Stout, and Charles Reagan Wilson, eds. *Religion and the American Civil War*. New York: Oxford University Press, 1998.

Miller, Samuel, Jr. *Report of the Presbyterian Church Case: The Commonwealth of Pennsylvania*. Philadelphia: Martien, 1839.

Mintz, Steven, and Susan Kellogg. *Domestic Revolutions: A Social History of American Family Life*. New York: Simon and Schuster, 1989.

Monaghan, E. Jennifer. *Learning to Read and Write in Colonial America*. Amherst: University of Massachusetts Press, 2005.

Moorhead, James H. "The 'Restless Spirit of Radicalism': Old School Fears and the Schism of 1837." *Journal of Presbyterian History* 78 (Spring 2000): 19–33.

More, Hannah. *Strictures on the Modern System of Female Education*. London: Cadell and Davies, 1799.

Morris, Thomas D. *Southern Slavery and the Law, 1619–1860*. Chapel Hill: University of North Carolina Press, 1999.

Morse, Jedidiah. *Elements of Geography*. Boston: Thomas and Andrews, 1795.

Mount Holyoke Female Seminary. *Tenth Annual Catalogue of the Mount Holyoke Female Seminary in South Hadley, Massachusetts, 1846–7*. Amherst, Mass.: Adams and Adams, 1847.

Muelder, Owen W. *Theodore Dwight Weld and the American Anti-Slavery Society*. Jefferson, N.C.: McFarland, 2011.

Murray, John E. *The Charleston Orphan House: Children's Lives in the First Public Orphanage in America*. Chicago: University of Chicago Press, 2013.

Murray, John E., and Ruth Herndon. "Markets for Children in Early America: A Political Economy of Pauper Apprenticeship." *Journal of Economic History* 62 (June 2002): 356–82.

Murray, Lindley. *English Grammar, Adapted to the Different Classes of Learners.* New York: Collins and Perkins, 1809.

———. *Sequel to the English Reader; or, Elegant Selections in Prose and Poetry.* New York: Collins, 1817.

Myers, Sandra L. *Westering Women and the Frontier Experience, 1800–1915.* Albuquerque: University of New Mexico Press, 1982.

Najar, Monica. *Evangelizing the South: A Social History of Church and State in Early America.* New York: Oxford University Press, 2008.

———. "'Meddling with Emancipation': Baptists, Authority, and the Rift over Slavery in the Upper South." *Journal of the Early Republic* 25 (Summer 2005): 157–86.

Nash, Gary B. *Forging Freedom: The Formation of Philadelphia's Black Community, 1720–1840.* Cambridge: Harvard University Press, 1988.

Nash, Gary B., and Jean R. Soderlund. *Freedom by Degrees: Emancipation in Pennsylvania and Its Aftermath.* New York: Oxford University Press, 1991.

Nash, Margaret A. "Rethinking Republican Motherhood: Benjamin Rush and the Young Ladies' Academy of Philadelphia." *Journal of the Early Republic* 17 (Summer 1997): 171–91.

———. *Women's Education in the United States, 1780–1840.* New York: Palgrave Macmillan, 2005.

Newell, Harriett. *Memoirs of Harriett Newell, Wife of the Rev. Samuel Newell, Missionary to India; Who Died at the Isle of France, Nov. 30, 1812, Aged 19 Years; to Which Are Added Memoirs of Her Life.* Edited by Leonard Woods. London: Booth, 1815.

Newman, Richard S. *The Transformation of American Abolitionism: Fighting Slavery in the Early Republic.* Chapel Hill: University of North Carolina Press, 2002.

New York (State). Assembly. *Documents of the Assembly of the State of New York, Fifty-Seventh Session, 1834.* Albany: Croswell, 1834.

New York (State). Superintendent of Common Schools. *Annual Report of the Superintendent of Common Schools of the State of New York.* Albany: Carroll and Cook, 1845.

Noll, Mark A. *America's God: From Jonathan Edwards to Abraham Lincoln.* New York: Oxford University Press, 2002.

———. *The Civil War as a Theological Crisis.* Chapel Hill: University of North Carolina Press, 2006.

North Carolina. *Acts Passed by the General Assembly of the State of North Carolina at the Session of 1830–1831.* Raleigh: Lawrence and Lemay, 1831.

———. Constitutional Convention. *Proceedings and Debates of the Convention of North-Carolina, Called to Amend the Constitution of the State, Which Assembled at Raleigh, June 4, 1835, to Which Are Subjoined the Convention Act and the Amendments to the Constitution, Together with the Votes of the People.* Raleigh: Gales, 1836.

North Carolina. Department of Public Instruction. *Biennial Report of the Superintendent of Public Instruction of North Carolina.* Raleigh: Barnes, 1898.

North Carolina. Superintendent of Common Schools. *First Annual Report of the General Superintendent of Common Schools of the State of North Carolina.* Raleigh: Holden, 1854.

———. *Second Annual Report of the General Superintendent of Common Schools.* Raleigh: Holden, 1955.

Norton, Mary Beth. "Eighteenth-Century American Women in Peace and War: The Case of the Loyalists." *William and Mary Quarterly,* 3rd ser., 33 (July 1976): 386–409.

———. *Liberty's Daughters: The Revolutionary Experience of American Women, 1750–1800.* Boston: Little, Brown, 1980.

Nye, R. Glen, comp. *A Genealogy of the Nye Family.* Vol. 4. Edited by Katherine Watson Nye. N.p.: Nye Family of America Association, 1967.

Oakes, James. "'Whom Have I Oppressed?': The Pursuit of Happiness and the Happy Slave." In *The Revolution of 1800: Democracy, Race, and the New Republic,* edited by James Horn, Jan Ellen Lewis, and Peter S. Onuf, 220–39. Charlottesville: University of Virginia Press, 2002.

Oast, Jennifer. "'The Worst Kind of Slavery': Slave-Owning Presbyterian Churches in Prince Edward County, Virginia." *Journal of Southern History* 76 (November 2010): 867–92.

O'Brien, Michael. *Conjectures of Order: Intellectual Life and the American South, 1810–1860.* 2 vols. Chapel Hill: University of North Carolina Press, 2004.

Odom-Reed, Peggy Regina. *Bonding and Bridging Social Capital in Collaborative Learning Networks.* Ithaca: Cornell University Press, 2007.

Olney, James. *Autobiography: Essays Theoretical and Critical.* Princeton: Princeton University Press, 1980.

Opal, J. M. *Beyond the Farm: National Ambitions in Rural New England.* Philadelphia: University of Pennsylvania Press, 2008.

———. "Exciting Emulation: Academies and the Transformation of the Rural North, 1780s–1820s." *Journal of American History* 91 (September 2004): 445–70.

Osterud, Nancy Grey. *The Lives of Farm Women in Nineteenth-Century New York.* Ithaca: Cornell University Press, 1991.

Ownby, Ted. "Church Discipline." In *Encyclopedia of Religion in the South,* edited by Samuel S. Hill, Charles H. Lippy, and Charles Reagan Wilson, 199–200. Macon, Ga.: Mercer University Press, 2005.

Ozment, Steven. *When Fathers Ruled: Family Life in Reformation Europe.* Cambridge: Harvard University Press, 1983.

Paley, William. *Boston School Edition. The Principles of Moral and Political Philosophy. By William Paley, D.D., with Questions for the Examination of Students, by John Frost, Principal of the Mayhew Grammar School, Boston.* 2 vols. in 1. Boston: Whitaker, 1828.

———. *Moral Philosophy: Abridged and Adapted to the Constitution, Laws, and Usages, of the United States of America.* Edited by Bethel Judd. New York: Collins and Hannay, 1828.

———. *Paley's Moral and Political Philosophy. As Condensed by A. J. Valpy, M.A.: To Which Are Added Notes from Popular Authors; Embracing Present Opinions in Ethical Science, and an Exposition of Our Own Political Institutions. The Whole Carefully Adapted to Schools of Both Sexes, and Accompanied with Questions for Examination.* Edited by Richard W. Green. Philadelphia: Hunt, 1835.

———. *The Principles of Moral and Political Philosophy.* Vol. 1. London: Faulder, 1785.

———. *The Principles of Moral and Political Philosophy.* Vol. 1. London: Faulder, 1799.

———. *The Principles of Moral and Political Philosophy.* 7th ed. Philadelphia: Dobson, 1788.

———. *The Principles of Moral and Political Philosophy.* 8th American ed. Boston: West and Richardson, 1815.

———. *The Principles of Moral and Political Philosophy.* New York: King, 1824.

Pangle, Lorraine Smith, and Thomas L. Pangle. *The Learning of Liberty: The Educational Ideas of American Founders.* Lawrence: University Press of Kansas, 1993.

Parish, Peter J. *Slavery: History and Historians.* New York: Harper and Row, 1989.

Parkhurst, John L. *Elements of Moral Philosophy: Comprising the Theory of Morals and Practical Ethics.* Concord, N.H.: Moore and Shepard, 1825.

Patterson, Homer L. *Patterson's American Educational Directory.* Vol. 15. Chicago: American Educational Company, 1918.

Perciaccante, Marianne. *Calling Down Fire: Charles Grandison Finney and Revivalism in Jefferson County, New York, 1800–1840.* Albany: State University of New York Press, 2003.

Perko, F. Michael. "Religious Schooling in America: An Historiographic Reflection." *History of Education Quarterly* 40 (Autumn 2000): 320–28.

Perlmann, Joel, and Robert A. Margo. *Women's Work? American Schoolteachers, 1650–1920.* Chicago: University of Chicago Press, 2001.

Phelan, Julie E., and Laurie A. Rudman. "Prejudice toward Female Leaders: Backlash Effects and Women's Impression Management Dilemma." *Social and Personality Psychology Compass* 4 (October 2010): 807–20.

Phelps, Almira Hart Lincoln. *Lectures to Young Ladies.* Boston: Carter, Hendee, 1833.

Phillips, Ulrich Bonnell. "The Course of the South to Secession: An Answer of Race." *Georgia Historical Quarterly* 21 (December 1937): 309–44.

Pierce, George Foster. "Why Women Should Be Well Educated." In *Bishop Pierce's Sermons and Addresses: With a Few Special Discourses by Dr. Pierce,* edited by Atticus G. Haygood, 90–109. Nashville, Tenn.: Southern Methodist Publishing House, 1886.

Pinckney, Darryl. Introduction to *Uncle Tom's Cabin,* by Harriet Beecher Stowe, vii–xxii. New York: Signet, 1998.

Polgar, Paul J. "'To Raise Them to an Equal Participation': Early National Abolitionism, Gradual Emancipation, and the Promise of African American Citizenship." *Journal of the Early Republic* 31 (Summer 2011): 229–58.

Porter, Roy. *The Creation of the Modern World: The Untold Story of the British Enlightenment.* New York: Norton, 2001.

Porterfield, Amanda. *Conceived in Doubt: Religion and Politics in the New American Nation*. Illinois: University of Chicago Press, 2012.

———. *Female Piety in Puritan New England: The Emergence of Religious Humanism*. New York: Oxford University Press, 1992.

———. *Mary Lyon and the Mount Holyoke Missionaries*. New York: Oxford University Press, 1997.

Portnoy, Alisse. *Their Right to Speak: Women's Activism in the Indian and Slave Debates*. Cambridge: Harvard University Press, 2005.

Powell, William S., ed. "The Diary of Joseph Gales, 1794–1795." *North Carolina Historical Review* 26 (July 1949): 335–47.

———, ed. *Dictionary of North Carolina Biography*. Vols. 1 and 2. Chapel Hill: University of North Carolina Press, 1979, 1986.

Powers, Jane. *The "Girl Question" in Education: Vocational Training for Young Women in the Progressive Era*. London: Falmer, 1992.

Presbyterian Church in the U.S.A. *The Constitution of the Presbyterian Church in the United States of America: Containing the Confession of Faith, the Catechisms, and the Directory for the Worship of God: Together with the Plan of Government and Discipline as Amended and Ratified by the General Assembly at Their Sessions in May, 1805*. Philadelphia: Aitken, 1806.

———. *The Constitution of the Presbyterian Church in the United States of America: Containing the Confession of Faith, the Catechisms, and the Directory for the Worship of God, Together with the Plan of Government and Discipline, as Amended and Ratified by the General Assembly at Their Sessions in May 1821*. Philadelphia: Towar and Hogan, 1827.

Presbyterian Church in the U.S.A. General Assembly. *A Digest, Compiled from the Records of the General Assembly of the Presbyterian Church in the United States of America*. Philadelphia: M'Culloh, 1820.

———. *Extracts from the Minutes of the General Assembly, of the Presbyterian Church in the United States of America, 1817*. Philadelphia: Bradford and Bradford, 1817.

———. *Minutes of the General Assembly of the Presbyterian Church in the United States of America, with an Appendix, a.d. 1831*. Philadelphia: Geddes, 1831.

———. *Minutes of the General Assembly of the Presbyterian Church in the United States of America, with an Appendix, a.d. 1835*. Philadelphia: Geddes, 1836.

———. *Minutes of the General Assembly of the Presbyterian Church in the United States of America, with an Appendix, a.d. 1836*. Philadelphia: Bailey, 1836.

———. *Minutes of the General Assembly of the Presbyterian Church in the United States of America, with an Appendix, a.d. 1839*. Philadelphia: Bailey, 1839.

Presbyterian Church in the U.S.A. (New School). General Assembly. *Minutes of the General Assembly of the Presbyterian Church in the United States of America*. New York: Molineux, 1846.

Presbyterian Church in the U.S.A. (New School). Synod of New York and New Jersey. *Minutes of the Synod of New-York and New-Jersey*. New York: Dorr, 1840.

Presbyterian Church in the U.S.A. (Old School). *Book of Public Prayer, Compiled from the Authorized Formularies of Worship of the Presbyterian Church, as*

Prepared by the Reformers Calvin, Knox, Bucer, and Others. New York: Scribner, 1857.

Presbyterian Church in the U.S.A. (Old School). General Assembly. *Minutes of the General Assembly of the Presbyterian Church in the United States of America*. Philadelphia: Martien, 1845.

———. *Minutes of the General Assembly of the Presbyterian Church in the United States of America, with an Appendix*. Vol. 15. Philadelphia: Presbyterian Board of Publication, 1857.

Presbyterian Synod (Ky.). *An Address to the Presbyterians of Kentucky, Proposing a Plan for the Instruction and Emancipation of Their Slaves*. Newburyport, Mass.: Whipple, 1836.

"President W. L. Lingle Finds Old Document." *The Davidsonian*, September 23, 1931, 6. Available at library.davidson.edu/archives/davidsonian. Accessed June 9, 2011.

Preston, Jo Anne. "Domestic Ideology, School Reformers, and Female Teachers: Schoolteaching Becomes Women's Work in Nineteenth-Century New England." *New England Quarterly* 66 (December 1993): 531–51.

———. "'He Lives as a Master': Seventeenth Century Masculinity, Gendered Teaching, and Careers of New England Schoolmasters." *History of Education Quarterly* 43 (Fall 2003): 350–71.

Prospectus of the Raleigh Academy, and Mrs. Hutchison's View of Female Education. Raleigh, N.C.: White, 1835.

Putnam, Robert D., and Lewis Feldstein. *Better Together: Restoring the American Community*. New York: Simon and Schuster, 2009.

Quarles, Benjamin. *Black Abolitionists*. New York: Oxford University Press, 1976.

Quinn, John. "Amenia: Arsenal and Larder for the Revolution." N.d. http://ameniany.gov/Orgs/AHS/quinnhistory.htm. Accessed January 10, 2010.

Quist, John W. *Restless Visionaries: The Social Roots of Antebellum Reform in Alabama and Michigan*. Baton Rouge: Louisiana State University Press, 1998.

Raboteau, Albert J. *Slave Religion: The "Invisible Institution" in the Antebellum South*. New York: Oxford University Press, 2004.

Raleigh Female Benevolent Society. *Revised Constitution and By-Laws of the Raleigh Female Benevolent Society, Adopted July 23rd, 1823*. Raleigh, N.C.: Gales, 1823.

Raleigh Female Tract Society. *Fourth Annual Report*. Raleigh, N.C.: Gales, 1820.

Ramsay, David. *The History of South-Carolina: From Its First Settlement in 1670, to the Year 1808*. Vol. 2. Charleston, S.C.: Longworth, 1809.

Reed, Newton. *Early History of Amenia*. Amenia, N.Y.: DeLacey and Wiley, 1875.

Reis, Elizabeth. *Damned Women: Sinners and Witches in Puritan New England*. Ithaca: Cornell University Press, 1999.

Rhodes, Jane, and Mary Ann Shadd Cary. *The Black Press and Protest in the Nineteenth Century*. Bloomington: Indiana University Press, 1999.

Richards, William Carey. "Editor's Department." *The Orion*, December 1842, 122–23.

Riley, Glenda. *Divorce: An American Tradition*. New York: Oxford University Press, 1991.

Rivers, Richard Henderson. *Elements of Moral Philosophy*. Edited by Thomas O. Summers. Nashville, Tenn.: Methodist Publishing House, 1859.

Robert, Dana Lee. *American Women in Mission: A Social History of Their Thought and Practice*. Macon, Ga.: Mercer University Press, 1996.

Roberts, Philetus. *Memoir of Mrs. Abigail Roberts: An Account of Her Birth, Early Education, Call to the Ministry, Varied and Extensive Labors, and the Success Which Attended Her in Several States, with Many Interesting Incidents of Her Life*. Irvington, N.J.: Cummings, 1858.

Robertson, Stacey M. *Hearts Beating for Liberty: Women Abolitionists in the Old Northwest*. Chapel Hill: University of North Carolina Press, 2010.

Romero, Lora. *Home Fronts: Domesticity and Its Critics in the Antebellum United States*. Durham, N.C.: Duke University Press, 1997.

Rothman, Adam. *Slave Country: American Expansion and the Origins of the Deep South*. Cambridge: Harvard University Press, 2005.

Rothman, Sheila. *Living in the Shadow of Death: Tuberculosis and the Social Experience of Illness in American History*. Baltimore: Johns Hopkins University Press, 1995.

Rothstein, William G. *American Physicians in the Nineteenth Century: From Sects to Science*. Baltimore: Johns Hopkins University Press, 1992.

Rucker, Walter C. *The River Flows On: Black Resistance, Culture, and Identity Formation in Early America*. Baton Rouge: Louisiana State University Press, 2006.

Rudman, Laurie A., and Peter Glick. "Prescriptive Gender Stereotypes and Backlash toward Agentic Women." *Journal of Social Issues* 57 (Winter 2001): 743–62.

Rudolph, Frederick, ed. *Essays on Education*. Cambridge: Harvard University Press, 1965.

Ryan, Mary P. *Civic Wars: Democracy and Public Life in the American City during the Nineteenth Century*. Berkeley: University of California Press, 1997.

———. *Cradle of the Middle Class: The Family in Oneida County, New York, 1790–1865*. New York: Cambridge University Press, 1983.

———. *Mysteries of Sex: Tracing Women and Men through American History*. Chapel Hill: University of North Carolina Press, 2006.

———. *Women in Public: Between Banners and Ballots, 1825–1880*. Baltimore: Johns Hopkins University Press, 1990.

Sabean, David Warren. *Power in the Blood: Popular Culture and Village Discourse in Early Modern Germany*. New York: Cambridge University Press, 1984.

Salmon, Marylynn. *Women and the Law of Property in Early America*. Chapel Hill: University of North Carolina Press, 1986.

Sandberg, Sheryl. *Lean In: Women, Work, and the Will to Lead*. New York: Knopf, 2013.

Schantz, Mark Saunders. *Piety in Providence: Class Dimensions of Religious Experience in Antebellum Rhode Island*. Ithaca: Cornell University Press, 2000.

Schouler, James. *A Treatise on the Law of Husband and Wife*. Boston: Little, Brown, 1882.

Schultz, T. Paul. "Returns to Women's Education." In *Women's Education in Developing Countries: Barriers, Benefits, and Policies*, edited by Elizabeth M. King and M. Anne Hill, 51–99. Baltimore: Johns Hopkins University Press for the World Bank, 1998.

Schwartz, Marie Jenkins. *Born in Bondage: Growing Up Enslaved in the Antebellum South*. Cambridge: Harvard University Press, 2000.

Scott, Anne Firor. "The Ever Widening Circle: The Diffusion of Feminist Values from the Troy Female Seminary, 1822–1872." *History of Education Quarterly* 19 (Spring 1979): 3–25.

———. *The Southern Lady: From Pedestal to Politics, 1830–1930*. Chicago: University of Chicago Press, 1970.

Segal, Ronald. *The Black Diaspora: Five Centuries of the Black Experience outside Africa*. New York: Macmillan, 1996.

Seller, Maxine Schwartz. "Retrospective: *A History of Women's Education in the United States*: Thomas Woody's Classic—Sixty Years Later." *History of Education Quarterly* 29 (Spring 1989): 95–107.

Shammas, Carole. "Re-Assessing the Married Women's Property Acts." *Journal of Women's History* 6 (Spring 1994): 9–38.

Sheldon English and Classical School. *The Annual Catalogue of the Officers and Students of the Sheldon English and Classical School*. Northampton, Mass.: Shepard, 1830.

Sievens, Mary Beth. *Stray Wives: Marital Conflict in Early National New England*. New York: New York University Press, 2008.

Sizer, Theodore. *The Age of the Academies*. New York: Teachers College Press, 1964.

Skemp, Sheila S. *Judith Sargent Murray: A Brief Biography with Documents*. Boston: St. Martin's Press, 1998.

Sklar, Kathryn Kish. *Catharine Beecher: A Study in American Domesticity*. New Haven, Conn.: Yale University Press, 1973.

———. "The Founding of Mount Holyoke College." In *Women of America: A History*, edited by Carol Ruth Berkin and Mary Beth Norton, 177–201. Boston: Houghton Mifflin, 1979.

———. "The Schooling of Girls and Changing Community Values in Massachusetts Towns, 1750–1820." *History of Education Quarterly* 4 (Winter 1993): 511–42.

Smith, Adam. *The Theory of Moral Sentiments*. London: Millar, Kincaid, and Bell, 1767.

Smith, Christian. *The Secular Revolution: Power, Interests, and Conflict in the Secularization of American Public Life*. Berkeley: University of California Press, 2003.

Smith, Daniel Blake. *An American Betrayal: Cherokee Patriots and the Trail of Tears*. New York: Macmillan, 2011.

Smith, Daniel D. *Lectures on Domestic Duties*. Portland, Me.: Colesworthy, 1837.

Smith, Margaret Supplee, and Emily Herring Wilson. *North Carolina Women: Making History*. Chapel Hill: University of North Carolina Press, 1999.

Smith, Mark M. *Debating Slavery: Economy and Society in the Antebellum South*. Cambridge: Cambridge University Press, 1998.

Smith, Timothy Lawrence. *Revivalism and Social Reform: American Protestantism on the Eve of the Civil War*. Baltimore: Johns Hopkins University Press, 1980.

Smith, Wilson. "William Paley's Theological Utilitarianism in America." *William and Mary Quarterly*, 3rd ser., 11 (July 1954): 402–24.

Snay, Mitchell. *Gospel of Disunion: Religion and Separatism in the Antebellum South*. New York: Cambridge University Press, 1993.

Solomon, Barbara M. *In the Company of Educated Women: A History of Women and Higher Education in America*. New Haven, Conn.: Yale University Press, 1985.

Spafford, Horatio Gates. "Cruelty and Executive Clemency in North Carolina." *American Magazine* 1 (November 1815): 223–26.

———. *A Gazetteer of the State of New-York*. Albany, N.Y.: Southwick, 1813.

Sparks, Randy J. *On Jordan's Stormy Banks: Evangelicalism in Mississippi, 1773–1876*. Athens: University of Georgia Press, 1994.

Staiger, C. Bruce. "Abolitionism and the Presbyterian Schism of 1837–1838." *Mississippi Valley Historical Review* 36 (December 1949): 391–414.

Stampp, Kenneth M. *The Imperiled Union: Essays on the Background of the Civil War*. New York: Oxford University Press, 1981.

Standenraus, P. J. *The African Colonization Movement, 1816–1865*. New York: Columbia University Press, 1961.

Stewart, George S. "Barlow Records." *New England Historical and Genealogical Register* 68 (January 1914): 105–7.

Stowe, Harriet Beecher. *A Key to Uncle Tom's Cabin; Presenting the Original Facts and Documents upon Which the Story Is Founded, Together with Corroborative Statements Verifying the Truth of the Work*. Boston: Jewett, 1853.

Stowe, Steven M. *Doctoring the South: Southern Physicians and Everyday Medicine in the Mid-Nineteenth Century*. Chapel Hill: University of North Carolina Press, 2004.

Stuart, James. *Three Years in North America*. Vol. 2. Edinburgh: Cadell, 1833.

Sturge, Joseph. *A Visit to the United States in 1841*. London: Hamilton, Adams, 1842.

Swan, Robert J. "John Teasman: African-American Educator and the Emergence of Community in Early Black New York City, 1787–1815." *Journal of the Early Republic* 12 (Autumn 1992): 331–56.

Sweet, William W. *Religion on the American Frontier: The Presbyterians, 1783–1840: A Collection of Source Materials*. New York: Cooper Square, 1936.

Taylor, Amy Murrell. *The Divided Family in Civil War America*. Chapel Hill: University of North Carolina Press, 2009.

Thompson, Earl, Jr. "Slavery and Presbyterianism in the Revolutionary Era." *Journal of Presbyterian History* 54 (Spring 1976): 121–41.

Thompson, George, Robert Jefferson Breckinridge, and Charles Calistus Burleigh. *Discussion on American Slavery, Between George Thompson, Esq., Agent of the British and Foreign Society for the Abolition of Slavery throughout the World, and Rev. Robert J. Breckinridge*. Boston: Knapp, 1836.

Tise, Larry E. *Proslavery: A History of the Defense of Slavery in America, 1701–1840*. Athens: University of Georgia Press, 1987.

Tocqueville, Alexis de. *Democracy in America*. Vol. 1. New York: Adlard, 1839.

———. *Democracy in America*. Vol. 2. New York: Appleton, 1904.

Tolley, Bruce. *Pastors and Parishioners in Württemberg during the Late Reformation, 1581–1621.* Palo Alto: Stanford University Press, 1995.

Tolley, Kim. "A Chartered School in a Free Market: The Case of Raleigh Academy, 1801–1823." *Teachers College Record* 107 (January 2005): 59–88.

———. "Joseph Gales and Education Reform in North Carolina, 1799–1841." *North Carolina Historical Review* 86 (January 2009): 1–31.

———. "Mapping the Landscape of Higher Schooling, 1727–1850." In *Chartered Schools,* edited by Beadie and Tolley, 19–43.

———. "Music Teachers in the North Carolina Education Market, 1800–1840: How Mrs. Sambourne Earned a 'Comfortable Living for Herself and Her Children.'" *Social Science History* 32 (Spring 2008): 75–106.

———. "Schoolroom Slavery: The Moral Philosophy Textbook as Discourse in Antebellum America, 1785–1859." Paper presented at the American Educational Research Association Annual Conference. San Francisco, 2013.

———. *The Science Education of American Girls: A Historical Perspective.* New York: Routledge, 2003.

———. "The Significance of the 'French School' in Early National Female Education." In *The Founding Fathers, Education, and "The Great Contest,"* edited by Benjamin Justice, 135–54. New York: Palgrave Macmillan, 2013.

Tolley, Kim, and Nancy Beadie. "Socioeconomic Incentives to Teach in New York and North Carolina: Toward a More Complex Model of Teacher Labor Markets, 1800–1850." *History of Education Quarterly* 46 (Spring 2006): 36–72.

Tolley, Kim, and Margaret A. Nash. "Leaving Home to Teach: The Diary of Susan Nye Hutchison, 1815–1841." In *Chartered Schools,* edited by Beadie and Tolley, 161–85.

Tompkins, Daniel Augustus. *History of Mecklenburg County and the City of Charlotte: From 1740 to 1903.* Vol. 1. Charlotte, N.C.: Observer Printing House, 1903.

Torres, Louis. *Historic Resource Study of Cape Hatteras National Seashore.* Denver: U.S. Department of the Interior, National Park Service, Denver Service Center, Branch of Planning, Southeast/Southwest Team, 1985. Available at https://archive.org/details/capehatterashistootorr. Accessed June 21, 2014.

Towle, Nancy. *Vicissitudes Illustrated in the Experience of Nancy Towle, in Europe and America, Written by Herself, with an Appendix of Letters.* Charleston, S.C.: Burges, 1832.

Trollope, Frances. *Domestic Manners of the Americans.* Boston: Whittaker and Treacher, 1832.

Turner, Frederick Jackson. "The Significance of the Frontier in American History." In *The American Intellectual Tradition,* vol. 2, edited by David A. Hollinger and Charles Capper, 54–62. New York: Oxford University Press, 2006.

Tyack, David. "The Kingdom: Protestant Ministers and the Educational Awakening in the West." *Harvard Educational Review* 36 (Winter 1966): 447–69.

Tyack, David, and Elizabeth Hansot. *Learning Together: A History of Coeducation in American Public Schools.* New York: Sage, 1992.

Tyler-McGraw, Marie. *An African Republic: Black and White Virginians in the Making of Liberia.* Chapel Hill: University of North Carolina Press, 2007.

Ulrich, Laurel Thatcher. *A Midwife's Tale: The Life of Martha Ballard, Based on Her Diary, 1785–1812*. New York: Vintage, 1991.

U.S. Bureau of Education. *Report of the Commissioner of Education for the Year 1888–89*. Washington, D.C.: U.S. Government Printing Office, 1891.

U.S. Bureau of the Census. *Seventh Census of the United States: 1850*. Washington, D.C.: Armstrong, 1853.

U.S. Department of the Interior. *Report on Statistics of Churches in the United States at the Eleventh Census*. Washington, D.C.: U.S. Government Printing Office, 1894.

University of Pennsylvania. Department of Medicine. Society of the Alumni. *Catalogue of the Alumni of the Medical Department of the University of Pennsylvania, 1765–1877*. Philadelphia: Collins, 1877.

Vanderpoel, Emily Noyes. *Chronicles of a Pioneer School, from 1792 to 1833, Being the History of Miss Sarah Pierce and Her Litchfield School*. Cambridge, Mass.: University Press, 1903.

Van Dyke, Rachel. *To Read My Heart: The Journal of Rachel Van Dyke, 1810–1811*. Edited by Lucia McMahon and Deborah Schriver. Philadelphia: University of Pennsylvania Press, 2000.

Varon, Elizabeth R. "Evangelical Womanhood and the Politics of the African Colonization Movement in Virginia." In *Religion and the Antebellum Debate over Slavery*, edited by John R. McKivigan and Mitchell Snay, 169–95. Athens: University of Georgia Press, 1998.

———. "Tippecanoe and the Ladies, Too: White Women and Party Politics in Antebellum Virginia." *Journal of American History* 82 (September 1995): 494–521.

Vaughn, Gerald F. "Teaching Moral Philosophy in the South during Slavery and Reconstruction: Edward Wadsworth of Lagrange College and Southern University." *Methodist History* 46 (April 2008): 179–88.

Vinovskis, Maris, and Richard M. Bernard. *Women in Education in Antebellum America*. Madison: University of Wisconsin Center for Demography and Ecology, 1973.

Waddel, Moses. *Memoirs of the Life of Miss Caroline Elizabeth Smelt: Who Died on the 21st September, 1817, in the City of Augusta Georgia, in the 17th Year of Her Age; Compiled from Authentic Papers Furnished by Her Friends, and Published at Their Request*. New York: Fanshaw, 1818.

Walbert, Kathryn. "'Endeavor to Improve Yourself': The Education of White Women in the Antebellum South." In *Chartered Schools*, edited by Beadie and Tolley, 116–36.

Walker, David. *David Walker's Appeal to the Coloured Citizens of the World*. Edited by Peter P. Hinks. University Park: Pennsylvania State University Press, 2000.

Wallace, Peter J. "'The Bond of Union': The Old School Presbyterian Church and the American Nation, 1837–1861." 2 vols. Ph.D. diss., University of Notre Dame, 2004.

Walters, Ronald G. *American Reformers, 1815–1860*. New York: Hill and Wang, 1978.

Warner, Deborah Jean. "Science Education for Women in Antebellum America." *Isis* 69 (March 1978): 58–67.

Waugh, Elizabeth Culbertson. *North Carolina's Capital, Raleigh*. Raleigh: Junior League of Raleigh, 1967.

Wayland, Francis. *The Elements of Moral Science*. New York: Cooke, 1835.

———. *The Elements of Moral Science, with Questions for Examination*. London: Religious Tract Society, 1858.

Weaver, Douglas. "Second Baptist Church, Atlanta: A Paradigm of Southern Baptist Identity in the Nineteenth Century." In *Distinctively Baptist Essays on Baptist History: A Festschrift in Honor of Walter B. Shurden*, edited by Walter B. Shurden, Marc A. Jolley, and John D. Pierce, 75–98. Macon, Ga.: Mercer University Press, 2005.

Weber, Max. *The Protestant Ethic and the Spirit of Capitalism*. London: Routledge, 1992.

Weiler, Kathleen. *Country Schoolwomen: Teaching in Rural California, 1850–1950*. Palo Alto: Stanford University Press, 1998.

Wells, Jonathan Daniel. *The Origins of the Southern Middle Class, 1800–1861*. Chapel Hill: University of North Carolina Press, 2004.

———. *Women Writers and Journalists in the Nineteenth-Century South*. New York: Cambridge University Press, 2011.

Welter, Barbara. *Dimity Convictions: The American Woman in the Nineteenth Century*. Athens: Ohio University Press, 1976.

Wesley, John. *The Works of the Reverend John Wesley, Containing, Twenty-Eight Sermons on Various Subjects*. Vol. 9. Edited by Joseph Benson. London: Cordeux, 1811.

Wesleyan Academy. *Catalogue of the Officers and Students of the Wesleyan Academy*. Wilbraham, Mass.: Wesleyan Academy, 1828.

Wessinger, Catherine. *Religious Institutions and Women's Leadership: New Roles inside the Mainstream*. Columbia: University of South Carolina Press, 1996.

White, Ann. "Counting the Cost of Faith: America's Early Female Missionaries." *Church History: Studies in Christianity and Culture* 57 (March 1988): 19–30.

White, Shane. *Somewhat More Independent: The End of Slavery in New York City, 1770–1810*. Athens: University of Georgia Press, 2004.

Whitman, Stephen. *The Price of Freedom: Slavery and Manumission in Baltimore and Early National Maryland*. New York: Routledge, 1997.

Wigger, John H. *Taking Heaven by Storm: Methodism and the Rise of Popular Christianity in America*. New York: Oxford University Press, 1998.

Willard, Emma. *An Address to the Public, Particularly to the Members of the Legislature of New York, Proposing a Plan for Improving Female Education*. Middlebury, Vt.: Copeland, 1819.

Williams, David. *The Georgia Gold Rush: Twenty-Niners, Cherokees, and Gold Fever*. Columbia: University of South Carolina Press, 1993.

Williams, Heather Andrea. *Self-Taught: African American Education in Slavery and Freedom*. Chapel Hill: University of North Carolina Press, 2005.

Wills, Gregory A. *Democratic Religion: Freedom, Authority, and Church Discipline in the Baptist South, 1785–1900*. New York: Oxford University Press, 1997.

Wilson, Elizabeth. *A Scriptural View of Woman's Rights and Duties: In All the Important Relations of Life*. Philadelphia: Young, 1849.

Wilson, James. *The Works of the Honourable James Wilson, L.L.D., Late One of the Associate Justices of the Supreme Court of the United States, and Professor of Law in the College of Philadelphia*. Vol. 2. Edited by Bird Wilson. Philadelphia: Lorenzo, 1804.

Winch, Julie. *Philadelphia's Black Elite: Activism, Accommodation, and the Struggle for Autonomy, 1787–1848*. Philadelphia: Temple University Press, 1993.

Withers, W. A., ed. *The Semi-Centennial Catalogue of Davidson College, Davidson, N.C., 1837–1887*. Raleigh, N.C.: Uzzell, 1891.

Witherspoon, John. *Lectures on Moral Philosophy, Carefully Revised, and Freed from the Errors of Former Editions, to Which Is Added, by the Same Author, an Address to the Students of the Senior Class, and Letters on Education and Marriage*. Philadelphia: Woodward, 1822.

Wood, Gordon S. *The Radicalism of the American Revolution*. New York: Vintage, 1993.

Wood, Kirsten E. *Masterful Women: Slaveholding Widows from the American Revolution through the Civil War*. Chapel Hill: University of North Carolina Press, 2004.

Wood, Nathan Eusebius. *The History of the First Baptist Church of Boston (1665–1899)*. Philadelphia: American Baptist Publication Society, 1899.

Woodbridge, William C., ed. "Motives to Study in the Ipswich Female Seminary." *American Annals of Education* 3 (1833): 75–80.

Woodworth, Samuel, ed. "The Female Character." *Ladies' Literary Cabinet* 1 (March 18, 1820): 147–48.

Woody, Thomas. *A History of Women's Education in the United States*. Vol. 1. New York: Science Press, 1929.

Wyatt-Brown, Bertram. "The Abolitionists' Postal Campaign of 1835." *Journal of Negro History* 50 (October 1965): 227–38.

———. *Lewis Tappan and the Evangelical War against Slavery*. Baton Rouge: Louisiana State University Press, 1997.

———. *Southern Honor: Ethics and Behavior in the Old South*. New York: Oxford University Press, 1981.

Wyly-Jones, Susan. "The 1835 Anti-Abolition Meetings in the South: A New Look at the Controversy over the Abolition Postal Campaign." *Civil War History* 47 (December 2001): 289–309.

Wyman, Andrea. "Dame Schools." In *Historical Dictionary of Women's Education in the United States*, edited by Linda Eisenmann, 113–14. Westport, Conn.: Greenwood, 1998.

Young, Jeffrey Robert. *Domesticating Slavery: The Master Class in Georgia and South Carolina, 1670–1837*. Chapel Hill: University of North Carolina Press, 1999.

Zaeske, Susan. *Signatures of Citizenship: Petitioning, Antislavery, and Women's Political Identity*. Chapel Hill: University of North Carolina Press, 2003.

Zagarri, Rosemarie. "Morals, Manners, and the Republican Mother." *American Quarterly* 44 (June 1992): 192–215.

——. *Revolutionary Backlash: Women and Politics in the Early American Republic.* Philadelphia: University of Pennsylvania Press, 2011.

——. "The Rights of Man and Woman in Post-Revolutionary America." *William and Mary Quarterly*, 3rd ser., 55 (April 1998): 203–30.

Zboray, Ronald J., and Mary Saracino Zboray. *Voices without Votes: Women and Politics in Antebellum New England.* Lebanon: University of New Hampshire Press, 2010.

——. "Whig Women, Politics and Culture in the Campaign of 1840: Three Perspectives from Massachusetts." *Journal of the Early Republic* 17 (Summer 1997): 297–314.

Zilversmit, Arthur. *The First Emancipation: The Abolition of Slavery in the North.* Chicago: University of Chicago Press, 1967.

Index

English subjects, 29, 38, 203 (n. 13). *See also* Curriculum

Enlightenment ideology, 40; and religion, 22, 39, 187, 192; and secularism, 23; and curriculum, 41–45, 48, 61–62; and emancipation, 65; and antislavery, 171

Enrollments. *See* Schools

Entrepreneurship: and female educators, 6, 129, 134, 156, 189; and Lunsford Lane, 75; and French schools, 129

Evangelism: and teachers, 7, 27–28, 36, 54, 191; in Litchfield Female Academy, 21; and Susan Nye Hutchison, 54–58, 62, 178–79; of slaves, 90–91; and Hutchison's descendants, 191–92

Examinations. *See* Schools

Family life, 85, 87, 88, 109–10; and "sending out" children, 107; and church oversight, 109–10; and church discipline, 109–13

Fayetteville, N.C., 34, 148

Fayetteville Academy, 34, 44–45

Female education: in colonial period, 18; in common schools and academies, 8, 18, 19, 37–39; motivation for, 19, 50, 132; and Enlightenment ideology, 22; and religious ideology, 22, 27, 62; expansion of, in the South, 29, 130; higher education, 37–38, 52, 138, 148, 149–53; Susan Nye Hutchison's views of, 136–40; Emma Willard's views of, 137–39, 152–53, 188–89; increasing rigor of, 144–45; and the Second Great Awakening, 188–91

Feminism. *See* Protofeminism

Finney, Charles G.: and female prayer meetings, 25, 62; and the New School, 166, 177–78; and antislavery, 166–67

First Great Awakening, 48

First Presbyterian Church, Amenia, N.Y.: Susan Nye's membership in, 20; formation of, 22; certificates in, 34–35; and the New School, 175, 178

First Presbyterian Church, Augusta, Ga., 83; and the middle class, 88–89; and community, 88–91; and women's political involvement, 89; and benevolence, 89; and revivals, 90; and slaves, 90; and discipline, 109–14, 125–26, 214 (n. 13); membership of, 112–13, 209 (n. 2); and marital separation, 119–20

First Presbyterian Church, Raleigh, N.C., 35, 60, 129

Franklin, Benjamin, 21, 50

Freedmen, in racially mixed congregations, 33

Freeman, Jonathan, 25

French schools, 38, 48, 129

Frontis, Stephen, 142, 146, 147, 217–18 (n. 38)

Gales, Joseph, 39–41, 52, 73, 151; and science, 44, 45; and religion, 46; and the American Colonization Society, 70; and the failure of Raleigh Academy, 135

Gales, Winifred, 44, 45, 46, 151

Garrison, William Lloyd, 159, 161–62, 167

Gaston, William, 46, 203 (n. 24)

Gender: and social mores, 12; and power relations, 26, 86, 120; and "separate spheres," 86; and the middle class, 88; and church discipline, 112–13, 120, 126; transgression of, 125–26; and views of intellectual ability, 138–39; and school leadership, 147–50, 157. *See also* Marriage; Presbyterian Church

Georgia Female College, 138, 148

Georgia Land Lottery, 93, 113–15

Gildersleeve, Benjamin, 172–73

Grace, 105, 114–15, 117

benevolence, 21; and evangelism, 21; and Enlightenment ideology, 22; and Timothy Dwight, 23–24; and curriculum, 38; and females' public speaking, 43; and moral philosophy, 73, 184; and "premiums," 97

Literacy: and the Second Great Awakening, 7; increase of among women, 48; and slaves, 76–78, 177, 180; and antiliteracy laws, 179–81

Lyon, Mary, 6, 149, 154

Mann, Horace, 152, 191

Manumission: in the early national period, 68–69; and North Carolina legislation, 180–81

Marcet, Jane, 48–49

Marks, Elias, and Female Collegiate Institute, 155

Marriage, 83–108; companionate, 84, 210 (n. 5); and English common law, 84–85; and men's authority over women, 85–86, 107, 115–16, 126; and men's duties, 87, 120; and family life, 88; and sociability, 88; and women teachers, 94; and women's work outside the home, 94–95; and women's obedience, 107, 120, 125–26; and community scrutiny, 107–8; and church discipline, 109–10; and marital separation, 118–19, 122; and the Second Great Awakening, 125–26; among slaves, 182, 183, 188

Massachusetts Anti-Slavery Society, 160–63

Mathematics education: in academies, 38; and Joseph Gales, 40, 44, 45; in Raleigh Academy, 49–52; and bookkeeping, 50; and cipher books, 50; and geometry, 51–52; in Miss Susan Nye's School, Augusta, 52; and Timothy Dwight, 52; and algebra, 52, 139, 143–44; and women's intellectual ability, 139; and trigonometry, 143

McPheeters, William, 42, 43, 53–54, 65, 76, 129, 134, 140–41; and founding of First Presbyterian Church of Raleigh, 34–35, 60

Methodist Church: and Susan Nye's church in Amenia, N.Y., 22; and male preachers, 22; and female preachers, 25, 26; and racially mixed congregations, 33, 76; and ecumenical collaboration, 40–41, 58–59, 65, 145–46; and revivals, 59; and emancipation and manumission of slaves, 68–69, 188; and women's obedience in marriage, 85; and church discipline, 110, 112; and women's higher education, 138, 148; and denominational competition, 146; in Salisbury, 146; and Charles G. Finney's "new methods," 166; division of, 177

Middle class: and women, 4, 48; development of, 6–7, 88–89; and curriculum, 44–45; and companionate marriage, 84; and household, 87; and women's work, 94–95; and "sending out" children, 101, 106; and education, 132; and views of teaching, 133, 152, 153; and slavery, 166

Migration: of northerners, 5, 29, 184; of women, 12, 16, 27; of Susan Nye's ancestors, 16–17; of teachers, 27, 64; of Susan Nye, 29–36; and the Second Great Awakening, 35–36

Miller, Stephen Decatur, 158

Miller, William, 67

Missionaries: female, 22–23, 55, 58, 191–92; missionary aspirations of Susan Nye Hutchison, 89, 128, 155; and marriage, 94; and American Colonization Society, 163; funded by sales of slaves, 169

Miss Nye's School, Augusta, Ga., 60–61

Moral philosophy: in Raleigh Academy's curriculum, 43, 44;

in Susan Nye Hutchison's schools, 61, 71, 116, 139–40; and the Enlightenment, 65; and emancipation, 65, 72, 163–64; and slavery, 71–75, 184; prevalence of in school and college curricula, 72; and southern textbooks, 74–75; and marriage, 85; in North Carolina female schools, 145; and proslavery, 158; and division of the churches, 192–93. *See also* Paley, William

More, Hannah, 40, 51, 56

Morse, Jedidiah, 47

Morrison, Mary Graham, 154, 187

Morrison, Robert H., 154, 187, 220 (n. 72)

Motherhood: and domesticity, 6; "republican", 21; southern views of, 94; idealized, 94, 106–7; and biological imperatives, 106–7, 125–26; and teaching, 141–42

Mott, Lucretia, 30

Mount Holyoke Female Seminary, 49, 64, 149

Mount Pleasant Academy, Va., 131, 147

Mrs. Adam Hutchison's School, Augusta, Ga., 84, 95–97

Mrs. Adam Hutchison's School, Beach Island, Ga., 116–17

Mrs. Susan Nye Hutchison's Academy for Young Ladies, Raleigh, N.C., 135–41

Murray, John, 31

Natural theology, 46–49

Ned, 181–82

Newell, Harriet Atwood, 22–23, 55, 58

New York City, 30–31

New York State: rural, 15–17; and farm families, 19, 28,

Nine Partners Boarding School, 30

Nullification Crisis, 160

Nye, Amanda: education of, 18–19; at Litchfield Female Academy, 20; in Raleigh, N.C., 60; in Augusta, Ga., 83, 87, 88, 97, 101, 105–6; in South

Amenia, N.Y., 123, 127, 129, 134, 136, 156–57, 185; opposed to Susan Nye Hutchison's return to the South, 128, 129; opposed to Susan's writing, 136; in Susan's will, 185; as assistant teacher, 205 (n. 59); in Sylvanus Nye's will, 224 (n. 2)

Nye, Meletiah, 105, 123, 154, 157, 183, 185

Nye, Sarah Louisa, 142, 191

Nye, Shubal, 154, 157, 224 (n. 2)

Nye, Sylvania Barlow, 16, 224 (n. 2)

Nye, Sylvanus, 16, 224 (n. 2)

Ornamental subjects. *See* Curriculum

Paine, Thomas, 21, 23

Paley, William, 46–47, 71–74, 85, 140, 163–65, 184. *See also* Moral philosophy; Natural theology

Panic of 1837, 147

Petitions. *See* Women

Phelps, Almira Hart, 6, 51; and domestic arts, 143, 197 (n. 11)

Philadelphia's Young Ladies Academy, 43

Pierce, George Foster, 138

Pierce, Sarah, 19–23, 73, 97

Pinckney, Charles Cotesworth, 158

Poughkeepsie, N.Y., 15, 16, 17, 18, 19, 30, 122, 194

Poughkeepsie Female Academy, N.Y., 184

Preachers, female, 25–27

Presbyterian Church: division of, 7, 158–59, 166–81; and discipline, 12, 110–13, 119–21; in South Amenia, N.Y., 20, 22, 34–35, 175, 184, 185; and women's prayer and ministry, 25–26; and gender roles, 25–26, 85, 126, 147–49, 150, 171–75; in Raleigh, N.C., 34, 35, 36, 59–60; certificates and testimonials of, 34–36, 121–22; and ecumenical collaboration, 40–41, 58–60; and Sabbath Day, 53, 56, 111; and charitable work, 56; in Augusta, Ga., 60, 83, 88–91, 109–13, 126; and slavery, 65–68, 82, 166–77, 189; and

mL   6-14